Living with Unmet Desires

EXPOSING THE MANY FACES OF JEALOUSY

Shawn Lantz

word

Nashville, Tennessee

Distributed by Word Books
© 2009 Shawn Lantz

Author photo on back cover courtesy of Chris Smith of Chris and Cami Photography, Charleston, South Carolina. www.chrisandcamiphotography.com

Book cover, interior formatting, and design courtesy of Jackie Mayberry, senior designer, at JCI Design of Dearborn, Michigan. www.jcidesign.com.

DEDICATION

To my beloved friend and sister-in-law, Karen Lowe:

You and I have been in each other's lives since I married your brother almost two decades ago. Our relationship was once a classic tale of competition and misunderstanding between two women who observed each other through jealousy's sightless and unmerciful eyes.

The Lord has healed what used to be broken between us. You were the first one to hear these ideas before they ever became lessons in a Bible study. You were not afraid to give me honest feedback with your questions as you lavished encouragement on me in the process. You were my sounding board, my prayer partner, and my friend through it all. I cannot pay the debt I owe you for the hours of intense prayer we have shared throughout the writing of this study.

It is because of what has happened between us that I know Jesus Christ can transform a relationship, once based on jealousy, to one which thrives on love and mutual respect. Because of you, I know that He is able to reconcile two people through His scandalous, extravagant grace and knit their once-distant hearts together. I know that you join me in giving Him all the glory. A marriage made us sisters-in-law, but you are now, and always will remain, my friend by choice.

I love you dearly, Karen,

Shawn

Now may the God of patience and comfort grant you to be like-minded toward one another, according to Christ Jesus, that you may with one mind and one mouth glorify the God and Father of our Lord Jesus Christ.

Romans 15:5-6 (NKJV)

Shawn's Gratitude List

I owe so much to the following persons for their support and encouragement:

My Lord Jesus Christ: Thank You for the gift of Your presence which I am learning to be jealous for more than anything I could possess in this life. Help me, dear Jesus, to continue to learn the truth that You are what I am seeking more than any temporary pleasure or possession this world could give me. You are the treasure—You and only You. Take this study and be glorified. Show us all what godly jealousy looks like and give us the hearts to pursue Your jealous love for us with Your power.

My man, Rob and my three children: Rob, the fact that this project has seen the light of day is due to your constant encouragement and belief that its message should be heard. Your confidence has overshadowed my timidity. Your loyalty has given me courage. I have been blessed beyond anything else in my life to be your wife. Whatever life throws at us, your coming alongside me through this process assures me that I have a true companion in you. I love you more than I can possibly express. You are the only one for me. Chase, Jordyn, and Jenna, you have been so patient with this process. I love you so much.

My parents, Jim and Nancy Smith: From my earliest memories, you had a relationship with Jesus that I envied. You are both the real deal. Anything good that comes from this study is fruit from your ministry to me as your daughter. You are examples of generosity and lives poured out as drink offerings. Thank you for the hours you spent in editing and praying for this study. I love you both.

My entire, extraordinary Word family: Special thanks to Mark Funderburg, Alan, Jim, Marty, Dusty, Ricky, Heather, Todd, Kevin, Tom, Josh, and John and three of the coolest college interns on the planet: Sarah, Mandi, and Garrett. You are my coworkers in the gospel and I cannot tell you how proud I am to stand shoulder-to-shoulder with all of you as we attempt to make Jesus famous.

My Bible study groups at Forest Hills Baptist Church and First Presbyterian Church of Trenton, Michigan: You ladies are so precious to me. Thank you for being willing to do this study to see if the material "worked." Your insight and input were invaluable in the process. I love you all so much!

My two spiritual teachers who, long before I took my first breath, were promoted to their heavenly reward, Matthew Henry and Charles Haddon Spurgeon: Meeting these two righteous men on the other side of eternity will be one of the greatest joys I can imagine. I cannot say it any better than Scripture regarding the debt I owe for the insight that God gave these two men who dedicated their lives to the Word of God:

"Those who are wise will shine like the brightness of the heavens, and those who lead many to righteousness, like the stars for ever and ever."   *Daniel 12:3*

To Jackie McClure and Jackie Mayberry of JCI Design: Thank you for making black words on a white page look so beautiful. You have made the process a delight. Thank you for your creative talent which makes a hard topic of study beautiful in its presentation. You are the best!

My wonderful participants: You are the reason for this study. I have prayed much for you through the writing of these lessons. Although I may never meet you in person, the Lord has allowed me to see your faces in my mind's eye as the inspiration for the nine weeks we will spend together in His Word. My prayer is that you and I will be voices who testify that Jesus Christ can empower us to live at peace with our unmet desires. I come to you as a sinner saved by grace and as your servant. Thank you for taking this journey with me!

CONTENTS

Living With Unmet Desires:
Exposing the Many Faces of Jealousy

INTRODUCTION

Jealousy

There are places emotionally and physically that I have not been able to empathize with in my life experience. Jealousy, however, has been something in which I have been both a perpetrator and victim, even at the same time. There have been seasons in my life in which I have allowed the green-eyed monster to take over my mind and control my every thought. I have noticed that no matter how much I may grow in my relationship to Jesus Christ, I have to battle jealous thoughts on a regular basis. Over the past two years, my struggle has been confirmed as universal through conversations with some of my dearest and most transparent friends. Through the vulnerability of our conversations, the Lord started putting this study on my heart. I am honored beyond measure to have you share this journey with me.

Have you ever set out to study a subject that intrigued you but, through the process of exploration, you discover that you will never exhaust the material? This is what I have found to be true with the topic of jealousy. I have found that jealousy wears many faces. In fact, without the light of God's Word illuminating this character flaw, I have often mistaken its face for a different sin.

A key discovery the Lord has allowed me to realize is that jealousy is a symptom of a broken heart. In the first week of this study, we will examine four core heart issues. I believe that unbelief in any one of these major areas beckons jealous thoughts through the door of our hearts. Jealousy is sinister because it covers up the true source of the problem. I think this is why we are puzzled and dismayed by our unwholesome thoughts and actions toward others. We can understand that we do not think well of others, but cannot necessarily understand why. Because we lack this knowledge, we can never really get to the root of the problem and deal with our feelings in a God-honoring way. The result is pure devastation in our relationships.

Our gracious God has given us story after story of real flesh and blood who engaged in this battle before us. Some have been blindsided with jealousy's cunning and have failed miserably in the fight. Some have been tripped up, but recovered, and were the wiser for the wounding. By looking at the narrative of a life story we will be able to ponder why the individual made the choices he or she did in the light of Scripture. We will meet up with several Biblical heroes and examine their own war against jealousy. Some overcame; others were overcome. We will look at their stories in depth and, hopefully, learn to make their victories our own.

Solomon, the wisest king of Israel, wrote the following words in Proverbs 4:23:

"Above all else, guard your heart, for it is the wellspring of life."

> Each week, you will have five days of homework to complete on your own. In each day of homework, you will notice a pink flower ✺ next to the key question of the day's lesson and a black mirror ♀ next to the reflective question. You can use these two questions to encourage discussion if you meet with others in a group setting. These activities are meant to help you apply the lesson being taught in each day's homework to your own life. These are only suggestions. Feel free to let the Holy Spirit guide your discussions with others about the material. You are always at liberty to share as much as you feel comfortable revealing to others.

I have begged the Lord to empower us to know how to obey Solomon's charge better as we seek to guard our hearts, with the realization that Jesus Christ lives inside of our hearts. I want my heart, His temple, to be one that is not as easily entangled by sin's deception. This is my prayer for all of us as we uncover the many faces of jealousy. May we start this journey with the following encouragement from Hebrews 12:1-3 (The Message):

Do you see what this means—all these pioneers who blazed the way, all these veterans cheering us on? It means we'd better get on with it. Strip down, start running—and never quit! No extra spiritual fat, no parasitic sins. Keep your eyes on Jesus, who both began and finished this race we're in. Study how he did it. Because he never lost sight of where he was headed—that exhilarating finish in and with God—he could put up with anything along the way: Cross, shame, whatever. And now he's there, in the place of honor, right alongside God. When you find yourselves flagging in your faith, go over that story again, item by item, that long litany of hostility he plowed through. That will shoot adrenaline into your souls!

Be glorified, Lord Jesus, and speak to each of our hearts!

Four Core Issues of a Jealous Heart

I was experiencing some frightening symptoms related to my stomach several years ago. I kept putting off going to the doctor because, frankly, I was terrified about what he might tell me was the cause for the painful burning sensation I felt daily. Finally, when I became more desperate to know the cause of the pain than to continue living in denial over the symptoms, I scheduled an appointment to find out what was wrong.

Jealousy is not the problem. Jealousy is a symptom of a broken heart. There are four core issues of a jealous heart that we are going to examine in depth this week in our study. If you, like me, are finally ready to get at the root of this destructive character flaw, God is ready and waiting to open our eyes. Within the pages of His Word, He has given us a fabulous flesh and blood example of a woman who struggled with jealousy's poison and was victorious in the fight. Although she may be a familiar figure to you, I pray that you will see her with new eyes this week.

We need more than our natural eye's ability to see as we embark on this very important foundational week of study. I would like to pray the words of the apostle Paul as we begin to uncover the real cause of our jealousy:

I keep asking that the God of our Lord Jesus Christ, the glorious Father, may give you the Spirit of wisdom and revelation, so that you may know him better. I pray also that the eyes of your heart may be enlightened in order that you may know the hope to which he has called you, the riches of his glorious inheritance in the saints, and his incomparably great power for us who believe...   *Ephesians 1:17-19*

 **Day One:** A Matter of Trust

It was October 27, 1984, and my sister, Nicol, and I were attending a school friend's birthday party. We all lived in the sub-Saharan African country of Zaire (now the Democratic Republic of Congo), where resources were scarce. Janet was turning sweet sixteen and what her parents lacked in resources, they made up for in creativity by way of games and food for the celebration. The party was full of laughter and the silly banter of adolescent girls.

Nicol and I were attending TASOK (the American School of Kinshasa), over four hundred miles away from the bush mission station where we had lived the four previous years with Mom and Dad and our brothers. Our parents had been forced to make the painful decision to send us away from them so that we could receive our high school education. We lived in one of three hostels. Our hostel had eleven other missionary children whose parents had also sent them to the capital city for school. Because Janet had invited some girls from the hostel just outside the gate and down the road from ours, we had decided to carpool. Our hostel parent dropped all of us off and their hostel parent would be picking us up after the party.

Our community was very small. Our worlds of youth group, school, and home life all blended together into one. Everyone knew everyone else because we did everything together. Like all small-town communities, this knowledge had both good and bad aspects to it. For the most part, everyone got along, simply because we had to see each other constantly and had no other choice.

Before we arrived at Janet's party, we had been made aware of a disturbing event that had happened earlier in the day. Cindy, the daughter of my hostel parents, had been out to the Zaire River for a day of swimming with her young adult friends. The Zaire River was a swift-moving body of water, infested with both crocodiles and hippopotami. There were rapids all along the wild course it took as it meandered through the country. Unexpectedly, a whirlpool with a powerful current came up on Cindy, threatening to sweep her away from the others in the group. Phil Braun, one of the party and a big brother-figure to so many of us teenagers, dove into the whirlpool after her with no thought of the risk to himself. He managed to push Cindy out of the raging current, but Phil was swept down the river.

We knew that the American Embassy dispatched planes and helicopters to look for Phil. In the past, others who had been swept away in the current had landed on the opposite shore of the river. I did not worry at all about the situation. After all, I reasoned, God couldn't take Phil, a young twenty-seven-year-old who loved Him so much and had come to Zaire to help his missionary parents in their work.

When Nancy, our girlfriends' hostel parent, came to pick us up from Janet's party, I just knew that Phil had been found. As she walked in the door, I asked her if the Embassy planes had found him. With tears in her eyes, she shook her head no. For the first time, I understood the gravity of the situation

**Four Core Issues
of a Jealous Heart:**

God, can I trust You?

God, do You love me?

God, are You good?

God, are You Just?

and burst into tears. All of us girls dissolved into heart-wrenching sobs as the realization that Phil may never be found hit us like a ton of bricks. Our big brother, our friend, was gone.

Sitting in the church sanctuary during Phil's memorial service, with Michael W. Smith's *Friends* playing over the sound system, I dared to think something I had never thought of before. With my mind reeling in shock, the most frightening question my sixteen-year-old mind had ever dared to ponder was suddenly shouting at me:

"God, can I trust You? How could you let this happen? How could you have taken Phil? He loved you so much, and… and… I loved him!" I thought to the sound of my own and others' sobs. I don't know what was more devastating to me—the fact that my beloved friend had drowned, or the thought that God may not be trustworthy.

Phil's death turned my world upside down. I did not know how to deal with the doubt and nagging questions I had. Being a "good" Christian girl, I thought I was being disrespectful by asking them. I was afraid God might kill me for daring to think them. Denial set in, allowing my foot, once so firmly planted in the soil of belief, to slip into the pit of doubt. It would be a long time until I would see light in the darkened, hurtful, and broken places in my heart caused by my unanswered questions.

I would like us to do an exercise to help us evaluate how important trust is to us. There are no right or wrong answers. Simply mark the answer which most closely resembles your feelings right now.

If I trust someone…

I can believe he/she took my welfare into consideration even when it is not apparent in his or her actions.

Strongly agree	Agree	Somewhat agree	Disagree	Strongly disagree

I can believe he/she loves me even if we have a strong disagreement or fight.

Strongly agree	Agree	Somewhat agree	Disagree	Strongly disagree

I can believe he/she will act fairly toward me.

Strongly agree	Agree	Somewhat agree	Disagree	Strongly disagree

I can more easily give the person control of the situation.

Strongly agree	Agree	Somewhat agree	Disagree	Strongly disagree

❊ What does Psalm 22:9 tell us about when our need for trust began and with whom?

"Yet you brought me out of the _____; you made _____ in _____ even at my mother's breast."

One of the most profound revelations to me as a mother was my young children's ability to believe whatever I told them. Rob and I have tried, not flawlessly, to follow the Bible's command to raise our children in the fear of the Lord. Each of my children has come to see his or her need for Jesus Christ to be his or her Savior before the age of five. There was no debate between my children and me over theological issues. They simply trusted that Jesus was who He said He was. That ability for a child to trust is a God-given gift, according to the Word of God. Trust is precious, beautiful, and vulnerable to be altered or shattered.

Try to remember the first time your trust in someone was broken. Use three words to describe the emotions you felt:

What does Psalm 140:5 liken those crushing life experiences to?

An empty well   A deserted house   A hidden snare/net   A flood

Since the day you were born, there has been a war waged against you to steal your God-given trust. The reason you may not have known that before now is because the war is fought by an enemy you cannot see with your eyes (Ephesians 6:11-12). Did you notice that the verse above pointed to proud persons as who laid it down? Pride was the reason for Satan's downfall

Since the day you were born, there has been a war waged against you to steal your God-given trust.

(Isaiah 14:11-17). He wanted to ascend to God's position and be worshiped instead of worshiping His Creator. John 10:10 depicts him as a thief who comes to steal, kill, and destroy. We may be able to trust in our Creator easily at birth, but Satan has deliberately laid a hidden net for us through disheartening and disappointing life circumstances with the goal of first stealing and then killing our trust. Satan stealthily uses what we cannot understand without faith to become the hidden net he uses to destroy our peace, our joy, and our very lives if we are not rescued by our Jesus.

Match the following verse with the correct reference:

"The LORD is good, a refuge in times of trouble.　　　*Psalm 22:5*
He cares for those who trust in him."

"Those who know your name will trust in you, for　　　*Psalm 56:11*
you, LORD, have never forsaken those who seek you."

"They cried to you and were saved; in you　　　*Nahum 1:7*
they trusted and were not disappointed."

"In God I trust; I will not be afraid.　　　*Psalm 9:10*
What can man do to me?"

Which area of trust are you having the most difficulty with right now in your relationship with God? Why?

The vacuum created by a lack of trust in our lives beckons jealousy into the empty space.

We do not have to live long to be caught in the hidden snare that Satan has carefully laid for us through unloving, unjust, or horrible circumstances that happen to us in this life. Those disappointments will cause us to look to things and people to put our hope in and be crushed by every single time. So what does jealousy in our lives have to do with our ability to trust God? Everything! The vacuum created by a lack of trust in our lives beckons jealousy into the empty space. Because so many of life's experiences cannot be accepted without the eyes of faith, we set our sights on acquiring earthly possessions or position to ease the ache of our bewilderment over what God has allowed to happen to us. We become prey dangling in the hidden net.

Life is hard, dear friend. There are questions in this life that we will never have answered to our satisfaction on this side of eternity. Maybe you have not heard anything else this lesson, but I am praying that you will hear this today:

"Trust in him at all times, O people; pour out your hearts to him, for God
is our refuge."　　　*(Psalm 62:8)*

As we close, would you be willing to pour out your heart to Him over today's lesson? Use the margin to record anything He has revealed to you about your level of trust as it may relate to jealousy in your life. May His peace flood your soul as you do.

Day Two: Have to Have It

What can you and I not buy or work for, but must have to live? We will sell our bodies and even our souls in an effort to possess it, but if we hold on too tight, we can strangle it. It must be freely given and received to be healthy. What is it?

L-O-V-E.

Scripture confirms how important our need to be loved is in Proverbs 19:22:

"What a man [or woman] desires is unfailing love; better to be poor than a liar."

Underline the adjective in front of love in the above verse and write it here: _____

Circle true or false for the following statement as you have experienced it in your own life:

True   False   "I have never been disappointed by someone who says he or she loves me."

We can have many people whom we feel deeply loved by in our lives. We can have loving relationships with our families and friends, but we cannot find *unfailing* love with any other human being, no matter how strong and vibrant the relationship. A loving person does not set out to hurt or disappoint us, but the disappointment will inevitably happen. None of us has experienced unfailing love, but the horrible dilemma we have as human beings is that this is the love we desire most.

What complicates our understanding of *love* even more is that we use the word so inappropriately. We *love* ice cream, summer days, and going shopping. When it comes time to describe our fervent emotions toward our spouse or children, we use *love* again. No wonder there is so much confusion about the word and its true meaning.

The Bible has a lot to say about the subject of love. Greek was one of the original languages used by men inspired by the Holy Spirit to express the different kinds of love. We are going to briefly look at three different definitions before delving into our study today.

Eros love

Eros (a greek word not found in the New Testament) love is the heart-racing, ardent, passionate love between a man and a woman. It is giddy, impulsive, and can make you do things you never thought you would. This love is carnal and fleshly. It seeks after self-pleasure rather than the welfare of others. Many of us women naturally think of this kind of love as what we desire. While we

Four Core Issues of a Jealous Heart:

God, can I trust You?

God, do You love me?

God, are You good?

God, are You Just?

16

may enjoy the rush of emotion we feel surrounding this kind of love, the downside is that we can subject ourselves to many forms of abuse because eros love can be manipulative and self-serving. If a relationship is only built on this kind of love, it runs the risk of never maturing and may eventually fizzle out.

Phileo Love

Phileo love describes the affection between two people drawn together in a relationship based on common interests. We enjoy this kind of love because this love is very rewarding. If you have a best friend, this is the kind of love you share. Unfortunately, if one person moves away or into another life stage, the common interests that drew you together initially may become no more. As a result, you may not be able to maintain the same level of closeness in your relationship as before.

Agape Love

Agape love is it, girlfriends. This is the unfailing, selfless love that every single one of our hearts longs for. This is the way that God loves us. This kind of love always considers the other person's best interests. This love remains strong and steady, no matter what the circumstance, and it never disappoints us. Sound impossible for human beings to love this way? You are right! We can not love this way unless we are empowered by the Holy Spirit.

The passage of Scripture we are going to study today is probably very familiar to you. Rob and I had one of the verses from this chapter printed on our wedding ceremony program. Turn to 1 Corinthians 13 and read the passage in its entirety. For today's lesson, we will concentrate on verses 1-7.

Verses 1-3

What does the apostle Paul equate the following to if not done with love:

The words of our mouths without love are like:

The gift of prophecy, knowledge, and/or faith without love make me:

The giving away of all my possessions or a self-sacrificial death done without love gain me:

Have you ever been on the receiving end of a blast of words spoken without love?

How can you relate to the gong or cymbal illustration above? How did it make you feel to be around someone extremely intelligent or knowledgeable in the things of faith who interacted with you without love?

None of us has experienced unfailing love, but the horrible dilemma we have as human beings is that this is the love we desire most.

Have you ever received a gift from someone you knew bought the gift merely out of obligation? Or did you grow up in a home where you were always reminded what a burden it was to clothe and feed you? How did that make you feel?

Any of those acts done above without love behind them cheapen love to us. Receiving something given by another without love not only makes us feel uncomfortable, but also unloved.

We can come to Christ for salvation and never grasp His agape love for us. Our understanding of love comes through the experience of being loved by fallible human beings. We confuse eros and phileo love for the agape love that we so deeply desire. Let's look at the definition of agape love as defined in 1 Corinthians 13:4-7:

Verses 4-7
Mentally evaluate yourself on the following characteristics of agape love. Check any area you feel you have mastered, remembering that agape love never falls short in these areas:

Love is patient.
Love is kind.
Love does not envy.
Love does not boast.
Love rejoices with the truth.
Love does not delight in evil.
Love always trusts.
Love always perseveres.

Love is not proud.
Love is not rude.
Love is not self-seeking.
Love is not proud.
Love never fails.
Love always protects.
Love always hopes.

Not one of us would argue that these characteristics make up the love we are longing for, but not one of us has come close to perfecting these attributes of agape love. Our hearts are on a relentless pursuit to be loved this way, but no human being is capable of loving perfectly in these areas. The reason why agape love is so hard to experience, girlfriends, is that agape love loves others! Those who love with agape love put the burden of loving on themselves, not on the other person. I would like to suggest that we will never feel loved until we love others this way. We will never perfect loving others with agape love during our lives on earth, but we can strive to love this way with the Holy Spirit's help.

※ We have a problem, however, if we do not trust that God is who He says He is. What does He declare Himself to be in 1 John 4:8? Write the verse out here:

> If we do not understand that unfailing love cannot be found in anything other than our relationship to Jesus Christ, we will be led astray by jealousy's lies.

God is love. A person who does not believe the depth to which she is loved by God will be jealous of love that is not love at all, the kind that continually disappoints us. How freeing to realize that we do not have to earn God's unconditional and limitless love for us. Such a realization makes us free to love others and experience a relationship with Him that we have never been able to find in anyone else.

What do the following reveal about God's love?
Match the following verses to the correct reference
(two verses will use one reference):

His love endures forever.   *1 John 4:19*

Everyone who loves has been born of God
and knows God.   *1 John 4:8*

Whoever does not love does not know God,
because God is love.   *1 John 4:7*

We love because he first loved us.   *Psalm 136:2*

Dear friends, let us love one another, for love comes from God.

I will tell you the most damaging misinformation I believed due to my lack of trust in my relationship with God. I could not believe He loved me as Scripture clearly said He did. I pictured Him as a righteous Judge waiting to zap me when I failed, which was constantly!

My sweet sister, do you have trouble believing that God loves you? If yes, why?

We all want to be the beloved one to someone. Listen! We will never find the love we are looking for in material possessions or another human being, because love comes from God. The need to be loved is a driving force in everyone's life. No one other than God can handle the depth of our need to be loved unconditionally.

When did God first demonstrate His love for you and me according to Romans 5:8?

Jealousy calls deceptively to the heart that feels unloved. It whispers that we need to strive to be loved, no matter what the cost to our dignity or integrity. If we do not understand that true love cannot be found in anything other than our relationship with Jesus Christ, we will be led astray by jealousy's lies. Those lies will ultimately destroy us as we seek to assuage a need for love in the wrong way. Jealousy's definition of love makes everything all about its needs, in contrast to agape love making it all about the other person's needs.

"I the LORD search the heart and examine the mind, to reward a man according to his conduct, according to what his deeds deserve."
Jeremiah 17:10

Let's ask the Lord to search our hearts and examine our minds to find out if jealousy's face has shown up in our lives because we believe the lie that we are unloved. May peace be your reward.

Day Three: His Presence or His Presents? [1]

One of the reasons we may assume we have a personality conflict with someone else is because we believe we have irreconcilable differences with that person in the way we handle life's biggest priorities. Someone who continually hurts my feelings in areas that are sensitive and of high value to me will get the label of not being nice or even hurtful in my mind. Have you noticed, however, that this same person who rubs you the wrong way can get along just fine with one of your dearest friends? That is maddening and a big cause of jealousy among us women!

But what do we do when the person who we believe has disappointed us the most in the area of being good to us is God Himself? Somewhere on the journey of faith, we have had a head-on collision with God's character not fitting our understanding of the goodness of God. If we do not come to a satisfying reconciliation of the character of God and the goodness of God, we can be tempted to throw the whole idea of faith out the window.

Identify a time when you could not easily reconcile the character of God as you understood Him to be with the goodness of God:

I want to present you with two scenarios. I don't want you to respond with your head. I want you to respond with your gut-level emotions. To make this even more personal, I want you to imagine that you are the main character in both scenarios.

Scenario One

Your husband's job requires you to move to a foreign culture. Being a girl from a small town and a very close-knit family, the fact that you cannot see your family and friends except once a year is traumatic for you. You soon learn that you are pregnant, however, and your joy knows no bounds.

After several months of feeling your unborn child's kicks, you are stunned to lose the dream of motherhood before it has begun. Although you become pregnant soon after, a wound of sorrow remains raw for a long time. After the birth of two sons, a cherished daughter is born. By the time she is eight years old, her laughter and girlish ways have helped to dull the pain of the first pregnancy you lost. But one faith-shaking day, your beautiful little girl dies in her bed.

Through it all, you and your husband continue to serve where you have been called. You humbly accept God's plan for you, although that plan was not what you wanted at all. Fifteen years into your marriage, you wake up with a searing pain in your abdomen. You wrestle through horrible fears for the twins you now carry in your womb. Because you do not have access to morphine or chemotherapy for your liver cancer, you scream your way into the arms of

Four Core Issues of a Jealous Heart:

God, can I trust You?

God, do You love me?

God, are You good?

God, are You Just?

Jesus shortly after you give birth prematurely to your twin sons. Through the entire agonizing process of losing your earthly life, your husband can only stand by and watch your suffering as he is left to wonder why.

Scenario Two

You are a child who grew up in a loving family with many friends. Your young life was full of opportunities: a home in which you wanted for nothing materially, private elementary and secondary education in the best schools, which led to a fabulous college application allowing you to be accepted at your prestigious university.

After pledging for the most envied sorority, you met your knock-out hubby at a party. He was the catch of the campus and wanted you! You almost fainted when he called the first time. And when he proposed, you could not regain your composure for several minutes. Your summa cum laude efforts, recognized at commencement, led to the job of your dreams. Both you and your husband made a seamless transition into your lucrative careers after graduation. Your husband's ambition reassured you that the lifestyle you grew up with was going to be yours as an adult. After three years of marriage, you became pregnant the first month you tried and delivered the first of your beautiful, healthy children nine months later. You had a boy first and then a girl.

Because of your husband's success and your sizable contribution to your joint income, you were able to buy your dream house, build an impressive stock portfolio, and stay home to raise your children. Vacations to exotic places were the norm every summer. Your savings account was well-cushioned. You nor anyone else in your family has ever had a major illness. However, you live within five minutes of one of the best trauma and cancer treatment hospitals in the country.

Which woman is more blessed of God in your opinion and why?

The next question is not one I want you to answer, but simply to ponder: How much do you and I equate the goodness of God with our personal happiness and comfort?

Somewhere on the journey of faith, we have had a head-on collision with God's character not fitting into our understanding of the goodness of God.

Unfortunately, the details of scenario one are the true life facts of my dearly loved friend, Suzanne Kapinga. Her husband, Gary, married her shortly after he became a staff member of my parents' mission work in the Democratic Republic of Congo. Congo is very tribal. When Suzanne moved to Nkara-Ewa, she may as well have been moving to a foreign country, even though her home village was only two hundred miles away. Being an outsider made her the object of other's scorn. The death of her first baby left her crushed. Her beautiful daughter, Diana, died of a disease that would not have necessarily taken her life had she lived here in the United States. The last eighteen months of Suzanne's life was exacted from a body filled with excruciating pain. Gary watched helplessly as the mother of his surviving children screamed out in anguish under the ravaging effects of liver cancer. Her illness caused the premature delivery of twin boys. Gary buried his beloved wife within weeks of burying his twin sons.

Growing up in the third world has forced me to come to the conclusion that God's goodness does not equal His presents to me. You and I live in a country that is the envy of the world. Our poorest live better than 90% of the rest of the world's population. How can God be good when more than a million people die every year from malaria? How can God be good if the average Congolese annual salary per household is one hundred dollars per year in buying power? You read that right—a year, not a day. I can easily spend well over that amount every week on groceries for my family.

Which Scripture passage is closest to your reaction when God's goodness appears hidden in your life's circumstances? Circle one.

"[Job] replied, 'You are talking like a foolish woman. Shall we accept good from God, and not trouble?' In all this, Job did not sin in what he said."
Job 2:10

"But Zion said, 'The LORD has forsaken me, the Lord has forgotten me."
Isaiah 49:14

❋ Why do you think we tend to believe that God has forgotten or abandoned us when bad things happen?

What do you tend to do emotionally when life starts getting difficult? Circle all that apply:

Become depressed	Lose sleep
Become controlling	Overeat
Withdraw emotionally	React with anger
Have little patience with loved ones	Pray more fervently
Spend more time in God's Word	Over-spend
Turn to addictive behaviors	

It has only been in the last three years that I have understood that I truly do have a choice to not react in a destructive way emotionally when my circumstances have become difficult. Hear me loud and clear: I do not always make the right choice! My first response is to react with anger and worry about what is happening around me. But God has patiently been teaching me that adversity and suffering are to be rejoiced over, not feared.

What are the benefits of trials according to the following verses:

Isaiah 30:20 _____

James 1:2-3 _____

I Peter 1:6-7 _____

Do we call ourselves blessed by God when we are experiencing His presence or His presents? Looking at the two scenarios I provided in this lesson, if our definition of God's blessing is favorable circumstances, one could argue that my friend Suzanne saw none of God's goodness in her short and pain-filled life. If that were true, then God could not have been good to Suzanne, her husband, or her surviving children.

How then do I explain the peace and joy that Suzanne continued to possess which defied her horrible circumstances? Perhaps the explanation is found in realizing that God's goodness is not limited to just the material blessings He lavishes on us. Instead, the true blessing of God is found in His presence. Many times, we will only search for a deeper relationship with Him because of the trials in our lives.

I came across a sermon by Charles Spurgeon, a British preacher from the nineteenth century. His perspective on trials has profoundly affected the way I look at my own circumstances:

"When the Lord finds a saint whom He loves—loves much—He may spare other men trials and troubles, but He certainly will not this well-beloved one. The more beloved you are the more of the rod you shall have… It is an awful thing to be a favorite of heaven. It is a thing to be sought after and to be rejoiced in, but remember, to be one of the King's council-chamber is a thing involving such work for faith that flesh and blood might shrink from the painful blessing… Sometimes when we plead for our adverse circumstances to change, God simply makes us content where we are. Many saints have found riches in poverty, ease in labor, rest in pain, and delight in affliction. Our Lord can so adapt our minds our circumstances, that the bitter is sweet, and the burden is light." [2]

Without the right perspective on the difficulties God has ordained in our lives, we can easily begin to envy the gifts God has given to someone else. With the wrong definition of God's blessing, we spend our lives in vain striving to attain material possessions that can be here today and gone tomorrow. We can lose precious family and friends in our frantic pursuit of what cannot satisfy and will only whet our desire for something bigger and better. Eventually we will come to the disappointing conclusion that our pursuit for soul satisfaction cannot be found in anyone or anything on this earth. His presence is where His goodness is found. The joy of the trial is experienced when we realize that without the pain, we would not know that His presence is what we desire more than His presents.

Do we call ourselves blessed by God when we are experiencing His presence or His presents?

You have made known to me the path of life; you will fill me with joy in your presence, with eternal pleasures at your right hand. **Psalm 16:11**

As we close today's lesson, have you allowed jealousy to cause you to desire God's presents more than His presence in your life? Use the space below to pour your heart out to Him about this:

Day Four: God, Are You Just?

Hey girlfriends! I am so excited about our lesson today and tomorrow.

Without looking back at your homework, list the three core issues of a jealous heart that we have discussed so far:

1)

2)

3)

I have found that in the narrative of a Biblical character I can more readily recognize valuable life lessons which help to illuminate my blindness regarding my own flaws. The Word of God provides story after story in the Old Testament of individuals who did life their own way or walked in obedience with Him. I get completely pulled into the story when the Bible provides multiple lessons in the life of one person—especially when that person is a woman.

Song of Solomon 8:6 is a passage of Scripture that will give us insight into the intensity of the situation in which the woman we will study today and tomorrow found herself. Hannah is a popular name to give a baby girl in the United States. The Biblical character Hannah is held up in Sunday school stories as the woman who did an unbelievable act in fulfilling her end of a request she made to God when He fulfilled His part to her. In a study that has yet to hold out an example in female form of handling jealousy correctly, it is my prayer that we will see Hannah as the worthy example to follow. If you are familiar with Hannah's story in Scripture, I am going to ask you to pray for new eyes as we look at her situation in the context of our study's subject of jealousy.

There is no subject that has been written or sung about more, in all languages of the world in all its many cultures, than the power of romantic love. Solomon was inspired by God to write an entire book about both the ecstasy and despondency that can be experienced originating from the love relationship between a man and a woman.

Please read Song of Solomon 8:6 and contemplate the following questions in light of our study:

What does this verse compare the strength of love to?

Our brokenness of spirit does not make Christ run away from us, but the first step of our healing comes in running to Him.

✳ What attribute following *love* is compared in its cruelness to the grave in this verse?

Do you agree that love is as strong as death and that its jealousy is as unyielding as the grave? If yes, please give a personal life example that illustrates this truth. You will not be called on to share this with anyone.

With your own experience fresh in your mind, let's read Hannah's story found in 1 Samuel 1:1-8. I can hardly imagine the household in which Hannah lived. I have often joked with my husband that he can only handle being married to one woman—that would be *me*. Would you agree that a one man, two women love triangle equals one volatile opportunity for jealousy to be involved? Domestic violence calls are those that have the most potential to be deadly because of the rage involved when a man and a woman cannot handle their disagreement in a constructive manner. Not only are those calls a danger to those involved in the relationship, but also to law enforcement who have been called on to intervene in the situation.

Hannah's problem was that she and her husband's other matrimonial partner had to share one man. How many of us have ever played second fiddle to another woman in a dating relationship? To feel like a fool in any area is painful, but when it involves love with all its complex emotions, coherent, rational decisions can be nonexistent. To have to share a husband is unthinkable. There were several complicating factors involved in Hannah's having to share a house with the other wife, Peninnah. Let's examine those together.

Please read 1 Samuel 1:4-8 again. In the first column, list the possible reasons for Peninnah's jealousy toward Hannah. In the second column, list the possible reasons for Hannah's jealousy toward Peninnah.

Peninnah toward Hannah   Hannah toward Peninnah

_____   _____

_____   _____

Jealousy is a symptom of a deeper heart issue. Looking at the three core issues we listed at the beginning of the lesson, which issue do you think was Peninnah's biggest area of brokenness and why?

Verse six gives us a clue as to why Peninnah provoked and irritated Hannah, but I believe that Peninnah's behavior came from a deeper problem revealed in verse five concerning the man they shared. What was that?

List the four things the earth trembles and cannot bear up under in Proverbs 30:21-23:

_____   _____

_____   _____

To feel like a fool in any area is painful, but when it involves love with all its complex emotions, coherent, rational decisions can be nonexistent.

People react differently to hurt. Some, like Peninnah, lash out and openly wound another. Hannah appeared to be more passive in her response to Peninnah's aggression toward her. I would like to share my own perspective on why she might have chosen to struggle through her hurt alone. My husband is the only person who truly sees all sides of me. It is unthinkable to me to lash out at a person to his or her face, not because I have a corner on righteousness, but because I feel that I would bring disgrace to myself. My pride and the fear of making a spectacle of myself restrain me in a confrontation with those outside of my marriage. I, like Hannah, might weep when confronted aggressively by someone, or I may even be able to keep it together until I feel I am safe to emote, but I do not tend to lash out. The hurt and rage I have, however, is just as real to me; I just do not show it outwardly.

I especially will not share my hurt if I feel hopeless to change the situation. Now let me apply this to Hannah's story. I hope that you included Hannah's infertility in the possible reasons for Hannah's jealousy toward Peninnah. For those of you who have never had fertility problems, it may be hard to imagine what that hurt does to a woman.

I will never forget the joy I had looking down at positive result in the window of the pregnancy test I took in February of 1996. I worked at a health department, which gave pregnancy tests to clients. I was alone in the bathroom when I took the test. My husband, Rob, and I had been married for three and a half years. I had wanted to try for a baby within the first year of marriage. Rob, the more practical of the two of us, thought it was important that we be able to provide for the baby. That meant we needed to eliminate both his student loans and mine, before we added a third member to our family. Two and a half years later, the loans were paid off, we had bought our first home, and he had come around to the idea of starting our family.

Four days after taking the pregnancy test, I woke up to the worst cramping and bleeding I had ever experienced. The temperature outside had drastically changed overnight. When the calendar says February in the Midwest, the thermometer outside rarely shows anything above the freezing point. A sudden heat wave with temperatures in the fifties had come through our suburb of Chicago while I slept. The result was fog so thick I could not see the street from the end of my short driveway.

Although I knew in my head that the amount of bleeding I was experiencing gave me little hope of keeping the baby, I called my doctor's office for an appointment. I felt as though I was on an alien planet as I tried to carefully drive through the fog. I had been crying ever since I had woken up and looked a mess by the time I arrived at the doctor's office. The doctor's bedside manner was horrible. "Mrs. Lantz, you have to stop thinking of this [embryo] as a baby. You were barely pregnant. It is just a ball of cells at this stage. There will be another opportunity for you to have another one." *Barely pregnant*—what did that mean? How could I be barely pregnant? *Just a ball of cells*—is that what this disconnected man had just said to try to ease my grief? *No!* My heart screamed.

Can you relate to the author's anguish in Psalm 88:6? How has struggling with a feeling of injustice put you there as you have become jealousy's victim or its perpetrator? Please share here:

The psalmist's words resonated with me at that time because the aftermath of my miscarriage caused me to fall into a pit of despair. The lowest and darkest depths of the pit were sounded in my soul at the frightening prospect that I might never be able to have a baby. This was a new fear. I had always assumed that my body would be able to carry a baby to full-term. Now I had to face the possibility that I may never get to carry a child in my womb, which was something I had wanted since my childhood.

Jealousy was something I felt profoundly after my miscarriage. Every time I would see a woman with a baby, I would resent the fact that she could be a mother. I realize now that my jealousy was so bewildering because I did not see then that my self-esteem had taken such a hit. I felt crippled, broken, inept, and helpless because I could not fix myself. There was no quick fix to my situation. I could do nothing to change my circumstances. Is it possible that Hannah felt the same way as I did?

What was Elkanah's response to Hannah's weeping in Samuel 1:8?

Four Core Issues of a Jealous Heart:

God, can I trust You?

God, do You love me?

God, are You good?

God, are You Just?

Hannah and Peninnah each wanted what the other wife had and felt helpless to have their unmet desires fulfilled. Both Hannah and Peninnah were victims of the cruelty of jealousy in different ways. Peninnah wanted Elkanah's love, but his love belonged to Hannah. Peninnah must have felt frustrated with her inability to win Elkanah's full devotion because she had given him children in a culture that judged a woman's value on the functionality of her womb. In other words, Peninnah had given him what her culture told her she must, and, yet, she did not receive the devotion she craved. Elkanah loved Hannah more. In contrast, Hannah had to face her possible feelings of unworthiness as a woman by herself because of Elkanah's inability to empathize with the pain of her infertility.

Do you think that feelings of jealousy in your life might originate from a feeling of brokenness in the area of believing that God is not just in the way He has ordained your circumstances? Thinking of today's lesson, can you see yourself in either Peninnah's or Hannah's position? Please use the space below to discuss that with the Lord.

So where do we go from here? We tell the Lord where we are struggling. If we are in the pit, we tell Him. He will hear our cry for mercy and turn His ear to us individually. He has found us worthy. Our brokenness of spirit does not make Christ run away from us, but the first step of our healing comes in running to Him. Hope is just around the corner, my beloved sister! Tomorrow we will examine the steps Hannah took on the road to wholeness. You and I can choose to walk the same path she chose in our own lives. I pray that we will.

Day Five: Making the Choice to Leave the Pit

I hate the pit that jealousy has forced me to live in. So how do I get out of it? We are going to continue with Hannah's story to see how she wrestled with jealousy and found a way out of her misery. Before we go any farther, we need to establish what we believe about the relevancy of Scripture in our lives. On a scale of one to ten, rate how relevant you feel God's Word is to your daily life. As part of your rating, please factor in how often you consult His Word for direction in life's struggles.

1	2	3	4	5	6	7	8	9	10

Not relevant at all

Relevant in some areas of life

Relevant in all areas of my life

Our failure or success in wrestling with jealousy will depend on whether we believe that what God says about His character is true or what our feelings tell us is true about Him. What does Scripture say about God in the following four core issues we have studied this week?

His **trustworthiness** in Psalm 143:8?

His **love** for us in Jeremiah 31:3?

His **goodness** in Psalm 22:5?

His **justice** in Deuteronomy 32:4?

Glancing back at 1 Samuel 1:1-8, how could Hannah's jealousy toward Penninah be the result of a lack of belief in God's sovereignty in her life in the following areas?

Hannah's trust in God:

Four Core Issues of a Jealous Heart:

God, can I trust You?

God, do You love me?

God, are You good?

God, are You Just?

31

Hannah's perception of God's love for her:

Hannah's perception of God's goodness to her:

Hannah's perception of God's justice toward her:

Let's pick up today's story in 1 Samuel 1:9-20 and carefully read through the passage. Please make a note of important observations to you on the margin of this page.

     I love to read. Nothing is worse to me, however, than becoming completely wrapped up in a story that ends badly. Thankfully, Hannah's story does not end that way. At first glance, we may glibly sigh with relief for Hannah as she names her firstborn son, this baby that she longed for so greatly. Before we say, "And mother and son lived happily ever after," we must examine the difficult work Hannah chose to allow God to do in her life before she held her baby boy in her arms.

1 Samuel 1:9 says, "Once when they had finished eating and drinking in Shiloh…"

Glance back at verse three of 1 Samuel 1. In what location did the ugliness of the rivalry between Hannah and Peninnah emerge?

In front of Elkanah   At Shiloh

Between Peninnah's children and Hannah

Strong's Concordance defines *Shiloh* as, ***"a place of rest."*** [3]

In fact, the Hebrew word from which *Shiloh* is derived expands the definition this way:

"he whose it is, that which belongs to him, tranquility." [4]

Can you think of a place in your own mind that always reminds you of a specific, traumatic experience no matter how time has past since you were last there? Some examples of this place may be a hospital corridor where you received devastating news, the location where a person you loved ended a relationship you wanted to continue, a courtroom where you said goodbye to your dream of living happily ever after with the one who is now your ex-spouse, or a funeral home where your mind reeled with the finality of death and all that its stinging consequences would mean to your future. You may have consciously or unconsciously made a mental note to never return to that particular place because of the anguish the associated memories resurrect in your mind.

> In the context of Hannah's possible association with her difficulty in Shiloh, where do you find unrest in a place where you should find peace (your own Shiloh)?

Every Israelite male was required by Levitical law to appear before the Lord during three annual festivals of praise and sacrifice (see Deuteronomy 16:16-17). The three mandatory festivals were the Feast of Unleavened Bread (the Passover), the Festival of Weeks, and the Festival of Tabernacles. *The NIV Study Bible* notes on our passage explains that Elkanah, Peninnah and her 5 children, and Hannah were most likely attending the Festival of Weeks, a seven day celebration. [5]

Please summarize the purpose of the celebration by reading Deuteronomy 16:14-15. Note especially the attitude that the participants were to bring to the celebration.

You and I may have the luxury of never having to return physically to those places that pull the scab off the wound of dreadful memories in our past, but Hannah had to face Shiloh in order to obey God's will for her life as an Israelite.

Look back again at 1 Samuel 1:3, 7. How often did Hannah have to revisit Shiloh and face Peninnah's provocation?

I hope that the irony was not lost on us that this particular festival was to be celebrated joyfully by all family members for seven days for the purpose of giving God thanks for His blessing on a year's bountiful harvest. Have you ever been forced to spend any period of time (perhaps Christmas) with a family member who made you feel uncomfortable, embarrassed, or angry… anything but joyful? Perhaps you can relate well to Hannah's having to return to this place every year because you, too, have been forced to revisit an unpleasant situation through no choice of your own.

After reading 1 Samuel 1:9-16, I believe we can assume that the state of Hannah's heart was anything but tranquil. After finishing yet another meal that she did not really taste, Hannah stood up. She had known the cruelty

Our failure or success in wrestling with jealousy will depend on whether or not we believe that what God says about His character is true or what our feelings tell us is true about Him.

and bitterness of her rival wife Peninnah's jealousy and the seeming unfairness of bringing a barren womb to a celebration of God's goodness to families year after year. After finally coming to the end of herself, this desperate woman realized there was hope being offered which would allow her to find relief from the constant pain of her infertility.

Hannah's character makes me think that she believed in the God of Israel, but the fact that Hannah's wounds were made over many years makes me wonder if maybe, until that point, she had never thought to ask Him to show Himself powerful in her pain. I can relate to Hannah. I have known Jesus as my Savior since age five, but I can fail to believe that He is powerful enough to make a true difference in the area in which I need to trust Him. In those broken places of my heart, I have chosen jealousy to reign. I have limited His ability to heal me because of my unbelief. Eleven years ago, I started standing up against the unbelief that God could not be trusted in the broken places that had brought me pain to revisit in my mind. Gradually, my head knowledge of His power started to become heart knowledge as my daily time with the Lord in His Word began to heal me.

❋ To whom did Hannah turn to for help (1 Samuel 1:12-13)?

Did you see that Eli the priest misjudged her? Instead of drinking from a cup of sorrow, what kind of cup did Eli think she had been drinking from (verse 15)?

How about you? Have you either misjudged someone or been misjudged by someone when you were in deep sorrow? How did you feel as the perpetrator and/or the victim of that judgment?

I have felt as foolish in my own misplaced judgments of others as Eli must have felt after he realized he had made such a mistake about Hannah. A wise woman, Hannah did not rebuke him in anger, but responded in humility. In response to her sharing her heart with him, Eli blessed her in the place of his former rebuke.

I believe Eli's response to Hannah is God's promise to us who choose to respond according to Proverbs 15:1a. Please write that verse below.

Let's now look at the final three verses of our story. After Hannah had received Eli's blessing, where did she go and what did she do?

Her appetite had come back! What can we account for the dramatic change in the Hannah of verse 18? I would like to suggest that the following passage contains the answer:

"The pains of death surrounded me, and the pangs of Sheol laid hold of me; I found trouble and sorrow. Then I called upon the name of the LORD: "O LORD, I implore You, deliver my soul!"

Psalm 116:3-4 (New King James Version)

Strong's Concordance defines Sheol this way: sheol, underworld, grave, hell, pit. [6]

The grave is devoid of any joy. Have you ever felt, like the writer of Psalm 116, that your soul has been left in the grave? I want us to look carefully at verse 4, because this was the remedy for Hannah's feeling as though she was in the grave. Where do we need to go to get out of the pit—the hell—we find ourselves in? Where is fullness of joy found?

Hannah's entering into His presence unleashed God's power to rescue her soul from the depths of despair. Do you remember that jealousy's cruelty was compared to the grave, the place of the dead (Song of Solomon 8:6) in yesterday's lesson? How does our soul leave the pit, the grave of jealousy behind? We practice His presence.

You may say, "Shawn, how do I do that? I don't know what that means." We are human beings, who will continue to struggle with jealousy until the day we leave this world for heaven, but we are not without a powerful defense.

Please write out our defense against jealousy found in 2 Corinthians 10:3-5 below:

We practice our fullness of joy in His presence by deliberately taking each jealous thought and, like Hannah, pouring out our bitterness of soul to the One who can rescue us from death (Hebrews 5:7). No psychologist or behavioral modification can save us. The way out of the pit is by taking Him at His word, and doing what it says. 2 Corinthians 10:3-5 may look like this to me:

In those broken places of my heart, I have chosen jealousy to reign. I have limited His ability to heal me because of my unbelief.

"Lord, the weapons that You have given me by Your Spirit are not weapons of the world that are useless. I believe that they have divine power to demolish this stronghold of jealousy in my life. Because of the authority Your shed blood has given me, I demolish this jealous way of thinking because dwelling on it sets itself up against what I know You would want for me. I now take this thought captive and make it obedient to You, Jesus. I will find what I desire most in Your presence. Give me fullness of joy in Your presence! Help me!"

Did Hannah ever feel the sting of Peninnah's words again? I can almost guarantee that she did, knowing that two women still lived under the roof of one man. Notice in 1 Samuel 1:20 that, "in the course of time Hannah conceived and gave birth to a son." Did Hannah ever feel the pit closing around her soul again? I am sure of it. But she learned, like you and I can, to leave our Sheol behind so that our Shiloh can be resurrected in a place that no longer makes us ache in its remembrance. Our Shiloh can become our place of rest.

I am asking the Lord to help us begin to see that jealousy is a symptom of a broken heart in one of the four core issues we studied this week. Although jealousy pulled Hannah into the pit of despair, she walked out of the pit with God's help. We can, too.

Straight Down A Twisted Path

Have you ever acted rebelliously toward your parents? That is a rhetorical question, of course! We all have. But have you ever been shocked when your parents granted their permission against their better judgment?

Peer pressure acts strangely on the best of us, pushing us to act or do what we have never done before. Sometimes, after warning us of the consequences of our actions, our parents have let us feel the sting of a decision we made out of the wrong motives. Unfortunately, we are not the only ones hurt for our rebellion.

We are going to see Israel ask for a king because they wanted to be like the other nations around them, without counting the cost of that decision. Although the events of this week's study happened thousands of years ago, we are going to see ourselves in the story line—painfully so, at times. As much as things change, some things stay the same. Let's meet Hannah's little boy, Samuel, now an old man. We may think that choosing obedience, like Hannah did, is only for the one who obeys. Listen to the precious promise God gives us:

But from everlasting to everlasting the LORD's love is with those who fear him, and his righteousness with their children's children-with those who keep his covenant and remember to obey his precepts.　　　*Psalm 103:17-18*

Thankfully, God's lavish grace also extends blessing far beyond the life of one individual. Hannah's choice to walk out of the pit of jealousy blessed not only her own life, but also the life of the beloved son she relinquished to God for His service. May we never see Samuel in quite the same way again after this week's study.

✺ **Day One:** The Beginnings of Trouble

I am fascinated with the history of others. I love nothing better than to sit on the couch at a new acquaintance's home and look through her photo albums. While some might think this is a boring activity, I love seeing an inside track of people's lives this way. I think the reason that I love to see snapshots of someone's past is because they give clues to help me understand the person I am encountering in the present. Looking through the old photo albums may give me insight into the following questions I have about my new friend:

Does she look totally different now than she did in high school? Did she act differently then? How old was she when she got married or had her first child? Why does she look sad in this picture?

We are going to spend the majority of our time in this study on the life of a man named Saul. The Bible does not tell us every thought or deed of Saul, but the book of 1 Samuel gives us snapshots of crucial periods and decisions made in his life—ones in which the Word of God gives enough detail for us to understand life-altering truths offered to us on the page.

My youngest daughter and I have spent months compiling her baby book. Jenna was my third child in three and a half years. Although I did a fair job writing down details about my first two children, I regret to admit that I did not even buy a baby book for Jenna. One day last year, Jenna's older siblings decided to pull out their baby books. After an anxiety-filled search in the built-in shelves in our living room, Jenna came to me with tears in her eyes wondering if her book had somehow gotten lost.

I gulped hard and sheepishly admitted that the reason she could not find the book was not because it had gotten lost, but was because it didn't exist. That was not one of my prouder moments of motherhood, let me assure you! She brought me the computer and asked me to remedy the situation right away. She picked out the baby book that caught her eye and I ordered it right then. The book came within the week. The process of putting together pictures and captions from her life has afforded some of the most precious times we have shared together as mother and daughter.

The first pages of Jenna's baby book are filled with pictures of her father and me, and her siblings—the key people that were here before the day of her birth. In the same way, our in-depth study of the life of Saul does not start with the first time he is introduced in the Biblical narrative, but with the individual that he replaced. We met and cheered on Hannah, this man's mother, through her victory over jealousy's pit last week. Saul will quickly become the central focus of our study before the end of this week, but we need to start by looking at life in Israel through the eyes of a judge named Samuel.

I have heard the painful crash in my ears as I realize that what has tumbled out of my mouth lies shattered in front of me with no way to pick up the broken shards.

To get an idea of who Samuel was, please read the following verses and write a short sentence about the information you find out about him:

1 Samuel 1: 21-22:

1 Samuel 1:27-28:

1 Samuel 2:11:

1 Samuel 3:19-21, 4:1:

1 Samuel 7:15

Samuel had faithfully served the Lord as both a prophet and a judge in Israel from early on in his young life under the high priest of Israel, Eli. We are about to meet him as an elderly man in 1 Samuel 8. I know that I do not share with Samuel the incredible feat of none of his words falling to the ground (1 Samuel 3:19). On the contrary, I have heard the painful crash in my ears as I realize that what has tumbled out of my mouth lies shattered in front of me with no way to pick up the broken shards.

Let's read all of 1 Samuel 8 now, paying special attention to the following insights:

Whom had Samuel appointed as his helpers to judge Israel according to verse 1?

Contrast verse 3 with 1 Samuel 3:19 above. What does verse three tell us about Samuel's sons?

Unfortunately, just because your father serves God, there is no guarantee that you will continue in his footsteps. There are a staggering number of young people leaving the church and never returning.

Can you relate to Samuel's sons, Joel and Abijah?
Have you ever left the faith of your parent(s) for a time?

Drawing from your own experience or someone you know, circle the factors which may have influenced yours or someone else's decision to leave the faith of his or her childhood:

Culture/friends' influence   Hypocrisy of church members

Faith never really took root   Church did not seem important

Other _____

Samuel was appointed by God to minister to Israel. Now he was old and broken down—long past the years of vigor and vitality. Those who had known him during his prime were replaced by a new generation led by two main constants in their lives. Idolatry and complacency had left them without the wisdom to fathom the danger of asking for an earthly king.

What were the qualifications of the new king that they required in 1 Samuel 8:5?

I can almost hear the Lord saying "Samuel, don't grieve for yourself. Grieve for Me, because I am the One they have rejected, not you!

If you couldn't find one, you would be right. The main motivation for wanting a king was to be like all the other nations around them.

How did Samuel receive this new request of the elders (verse 6)?

What did God clarify to Samuel that indicates to us what emotion Samuel was feeling because of the peoples' rejection (verse 7)?

Girlfriends, it is crucial that we learn something from God's answer to Samuel's hurt. Horrible situations happen in our lives that we do not deserve. In our humanness, we can become so wrapped up in the rejection of others that we start believing we are being punished by God through their actions toward us. Let me be quick to say that we must examine our hearts before God frequently to make sure that there is no offensive way in us (Psalm 139:23-24).

✳ If, however, the Spirit of God does not reveal that the problem lies with us, what may we be encouraged by in I Peter 4:13-14 as a possible cause for others' rejection?

God shone a light in Samuel's mind on the true reason why Israel had rejected him when he had done no wrong to anyone. I can almost hear the Lord saying, "Samuel, don't grieve for yourself. Grieve for Me, because *I am the One they have rejected, not you!*"

Is this a comfort to you in a difficult life situation you may be facing or have faced in the past involving rejection by others? Share here.

Have you ever wanted something simply because of its appearance and not necessarily because it was the right choice for you? Expound in the following areas:

Dating and/or marriage partner:

Something you couldn't afford:

Material possessions:

> Discontentment is a breeding ground for all things evil.

The prominent eighteenth century theologian, Matthew Henry, pointed out that God had a king for Israel that was after His own heart, if Israel would have been willing to wait for the king God would have given them [1]. They were not willing to wait.

What were some of the warnings Samuel gave to them about a king in verses 11-18? Underline the warnings that would have made you reconsider wanting an earthly king:

Still, Israel wouldn't be satisfied. An old man with a broken heart was now given the unenviable task of finding his own replacement. Maybe that has happened to you, too. Maybe in a friendship, maybe in a position at work. To be able to handle rejection with grace is amazing.

Note here where you and I might see the first signs of jealousy raising its ugly head even in this stage of the story.

My dear sisters, we cannot separate ourselves from Scripture. God promises that His Word will not go out and return void. There is a lesson for each one of us today.

Who do you most closely identify with today in your life experience—Samuel the rejected or the elders itching for something new without having really counted the cost? Please share why here:

The atmosphere in Israel was ripe for the ugly green monster of jealousy to raise its head: dissatisfaction with God's will, a God-appointed leader rejected, and a flippant people whose eyes were focused on what someone else had (pagan nations, in this case). Discontentment is a breeding ground for all things evil. Israel made a critical choice to rebel against God being her King. In the weeks to come, we are going to see what a huge mistake that decision would be.

Day Two: A Dire Warning Unheeded

We are going to spend one more day with Samuel today before he steps down from his position. Samuel is going to go peaceably, but not without a thorough chastisement of the people for their rejection of God as their King. This could not have been an easy thing for Samuel to do. Who wants to leave their position, even if they have been forced out of it unfairly, possibly leaving a bad taste in the mouths of those being left behind? I love elderly people. One thing they are not afraid of is warning those around them of the impending consequences of certain actions.

How does the Bible describe godly, elderly people? Match the following (paraphrased) Scriptures with their correct references:

We are to rise in respect of the elderly.   *Leviticus 19:32*

God Himself is the One who sustains.   *Psalm 92:14-15*
the elderly

We are not to speak disrespectfully   *Isaiah 46:4*
to the elderly.

The elderly continue to bear fruit   *I Timothy 5:1*
in their old age.

I lived in the country of Zaire, now the Democratic Republic of Congo, during my childhood and adolescent years. Anyone with gray hair was highly respected. Gray hair meant that the individual had survived the overwhelming odds of living past the age of forty-seven—the life expectancy of the country. There was an unspoken, but very real, code of conduct among the Congolese with those who were elderly. The grandparents were treated as royalty. An elderly man or woman's advice was to be listened to and thoughtfully considered. I never saw a hint of disrespect among family members with the aged—not unless those that were younger wanted to receive a severe tongue lashing. We Americans have a lot to learn from the Congolese family dynamic.

> An elderly man or woman's advice was to be listened to and thoughtfully considered.

Do you think our culture treats the elderly as Scripture has instructed us to? Why or why not?

For our study today, we need to go back to 1 Samuel 8. Let's back up a little to include yesterday's portion of Scripture for context as we read 1 Samuel 8:6-22.

43

What did the Lord want Samuel to do before He gave them an earthly king according to verse nine? Underline the correct answer.

punish them   plead with them

warn them   hide information from them

I want us to hear how strongly this verse reads in the original Hebrew. Sometimes the seriousness of the tone in which something is said gets lost when translated from one language to another. Here are some other instances where the same derivative of the word *warn* is used:

*"I will **summon** as my reliable witnesses…"*   Isaiah 8:2

*"For I **solemnly warned** your ancestors to obey me. I warned them again and again, ever since I delivered them out of Egypt until this very day."*
Jeremiah 11:7

*"Today I **invoke heaven and earth** as a witness against you that I have set life and death, blessing and curse, before you. Therefore choose life so that you and your descendants may live!"*   Deuteronomy 30:19

The Lord was going to give Israel a king, but not before the people heard what their decision would bring down on their heads. The Lord was going to call this day of rejection of Him as a witness against Israel. As much as we might deny the truth, God always gives us warnings before we sin. Always. Israel would have their way, but not without fully knowing and accepting the consequences for their actions.

> *What verse in this passage we just read indicates that the people were fully aware of these consequences? Write it out here:*

Briefly skim 1 Samuel 8:11-18 again. Imagine that you were one in the crowd that day. What three warnings would been awful enough to have considered changing your mind about replacing God with an earthly king?

1)

2)

3)

As much as we might deny the truth, God always gives us warnings before we sin. Always.

Why do you think the people of Israel were so stubborn?

It is so easy to look at the Israelites and point a judgmental finger at them. If you are familiar with the story of the kings of Israel, you will remember that this day's decision was the origin of unbelievable destruction. What the people could not see that day was how grieved God's heart would be over their love affair with pagan nations. Their rejection of Him that day would ultimately lead to one horrible king after another, with a few godly ones in between. Israel would ultimately split over a civil war and cease to be a united kingdom. And tragically, the nation's two kingdoms would be exiled for their sin.

Name a time when you deliberately disobeyed God's commands for your life. How would you characterize your emotional health after making that decision? (e.g. peaceful, stressful, etc...)

What is the lesson here for us? I want us to think about a time when we deliberately disobeyed God, having been warned that there would be a price to pay for our rebellion. The stiff-necked betrayal of God's people is what continues to plague followers of Christ today. We do not have a king or a judge over us now, but we still have God-given authority through the Scriptures. As believers in Christ, we are to be in submission to our pastors and his staff as well as lay people of our congregations.

My dear sister, are you still in the pit? God's will often looks unappealing compared to our own selfish desires. A life of obedience to God's commands can seem to be a life of restrictions with little fun. Nothing could be further from the truth. The pathway of obedience leads to joy, peace, and sweet sleep at night. Still, if we insist on our own way, God will relent. He will give us what we think we want. And then, after we realize the miry pit we have placed ourselves in, He will rescue when we repent and turn away from that behavior.

If the Holy Spirit is prompting you to face something you need to repent of, please use the space below to write out your confession. This will be for no one's eyes except yours and the eyes of your God who loves you so much.

The stage was set for the dawn of a new type of ruler. God had been rejected as Israel's king, their leader Samuel has been profoundly hurt, and Israel was flippant about the burden about to be thrust on their shoulders because of their rebellion. Is it any wonder that there was going to be many a bump along the way?

The pathway of obedience leads to joy, peace and sweet sleep at night.

❋ **Day Three:** The Donkey Wrangler

"And these beginnings [of Saul] would have been very hopeful and promising if it had not been that the sin of the people was the spring [board] of this great affair." [2]
– Matthew Henry

Israel had deposed her righteous leader, Samuel, and waited for the announcement of her first king. Let's refresh our memories.

What were the three reasons Israel rejected Samuel as her leader (see 1 Samuel 8:5)?

1)

2)

3)

Some distance away from the commotion of Samuel and the people, two men set out on a mission, neither one realizing how life-changing the trip would be for one of them. Samuel has been the main character of our study this week thus far. From this point on, the rejected judge will fade into the background of the story only to be seen briefly.

I was a voracious reader at age ten when my family became missionaries to Congo. We did not have a library nearby to provide a variety in books so I read the same ones repeatedly. Hands down, my favorite books were biographical in nature. If the story was true and exciting, that made it all the more enjoyable. Scripture is a treasure in providing us with an inside look at the workings of an extraordinary God moving in the lives of ordinary people. Our first introduction to these people can be less than memorable if we did not realize that the Author lived and breathed in the written words.

Let's read 1 Samuel 9:1-20 and be introduced to the main protagonist of our study. How does 1 Samuel 9:1-2 describe Kish and his son Saul?

The community that I lived in during my high school years was very small. The number of students from seventh to twelfth grade barely numbered two hundred altogether. Although we were on the African continent, the characteristics of an American small town were very evident. Perhaps some of us grew up in a thriving metropolis or urban setting. It doesn't matter. Every small community (youth group, sports team, choir, Sunday school class) has its "star." This is the person that is looked to as being "head and shoulders above the rest."

Scripture is a treasure in providing us with an inside look at the workings of an extraordinary God moving in the lives of ordinary people.

Let's have some fun. I know exactly who was "head and shoulders" above the rest of the crowd in my high school and all those smaller groups.

Give the first name of the person who was considered above the rest of the crowd and why he or she was given that honor (athletic, intelligent, charismatic, physical attractiveness, etc.):

No matter how close or far away in time or distance we are from those days, we can instantly think of the person who was our school's hero or heroine. I can bet that the reasons that the person was given that position in our eyes was, almost without exception, due to some quality that human beings esteem, not necessarily because he or she possessed the qualities God esteems.

✳ What is the danger of exalting someone based on his/her outward appearance and/or charisma?

What was the reason for the long trip taken by Saul and his father's servant according to 1 Samuel 9:3-4?

When they couldn't find what they were looking for, what did the servant suggest to Saul that they do (verse 6)?

What was Saul's response to his servant's suggestion in verse 7?

Have you ever known anyone who looked to money as the solution for everything? It is so interesting to me that Saul's servant knew that the man of God, Samuel, lived nearby. Yet Saul was unwilling to seek out Samuel's wisdom because he did not have any money in his pockets. It would seem apparent that Saul was unfamiliar with the person of Samuel by his response to the servant's suggestion. Only after learning that the servant had some silver in his possession was Saul ready to find this man of God.

If Samuel had not decided that obedience to the true King of Israel was more important than his pride, Saul could have found himself at the receiving end of a curse rather than the blessing he was about to hear.

Our God does not need anything we give Him. He is the owner of everything. Share an experience when money really helped you out of the difficulty of an unforeseen circumstance and when it did not.

What did the young women inform Saul and his servant about Samuel's presence in their town according to 1 Samuel 9:12-14? Circle all that Samuel was going to do there:

Offer a sacrifice.   Eat a special meal with invited guests.

Receive his wages.

Looking at 1 Samuel 9:15-17, how did Samuel know who Saul was as he came toward Samuel?

Last week in our lesson on Hannah, we discovered that every Israelite male was required by Levitical law to appear before the Lord during three annual festivals of praise and sacrifice (see Deuteronomy 16:16-17). Saul and his family should have been at those festivals. Saul should have known who Samuel was, even if he had never personally met him before.

What do 1 Samuel 3:19-21; 4:1 tell us about Samuel's standing in Israel? Put a check mark next to all that God had blessed Samuel with:

        God's favor since boyhood.

        All of Israel knew Samuel as a prophet.

        God revealed Himself to Israel through Samuel.

        Samuel's words were known to all Israel.

In other words, Samuel was well-known to all Israel! He was the human being that Israel as a nation had looked to for guidance and spiritual insight.

Briefly reread 1 Samuel 9:15-21. The Word of God has allowed us to be in on the anguish Samuel had to wrestle through privately as he faced Israel's rejection of his lifelong service to them as a nation. In between the painful revelation of God to Samuel in verses 15-17 and Samuel's obedient actions to God in verses 19-21 was Saul's reaction to Samuel in verse 18.

How would you characterize Saul's reaction in this verse?
Circle your answer:

Saul honored Samuel.　　Saul recognized Samuel.

Saul was clueless.

Have you ever had to relinquish something to someone who had no idea how much it cost you personally? How did that make you feel?

Girlfriends, this is real life. Saul could not possibly know how difficult his ignorant response was for Samuel to hear. If Samuel had not decided that obedience to the true King of Israel was more important than his pride, Saul could have found himself at the receiving end of a curse rather than the blessing he was about to hear.

Although Saul was completely clueless as to what God had revealed to the man of God he and his servant were looking for, Samuel knew what each step towards Saul would mean—the end of a life he had always known. With each footprint in the dust, life was changing forever. It could not have been an easy walk. Maybe you have taken a similar walk in life—one that you knew you had to make, but dreaded each step you took. Those footsteps might have led you to:

- divorce court
- the funeral of a family member or friend
- a painful conversation with a family member or friend
- a new home in a new town or country
- a demotion in a job

Obeying God and anointing Saul as king had to be one of the hardest acts of the will Samuel ever had to carry out in his lifetime. He had been in faithful service to Jehovah as soon as he was weaned from his mother. Now he had been cast off by those he had served faithfully his whole life.

Sometimes God gives us what we want. Sometimes that is the worst thing possible and the farthest thing from what would be the best for us. Saul was chosen at a time when Israel's apathy toward following the law of the Lord was at a feverish pitch. Israel wanted a king just like the nations around them. Sadly, as we will see in the next several weeks, they got just what they wanted, but certainly *not* what they needed.

Sometimes God gives us what we want. Sometimes that is the worst thing possible and the farthest thing from what would be the best for us.

Day Four: Humble Beginnings

In our last lesson, we left a clueless Saul stammering in front of Samuel, the one who had faithfully led Israel only to be rejected by the people when he became old. As a quick review, let's go back to 1 Samuel 9:19-20.

List the three things Samuel revealed to Saul that Samuel could not possibly have known without God's revelation:

1)

2)

3)

This is where we see the incredible mercy of God. Remember, Saul would never have sought Samuel out had the servant not had the "fee" that Saul believed Samuel would require for the knowledge of finding the donkeys. But God had already known what was going to happen according to 1 Samuel 9:15. God had prepared everything for Saul to step into the kingship, even though when stacked up next to Samuel, arguably, Saul did not deserve it.

Has that ever happened to you? Did something you worked really hard for go to someone whose moral character you questioned? Did it seem as though God had just laid out the red carpet for them and knocked down mountains He made you climb? Share here.

Had Saul remembered in later years who put him on the throne, perhaps he could have saved himself and his family heartbreak later on.

Saul, the donkey wrangler, has had the encounter of his life, though he does not yet know it. He thought the journey from home would merely include a sightseeing trip within the borders of the tribe of Benjamin to which he belonged. But those donkeys could not be found and Saul, thinking he could pay to have the seer of Israel "divine" where the beasts might be, ended up being placed in the seat of honor at Samuel's banquet.

Samuel has assured Saul that the donkeys have been found and that all of Israel is turned toward him in their hearts. Saul has not worked for the position about to be given to him. Circle his response to Samuel's words in 1 Samuel 9:21:

Boastful   Humble   Angry   Immediate acceptance

It's very important that we take a moment to stop here and see Saul's response. Later on in the study, we will see this response in great contrast to what Saul becomes. I do not know the motive behind the humble response, but Saul clearly feels inadequate for the job, even if he did come from money and was head and shoulders taller than everyone else. Although he stood out physically, he would rather stay in the background.

When my husband turned thirty, I had a group of our friends secretly meet at a park within walking distance of our apartment. One couple came over under the guise of borrowing our charcoal grill for their own cookout. After we got to the park, we passed another couple on their way to the place we had designated for the party. We briefly conversed while I sweated in my tennis shoes hoping the secret wouldn't be ruined. Twenty minutes after we left them, I casually turned us toward the designated spot. As we approached the table, I could see that everyone was in place. I walked us toward the group and, on my cue, everyone shouted, "Surprise! Happy birthday, Rob!" My husband looked like a deer caught in headlights. As we were munching on our burgers, cooked on our grill, he turned to me for the third time and said, "Is this really for me? I can't believe it!"

Has something happened unexpectedly to you that resulted in you being the center of attention? If yes, what were some of the emotions that you experienced? Were they all happy or comfortable?

But the surprises were not to end there. Go back to 1 Samuel 9:25-27 and list the order of events that Saul experienced with Samuel:

We need to see something very important in verse 27. The message that Samuel was about to relate to the shocked guest of honor came from God Himself. Had Saul remembered in later years who put him on the throne, perhaps he could have saved himself and his family heartbreak later on. Scripture is silent on the exact conversation that Samuel had with Saul into the night and the next day, but Israel's desire for a king had been fulfilled.

I firmly believe that Samuel was faced with one the greatest challenges of his life—to honor someone whom he did not think deserved to be honored and place Saul in the highest seat at the banquet. His graciousness to Saul gave no hint of the inward struggle Samuel may have felt over Saul being given the best cut of meat.

My daddy always sat at the head of the table. Before we moved to Congo, we had a rectangular shaped table. It didn't matter which end of the table he sat, my mom always sat opposite him and we children were seated on the sides of the table between them. Wherever Daddy sat was the head of the table. No question. His was the seat of authority. I never felt that it should be any other way. My father never pushed his authority down any of our throats. He gained our respect. My mother was very careful to encourage Dad's position as head of the household. It never entered my mind to begrudge my father the seat of authority at the table.

But I have been at other tables where I have fumed over who was in the seat of honor, questioning the person's right to be there. I find that it is by no mistake or coincidence that Samuel was the organizer of the dinner party. God had called Samuel to die to his own will even more.

With that in mind, answer the following questions as we look at 1 Samuel 9:22-24 and answer the following questions:

Who brought Saul and his servant into the hall?

Where was Saul seated and who gave him that place?

It is one thing when we believe that the other person deserves the honor, but what about when we question what in the world God is doing?

What portion of meat had been laid aside for Saul?

When was this portion of meat set aside for Saul?

We need to stop right here and learn something about the Jewish culture that may not be a part of ours. Listen to what Matthew Henry points out in his commentary about the symbolism of the table that Saul was honored at:

"Samuel treats him not as a common person, but a person of quality and distinction, to prepare both him and the people for what was to follow. Two marks of honour he put upon him:

1. He set him in the best place, as more honourable than any other of the guests, to whom he said, Give this man place, (Lu. 14:9). Though we may suppose the magistrates were there, who in their own city would claim precedency, yet the master of the feast made Saul and his servant too (who, if Saul was a king, must be respected as his prime minister of state) sit in the chief place, (v. 22) Note, Civil respects must be paid to those who in civil things have the precedency given them by the divine providence.

He presented him with the best dish, which, having had notice from heaven the day before of his coming (v. 16), he had designed for him, and ordered the cook to secure for him, when he gave orders for inviting the guests and making preparation for them. And what should this precious dish be, which was so very carefully reserved for the king-elect? One would expect it should be something very nice and delicate. No, it was a plain shoulder of mutton (v. 23,24).

The right shoulder of the peace-offerings was to be given to the priests, who were God's receivers (Lev. 7:32); the next in honour to that was the left shoulder, which probably was always allotted to those that sat at the upper end of the table, and was wont to be Samuel's mess at other times; so that his giving it to Saul now was an implicit resignation of his place to him. Some observe a significancy in this dish. The shoulder denotes strength, and the breast, which some think went with it, denotes affection: he that was king had the government upon his shoulder, for he must bear the weight of it; and the people in his bosom, for they must be dear to him. "³

I believe that the wrestling and grief of Samuel over his ousted position as the leader of Israel under God had been dealt with before the day that Samuel and Saul dined together. My beloved sisters, what would happen if we could do the same—if wrestling with our carnal nature and finding contentment in our unmet desires was settled before God so that we were enabled to treat others with the same honor He does? It is one thing when we believe that the other person deserves the honor, but what about when we question what in the world God is doing? That is the stuff faith is made of. What truth will quell the anger and the hurt in those times we must blindly trust and obey God's direction, even when bowing our will to His confuses us to the core? I believe the answer is found in Isaiah 49:4-5 (New International Version)

> *But I said, "I have labored to no purpose;*
> *I have spent my strength in vain and for nothing.*
> *Yet what is due me is in the LORD's hand,*
> *and my reward is with my God."*
> *And now the LORD says—*
> *he who formed me in the womb to be his servant*
> *to bring Jacob back to him*
> *and gather Israel to himself,*
> *for I am honored in the eyes of the LORD*
> *and my God has been my strength*

❋ According to these verses, where is what is due me?

What else belonging to me is with my God?

Who honors me and who has been my strength (or can be, by my choice)?

So often, our eyes believe only that which we can see. We forget that what is unseen is eternal. Whatever struggle Samuel may have had with God over what was happening, he ultimately made the decision to obey and leave his reward with the One he wanted to be honored by more than anyone else. When things seem so unfair after we have done everything right, we have to remember Who is keeping score. In the end, obedience always wins out, even if we have to wrestle through the experience kicking and screaming. Obedience puts us in the seat of honor when we have to honor someone as an act of sheer obedience to God. Samuel might have eaten a lesser portion of meat that day, but the true King's favor made it the most sumptuous fare he had ever tasted.

Obedience puts us in the seat of honor when we have to honor someone as an act of pure obedience to God.

Day Five: A Prophet's Final Instructions

I can hardly wait to dive into today's lesson. I hope that by this point in the study, you have had some "a-ha" moments. I used to overlook the humanness of Biblical characters exalted in Scripture because of the supernatural ways God used them. I thought these individuals always chose to do the right thing. I failed to look closely enough. Because of that, I would leave my quiet time with little hope, convinced that there was no way that God could ever use me in the ways He used some of them.

Eleven years ago, my husband brought into our house the single-most revolutionary spiritual tool I have ever laid my hands and mind on—the *One Year Chronological Bible* published by Tyndale [4]. I had never had the courage to study much of the Bible before that time—period. I would realize with dismay, as each Sunday rolled around, that I had not cracked the Bible a single time since the last Sunday I had sat in church. I am not excusing my lack of self-discipline, but I have come to realize that I was genuinely intimidated by Scripture. My lack of knowledge made me come to the conclusion that I was a hopeless case when it came to understanding what certain passages meant. Spell it out for me and tell me what it means. That's what I wanted. The order of the Old Testament was impossibly confusing. Who were these prophets called Obadiah, Nahum, and Habakkuk anyway? And there was no way I was going to swim in the quicksand of ignorance and crack open Revelation!

I cannot say this more strongly, sisters. If we are only students of certain books of the Bible, we are not receiving the whole counsel of God. We cannot understand New Testament teachings in their fullness without uncovering the foundation of those teachings in the Old Testament. Satan would like nothing better than to keep us from the Word of God through intimidation. We cannot let our personal fears or insecurities keep us from Scripture. When we feel as though we are not intelligent enough to understand what is on those pages, we have the wonderful Counselor to go to with our questions. Our God is so generous. He never faults us for not having wisdom of our own and gladly gives His own when we have the courage to ask for insight (James 1:5).

Please read Psalm 138:2 and fill in the following blanks:

"…for _____ have _____ above _____ things your _____ and your _____."

> If we are only students of certain books of the Bible, we are not receiving the whole counsel of God.

All Scripture is God-breathed and useful to us.   *Joshua 1:8*

Jesus said that He had not come to   *Psalm 119:105*
abolish the law, but to fulfill it.

Without the law, I would not know what sin was.   *Matthew 5:17*

God's Word is a lamp to my feet and a   *2 Timothy 3:16*
light to my path.

Meditating on God's law helps us to be   *Romans 7:12*
prosperous and successful.

Have you ever read the entire Bible from Genesis to Revelation? Why or why not?

Today's lesson is going to be an example of the value of knowing God's character and others through portions of Scripture outside of 1 Samuel 10. Buckle your seat belts and get ready for a ride through God's Word today.

The first place we are going to stop is 1 Samuel 10:1-8. Please read these verses carefully and take note of anything that jumps off the page at you with this as your focus:

How could Saul know that his becoming king was God's doing?

Verse one shows Samuel's stellar character again. What two things did he do for Saul?

We are going to discover the importance of the anointing oil. Thus far in the history of Israel, this oil was only used in connection with the high priest of Israel.

Write down the significance of the oil in each of the following passages:

Exodus 29:7-9:

Exodus 29:21:

Leviticus 10:7:

Leviticus 21:11-12:

Saul was not the high priest, but he was the king of Israel, an office so sacred that the king's ordination was to be sealed with the anointing oil, known for its solemn significance. If Saul had any idea of the seriousness of what Samuel was doing, he may have refused the oil bath on his head. Saul was ordained, consecrated and dedicated to the office of kingship. The warning he received at his anointing should have left no doubt in his mind how very serious and sacred his position over Israel was in the eyes of God. If that was not enough to satisfy Saul's wondering if all Samuel was doing was to be believed, Samuel gave him three specific signs as proofs that he was speaking the truth.

Satan would like nothing better than to keep us from the Word of God through intimidation.

What were those signs in verses 1 Samuel 10:2-6?

1)

2)

3)

Without getting an understanding as to what prophesying means in this context of the story, we will struggle with troubling events later in our study. Again, I go to Matthew Henry for the explanation.

"These prophets were not (as it should seem) divinely inspired to foretell things to come, nor did God reveal himself to them by dreams and visions, but they employed themselves in the study of the law, in instructing their neighbors, and in the acts of piety, especially in praising God, wherein they were wonderfully assisted and enlarged by the Spirit of God. It was happy for Israel that they had not only prophets, but companies of prophets, who gave them good instructions and set them good examples, and helped very much to keep up religion among them... The Spirit of God, by his ordinances, changes men, wonderfully transforms them; Saul, by praising God in the communion of saints, became another man, but whether a new man or no may be questioned." [4]

In other words, this example of prophesying emphasized praise and worship rather than predicting the future. I had always assumed that one who prophesied was a divinely inspired person who foretold dreams and visions and things to come. Matthew Henry's perspective lends a different meaning to prophesying in this context. Let me say here that no one can possibly know what was truly in Saul's heart at the moment this third sign played out in his life. Only the Holy Spirit can truly know our hearts (1 Corinthians 2:11) when we worship with others. I remember attending youth camp when I was in high school. I came back from that week encouraged and determined to change the world for Christ. I believed with my whole heart that I was going to feel as in love with Jesus from then on as I did when I made that commitment at the altar at youth camp. My tears and sincerity were real. However, without that encouraging environment, I soon fell back into my old patterns.

Matthew Henry's explanation for the prophesying that Saul did here denotes not a foretelling of future events, but a lavish praise service in which Saul participated in with other worshipers from the company of the prophets. Saul had an opportunity to become a different person by joining in with those who had spent their lives making God's Word the source of their praise helps me to reconcile Saul's behavior here in light of future events. Was Saul only caught up in the emotion produced in him by being in the company of those who made praise their way of life, or was he actually being transformed by the worship he offered? Only time would tell.

In your opinion, what is the difference between a spiritual "high" and a true worship encounter that brings lasting change. Give an example in your life experience of both.

We have been ordained and consecrated by God Himself for extraordinary lives. But with the extraordinary opportunities that this may bring, we must be diligent to never leave the presence of the God who gave those opportunities to us. Sometimes we get caught up in the emotion of worship rather than in true worship that demands a heart change. We can fool ourselves and everyone around us by getting caught up in a group of people who are praising when our own hearts are far from it. The danger of this is that it is just a spiritual high that we are destined to fall from because the change is not real. The heart change can last only if we continue being diligent in the reading of the Scriptures and living out a life of praise.

Hard times are bound to come and we will then show what our worship has produced in our lives.

Saul has been told to look for three specific signs to come true that very day to confirm everything Samuel has told him. Don't you and I wish we had it that good? I would love for God to make His will so clear to me about taking on a new level of leadership. At this point in time, Saul had everything he could possibly need to rule Israel well.

What was to be the occasion of their next meeting and when according to verse 8?

Samuel and Saul part ways here for a week, but only after they establish a tradition between the two of them. Samuel would meet Saul at the designated time and place and prepare a sacrifice to the Lord for him. We are given every reason to believe that Saul obeyed the instructions this time. Stick that fact in the back of your mind to recall later. We are going to see the importance of waiting in obedience as it relates to this tradition between the two of them later on. So the deposed judge moves over for the new king of Israel. Hang on, girlfriends! We are in for quite an adventure in the weeks ahead. I am so thankful that you are my companion!

When we feel as though we are not intelligent enough to understand what is on those pages (of Scripture), we have the wonderful Counselor to go to with our questions.

Portraits of a King

After three and a half years of anticipation of being reunited with family and friends in the United States, our family boarded a Swiss Air 747 jet for the first leg of the journey home. My parents had decided to include a family vacation as part of the trip. Our first stop was Geneva, Switzerland. We spent three days in the chalet town of Beatenburg. The Swiss Alps towered in the background of our accommodations. Snow was still on the ground—something we had not seen in almost four years. Although the snow was beautiful, the sleepy tranquility of the tiny Swiss town was one that I was ready to leave on the appointed day and board another flight to London, England.

London was anything but boring. Centuries older than our capital, Washington D.C., history was everywhere. After the excitement of riding a red double-decker bus and visiting Westminster Abbey, the highlight of the trip, in my opinion, was the day we saw Buckingham Palace and the Tower of London. The crown jewels were kept in the Tower and were dazzling beyond anything I could ever imagine. Beautiful oil paintings lined the walls of former kings and queens who had ruled the British Isles. The only way for my family to get an idea of what those who had lived before the middle of the nineteenth century looked like was through these old portraits.

In much the same way, the story of Saul can best be understood through the portraits of the man in his early kingship given to us in the various chapters of Scripture in this week's study. We are going to see a dramatic change from the beginning days of his reign as a humble, even timid, man to a warrior, fully established in his role as ruler over God's beloved people, Israel.

Day One: Instructions for a King

My in-laws had graciously given my husband and me money to fly our family to Savannah, Georgia from our home in the Chicago area. Our two children were under the age of three and did not do well with traveling in the car. I was so grateful to know that the length of the upcoming trip was only two and a half hours instead of the eighteen hours that would normally be required on the road by vehicle. I thanked my mother-in-law profusely and almost pinched myself with happiness.

What happened next is vague in my mind because the experience caused such a shot of adrenalized fear to flow through my veins. The tickets for the four of us were going to cost over $500. Somehow, I double-booked nonrefundable tickets! Instead of ordering three tickets for Rob, Chase, and myself (my daughter was young enough to fly as a lap child), I ordered six! I owed the airlines over one thousand dollars with no way to get a refund for the unnecessary tickets. My knees started shaking so badly I had to sit on the floor. I had just started becoming more disciplined in my Bible reading and begged God to intervene through my sobs.

"Oh, Jesus! How am I going to get out of this? We do not have the money to pay for what I have just done! Help me, Lord, please help me out of this mess I have made!"

Girlfriends, who of us has not made a colossal mistake of which we can see no way out? I don't know what is more terrifying—realizing a mistake I have made immediately or learning about my blunder slowly over time. I realized, as I sat in the muck of the despair of my costly mistake, that only a miraculous intervention would rectify what I had done.

Share a mistake that you could not see your way out of without a miracle happening. What was the outcome?

My beloved sister, you and I have so much more than a Savior in Jesus Christ. What names does Isaiah 9:6 attribute to Christ:

Wonderful _____

Mighty _____

Everlasting _____

Prince of _____

Identify a life situation where you have personally experienced each of those names above to be true:

WEEK THREE • PORTRAITS OF A KING

I have known God to be my counselor...

I have known God to be mighty...

I have known God to be my Father...

I have experienced God as my peace...

Not able to fill out one or two of the names with a life experience? Do not despair, my sweet friend! That is the stuff that faith is made of! Our lives with our heavenly Father are marathons, not sprints. If you have not fully experienced Him in some way above, I can assure you, on the authority of God's Word, that He is all that He says He is.

There are times, however, when we do not utilize the blessing of Him being everything we need. Israel had not asked for God's counsel as to whether they should ask Samuel to step down as their leader. Neither had they chosen to remember that He was mightier than any human being. They rejected His everlasting tenderness as their Father, and were going to soon forfeit His peace as a result of the decision to anoint a human being as king over them. Right now, however, the people were giddy with their choice of the tall, dark, and handsome man that stood head and shoulders above all the rest of them. Their decision seemed flawless without a hint of foolishness.

> What can we foolishly believe when God does not seem to immediately react to our disobedience according to Psalm 50:21?

God's silence on a matter does not always equal His approval.

God's silence on a matter does not always equal His approval. The frightening truth about our easily deceived hearts is that you and I can become prideful when we think our disobedience goes unnoticed by Him. We can arrogantly think, I must be right. God hasn't struck me dead yet! Girlfriends, God's timing is not our own! He is as merciful as He is just. Although we may be tempted to think mercy and judgment are not related, judgment over the sin that will destroy us and others is, in many cases, His mercy to us. We will do well to remember that during those times we have not heeded the conviction of the Holy Spirit about a matter and have acted out of rebellion as the Israelites had in asking for Saul as their king.

What does Colossians 2:13-14 promise that Christ did for us while we were still dead in our sins?

God is always big enough to work inside of our mistakes. No matter what the size of the problem we have gotten ourselves into, His ability to rescue us is bigger still. In the middle of the mess of our lives, our God has a plan of redemption for us. Although Israel had rebelled against Jehovah in asking for a king, God had given a way for His wayward children to thrive despite their rebellious choice. Centuries before Saul's coronation, God had given a plan of hope for this very situation laid down in the law He had given to Moses. Those who were students of the words of Jehovah would have been familiar with the following passage:

Let's read Deuteronomy 17:14-20 to find out how Israel's king was to govern Jehovah's people.

Was God caught off guard by the peoples' request that day according to this passage? What word in verse 14 gives you the answer?

What was to be the nationality of the king according to verse 15?

Circle three of the four things he must not do according to vv. 16-17:

Have many horses   Have great amounts of gold or silver

Take many wives   Not make treaties with other nations.

Let's stop right there. What do two out of three choices have to do with each other—wealth. Great wealth has the capacity to make us feel superior to others. We can forget that it is God Himself who has given us the ability to acquire wealth through talents He has bestowed on us or through prospering our families.

Without being dishonoring to anyone, have you known someone who felt superior to others because they were wealthy? Write the first initial of that person here. Were you impressed or repulsed by this person's behavior?

God is always big enough to work inside of our mistakes.

Not many individuals can rightly handle power and wealth. Girlfriends, it is a very rare individual who can step into the head-spinning position that fame and riches bring and come out unscathed. Look at Hollywood's victims. One starlet recently complained that she cannot have a normal life because she has no privacy. Fame and fortune often come with a terrible price. Anonymity is a gift, although the jealous heart cannot see that truth.

Have you ever wanted fame or fortune or been jealous of someone who had it? Which core issue from week one do you think could have been the cause of your jealousy in that situation?

What was the key for the earthly king to rule with justice according to Deuteronomy 17:18-19?

How often was the king to read this and where was it to be?

What was the promised result if the king followed the Lord in this manner?

Do we see that the Israelites had a way out by digging into the ancient law of Moses? More importantly, do we realize that their choice to obey God's Word is ours, too? My sweet sister, are you smack dab in the middle of the consequences of that mistake? Perhaps you are painfully aware of how greatly you have ignored the Word of God. Or maybe you are just starting on this glorious, difficult journey with Christ, and no one has ever told you how important God's Word is to your spiritual health. One of the greatest benefits we have as children of our heavenly Father is realizing, through meditating on God's Word, that Jesus Christ is more than just a Savior to us. Whatever pit we find ourselves in, our God is able to rescue us there. The way out of the pit is through the power of God's Word lived out obediently in our lives.

Saul was chosen to be king in an atmosphere fraught with rebellion and disobedience. But that did not have to be the doom of Israel. The reluctant ruler had the choice to become a righteous ruler through his own daily meditation on God's Word. If Saul had chosen that path, he and all Israel would have seen God's mercy triumph over the judgment of their sin.

I despise loose ends. I left you wondering how my issue was resolved with the double-booked plane tickets I had purchased. After fervently praying, I resigned myself to talk with whomever I needed to at the airline to plead my

sad predicament. I mentally prepared my best heart-wrenching case. To my amazement, the story was not needed. The airline that I had called back was going on strike and had made allowances for ticket refunds for a certain block of time. Our vacation fell within those dates. The airline cheerfully refunded the full amount of the tickets, no questions asked. I danced a happy jig of ecstatic praise the rest of the evening to my God who had heard my cry and rescued me.

Oh, my sweet friend, God's Word has absolutely changed my life. His Word is the biggest delight of my life. It has brought me such healing in so many places—places I didn't even know needed healing. I respected Christ before, I was even afraid of Him and His wrath, but I have since fallen in love with Him. The most profound wonder is that loving Him doesn't take any love away from anyone else in my life. It's the only relationship I have that gives me more to give to everyone else. I can never get to the bottom of Him. He is the most exciting, creative, beautiful, romantic, holy Being I have ever encountered and I am crazy about Him.

Jesus Christ is more than a Savior to me. He is my everything. I pray that He is for you, too. Life is hopeless without Him and hard, but wonderful, with Him. Let's praise Him for being more than a Savior to us in the space below.

God's Word has absolutely changed my life.

65

Day Two: A Reluctant Ruler

I am eager to get back into the story of our protagonist.

Before we start on today's lesson, briefly summarize what has happened to Saul up to this point in our story.

Although the Bible is silent on the subject, what kind of emotion do you think Saul might have been experiencing at this point?

I had a very lonely sophomore year of high school. The result of that experience was my feeling rejected and like a loser. On a whim, I tried out for the high school play. I honestly did not think I would get a significant role at all. I would have been all right with an ensemble part. I walked up to the board in the locker area where the cast was displayed to find out I had gotten the lead role! Yes, I was Dorothy Gale of Kansas destined to wear the ruby red slippers. You could have knocked me over with a feather! Never in my wildest dreams did I expect that! I had dreamed about it, but now that the role was really mine, instead of feeling exhilaration, my overwhelming emotion was... *is this some kind of a joke?*

I have to believe that Saul was completely overwhelmed by what had happened to him in the last day or two. The donkey wrangler had begun the journey looking for his father's animals and had, unwittingly, walked smack dab into his future. With that as the context of the possible emotional state of Saul, let's read 1 Samuel 10:9-26 for today's lesson.

Let's take verses 9-16 and mull them over together as we answer the following questions:

What happened to Saul in verse 9? Circle all that apply:

He found the lost donkeys.   The three signs were fulfilled.

God changed Saul's heart.

I came to accept the gift of salvation through Jesus Christ when I was five years old. What happens to us the moment we are saved out of our old life through our acceptance of Christ according to the following verses?

2 Corinthians 5:17

The donkey wrangler had begun the journey looking for his father's animals and had, unwittingly, walked smack dab into his future.

John 5:24

Romans 6:4

Romans 8:1-2

The Bible declares that at the moment of salvation, we have a new heart given to us. Although I could not fully comprehend what these verses meant when I was five years old, the fact remained that I now had the ability to become a new person experientially.

I come from a very musical family. All three of my siblings have made their livelihoods from their musical abilities. My sister has told me more than once that I had the raw talent to be able to do what she and our brothers have done. However, instead of being energized at the thought of performing like the three of them were, waves of nausea would sweep over me at the thought of others hearing my voice. As a result, I never capitalized on the potential that I may have had to develop my voice at a level that was profitable for me as my siblings have.

God fully equipped Saul with a new heart that day. The choice was Saul's what he was going to do with that heart, just as it was my choice whether I would train my voice to sing. We each have been given the promise of abundant life in Christ while living on this sin-sick planet. The choice is ours, however, whether we will take Him up on making that a reality in our lives by choosing obedience and wholehearted devotion to Christ or never seeing the promise fulfilled by becoming complacent in our Christian walk.

Saul had everything he needed at this point in our study to experience the difference between merely being told by Samuel that he would be a different person with a new heart and experiencing that promise as a reality in his life. The choice was Saul's to believe God was equipping him for the kingship or to cling to his old way of life lived out of a heart of fear. Saul's choice is yours and mine, too. We can miss the abundant life because we never believe that we have been given a new heart through Christ to live an extraordinary life of purpose to which He has called us. The difference between never realizing the reality of our new heart and living out a life full of God's power and overcoming our timidity is whether we believe God has equipped us or not.

> The Bible declares that at the moment of salvation, we have a new heart given to us.

Sweet sisters, our God prepares us for the things He wants us to do by changing our hearts. Has God ever asked you to do something you dreaded and changed your heart to be able to do it? Share here.

In 1 Samuel 10:10-13, what was Saul doing and what was the reaction of those who saw him participating in it?

If we don't stop, we are going to miss something huge that is going to give us another clue about the kind of man Saul had been known to be in his hometown. The people who were commenting on this strange turn in Saul were those who had known him before. Remember Matthew Henry's explanation of prophesying here. Prophesying in this verse does not mean someone who is foretelling the future, but one who is praising God and was familiar with the Scriptures. I think it is necessary to understand that this behavior that Saul was exhibiting was one that those who knew him had not seen before. Saul's spiritual experience in these verses raised questions in the minds of those who watched him so that they even said, "What is this that has happened to the son of Kish? Is Saul also among the prophets?"

I am not saying at all that God cannot radically change a person's heart. But we must remember something very important. Those in the Old Testament did not have the Holy Spirit as we do now. What reality did those who lived before Christ's death have to deal with as a consequence of their unconfessed sin?

Let's look up the following Scriptures for the answer to that question:

Psalm 51:11

Isaiah 63:10

Now let's contrast that reality with the new role of the Holy Spirit as a result of Christ's death and resurrection:

Romans 5:5

Ephesians 1:13-14

Ephesians 4:30

Living on this side of the cross, we will never have to plead with God to not take His Holy Spirit away from us as King David did. We can grieve the Holy Spirit. We can quench the Holy Spirit. But if we have accepted Jesus Christ as our Lord and Savior we are sealed by the Holy Spirit forever until the day we go to heaven. He does not come and go like He did before Christ's death and resurrection.

Glance back at 1 Samuel 10:14-16. This is a completely subjective question, but why do you think Saul did not tell his uncle about what Samuel had relayed to him?

I wonder if Saul realized that the praise service was over and reality was staring him in the face. The signs given to Saul through Samuel had all come true and he had done something completely out of character with the company of prophets.

What insight does Proverbs 17:28 provide as a possible explanation for someone's silence?

Only time would tell if the changed man had really made a change.

We do not have enough information on Saul at this point. Scripture does not specifically give the reason Saul did not share this momentous life event that had just happened to him with his uncle. Not to be too harsh on Saul, I do think that there may have been true humility or just fear of being laughed at by his uncle as the reason for Saul's silence. Only time would tell if the changed man had really made a change.

Saul was chosen to be king in an atmosphere fraught with rebellion and disobedience. But that did not have to be the doom of Israel. Saul had the choice to become a righteous ruler through his own daily meditation on God's Word. The choice was Saul's whether he and all Israel would see God's mercy triumph over the judgment of their sin. Would the reluctant ruler prove to be a fool or a new man empowered by God's Spirit? The weeks to come will answer that question for us.

Day Three: Cast By God

One of the most difficult adjustments to missionary life as a child was learning to value what Congolese culture valued. I had lived in the United States for ten years and had my own ideas of how a church service should be organized and how long the Sunday morning service should last. The churches that I attended in my home country were havens of personal comfort. I sat in padded pews in a sanctuary cooled to a temperature that defied the blazing heat of an August sun. I had a church program that I could glance at every Sunday morning to know exactly how far the service had progressed and to estimate how much longer I had to wait before I could satisfy my rumbling stomach. The pastor never preached beyond an hour unless our family was attending some kind of special service at church camp or a revival service. If I was fidgety, I could draw with paper and pencil that my mother always had in her purse.

The first Sunday after we arrived at our mission station of Nkara-Ewa in Congo, I was expecting the service to follow somewhat the same pattern. There was fascination and even excitement at the thought of attending a Congolese church service. My parents explained to us children that this was a welcoming service for us by our new neighbors. I had visions of an award ceremony flash through my head of a sea of eager faces hanging on to my every word as I thanked our new friends for coming to the service.

Three and a half hours later, after constantly wiping the sweat mustache from my upper lip and hearing twelve verses to each of the twenty songs that were sung by various choirs (of which I could only understand a word here and there), the pastor was one and a half hours into his sermon with no end in sight. My bottom had long since fallen asleep and my hunger had given way to intense thirst. I kept glancing at my mother with pathetic eyes, pleading with her to end my torture. Not wanting to offend anyone, she whispered that I was going to have to endure my misery until the end. The service finally ended forty-five minutes later. Although there had been no awards given out, I was convinced I deserved one for enduring the most torturous hours any ten-year-old girl ever had lived through in the history of the world.

I would come to realize that the welcome service was more a true representation of a Congolese worship service than the thirty to forty-five minute sermons I was used to in America. I must admit that I never did enjoy the length of those services, but I miss the profuse adoration of Jesus Christ by a people who did not need to be entertained by a church staff on a Sunday morning. In a life which most eked out an existence, Sunday worship was a time of offering sacrifices of praise to the only One who made life bearable. With no technology to wow them, they brought intense praise to the feet of their Savior. That is what I miss.

Today we are going to talk about something as unfamiliar to you and me as my childhood experiences in a foreign country. Our unfamiliarity with something we don't understand can make us question its validity. The Old Testament is full of such practices: sacrificial animal killings for the atonement of sin, mandated festivals, men and women who forth-told the word of the Lord as prophets, and the casting of lots to determine the will of God.

One of the most difficult adjustments to missionary life as a child was learning to value what Congolese culture valued.

70

We are going to pick up our story in 1 Samuel 10:17-25. Please read these verses, paying special attention to verses 19-21.

My NIV translation does not use the word lot in verse 20, so I wanted to include the translation of this verse here from the NASB version:

*"Thus Samuel brought all the tribes of Israel near, and the tribe of Benjamin was taken by **lot**."*

Nelson's New Illustrated Bible Dictionary tells us what the casting of the lot entailed: "[The lot was] a way of making decisions in Bible times, similar to drawing straws or casting a pair of dice to determine what course or direction to follow." [1]

Americans live in a democratic country. Congress establishes laws for the citizens of the United States. It may be hard for us to wrap our brains around establishing a king by lots. The unfamiliarity of the process can make it sound foolhardy and a bit superstitious. There was a good reason, however, why Samuel chose this method to publicly ordain Saul as king over all the tribes of Israel, we have to see the process through the Israelites' eyes to understand its importance and finality.

Read through the following Scriptures and summarize what was established by the casting of the lot in each one:

Numbers 26:55

Leviticus 16:7-9

Psalm 16:5

What does Proverbs 18:18 further reveal about the finality of the lot cast?

The lot was the final vote cast by God Himself. After it had been cast, there was no disputing the answer that it revealed. Samuel's word would not have been enough for the people to accept Saul as king. We humans are fickle creatures. We will nullify anything that is not written in a contract. The lot was the contract. Never could the people question whether Saul had been chosen by God to lead them. Jealousy would have been far too easy to take root and fester had the lot not settled the matter.

There was something that the people who had asked for a king may not have remembered. God is always faithful to His covenant. As much as the people of Israel may have justified their actions in deposing Samuel because of his age or the lack of character in his sons, their motive behind asking for a king was that they had rejected Jehovah as their righteous Ruler. We can easily forget what God has commanded in the past when what we want in the present screams the most loudly to us.

Which of the twelve sons of Jacob received the promise that royal descendants would be part of his heritage in the blessing spoken over him according to Genesis 49:10, 27?

Matthew Henry lends his insight on the casting of the lot:

The disposal of the lot is of the Lord. It would also prevent all disputes and exceptions; for the lot causeth contentions to cease, and parteth between the mighty. When the tribe of Benjamin was taken, they might easily foresee that they were setting up a family that would soon be put down again; for dying Jacob had, by the spirit of prophecy, entailed the dominion upon Judah. Judah is the tribe that must rule as a lion; Benjamin shall only ravin as a wolf. Those, therefore, that knew the Scriptures could not be very fond of the doing of that which they foresaw must, ere long, be undone again.[2]

Okay, so what does all that mean? The lot was an unmistakable sign to the people of Israel that Saul had been appointed king by God. The troubling factor was that the tribe of Benjamin was not to have a king come from it, but the tribe of Judah. The remnant of Israel that still wanted Jehovah—and there always is a righteous remnant whom God has saved for Himself—would have realized that something was not right with what God was allowing. Behind the ceremony could have been an unsettling feeling that the tribe of Judah should have produced a king, not Benjamin, Saul's tribe.

> The troubling factor was that the tribe of Benjamin was not to have a king come from it, but the tribe of Judah.

Have you ever gone against a check in your spirit because something did not seem to add up and regretted the outcome? If yes, share here.

What troubling truth does Proverbs 16:33 reveal about the lot? Circle one.

It is controlled by circumstances.

It could only be cast by a righteous man.

The Lord controls the outcome.

And here, my beloved sisters, is where we can be so thrown off by the enemy. Satan knows that God cannot be anything but faithful to His promises. But if Satan can get us to believe otherwise, then he can lead us right down the pathway of destruction. The Holy Spirit will be faithful to warn us of trouble ahead, but Satan and our own fleshly desires can overrule His still, small voice leading us away from danger. We can forget what God has clearly said to us in Scripture. I want us to personalize this for a moment. Have you ever been promised something by God through His Word, a song, a sermon, or godly mentors whose luster has grown dim because some huge obstacle has raised its head between the time the promise was given and its fulfillment? What happens, my beloved sisters, when what God has promised seems blocked by circumstances? Our faith will never have to exercised more than when we are blindsided this way.

> ✳ After a reminder filled with warning to the people about whom they had really rejected, list the steps of the process to identify the new king in 1 Samuel 10:20-24.

What was Saul's reaction to his new position over all of Israel? Circle the correct answer.

Arrogant	Humble
Fear that caused him to hide	Other_____

Saul may have been so swept away by the praise of God by others that he had to join in so that people wouldn't have even been able to recognize him, but the show was now over. If it was merely a spiritual high, the emotions that had reached such a peak had to come down. Saul was so overwhelmed by everything that he hid himself from what the lot revealed.

Have you ever needed to be really brave in front of others, even when you were terrified inside? Saul's terror over what was happening to him stripped him of all pride over caring what others thought. He hid himself so well that he could not be easily found.

What does Philippians 2:12-13 point to as the source of our strength in fear?

There are times when we will be faced with a tremendous amount of fear in our obedience to God.

There are times when we will be faced with a tremendous amount of fear in our obedience to God. He will call us to a task that we know we are simply unqualified to take on in our own strength. If He has called us to the task, He will also work in us to will and act according to His good purpose. We must never let the size of the task overwhelm us and run for the luggage. I believe that Saul had that same kind of strength of God at his disposal. Fear got the better of him, however, and he hid from the people.

After glancing back at 1 Samuel 10:23-25, respond to these questions:

Who was the revealer of Saul's location to Samuel and his new subjects?

What was the people's reaction to Saul after he was brought out before them?

What did Samuel do in verse 25?

The lot had been cast. Although the people may have falsely believed that they were in control of who was the leader over Israel, God had never been more securely in charge of the lot. Saul had indisputably been chosen king over Israel.

I wonder how Saul slept that first night as Israel's first king. He had no throne, no palace, or other outward sign of his kingship. Yet the fact remained that he was the divinely chosen king of Israel. The question to be answered, however, was who was the real Saul?

Day Four: To Prove His Mettle

It was June 19, 1993. I woke up out of a sound sleep with the feeling that something monumental was about to happen to me. In the fogginess of sleep, I could not remember the reason for my excitement for a split second. I stared up at the ceiling of my rented basement room in the house that I shared with three other girls. Suddenly, I remembered the reason I felt like I was going to jump out of my skin with happiness. This was my wedding day—the day I had dreamed about for as long as I could remember.

Let's have a little fun here. When was the last time you woke up happy, knowing that the world was never going to be the same again for you? (e.g. anticipated first date, wedding day, scheduled C-section, graduation day, etc.). Share briefly some of the emotions that you experienced that set that day apart in your memory.

I believe that Saul must have woken up on the first morning as his royal highness with very mixed emotions, much like me on my wedding day. Along with the wonder and anticipation of my new life with my soon-to-be husband, I had a certain amount of dread and anxiety over leaving all that I had known as a single person behind. I had on beautiful, rose-colored glasses that day, but even I could spot inevitable conflict on the other side of the words, "I do."

Let's start today's lesson by reading 1 Samuel 10:26 to the end of 1 Samuel 11.

What was the immediate problem facing Saul in 1 Samuel 10:26-27? What was Saul's reaction to these men?

Guess what girlfriends? My beautiful, rose-colored glasses came off quickly— on the honeymoon! It's funny in an odd way, but no one had to tell me how to be selfish. I just never realized how selfish I was until I started sharing life with another person.

If human nature is anything, it is fickle. The people wanted a king. In hindsight their reasoning for a king seems lame. But isn't that the thing about poor decisions? Don't they always seem urgent and critical at that moment? God granted them their wish, they got rid of their spiritual leader, and witnessed the indisputable casting of the lot as to who their king should be. Notice that after the assembly of Saul's subjects were told he was king, Saul went back home. Everyone was new to this idea of having a king. And although some valiant men jumped on board immediately, some were not so friendly.

If human nature is anything, it is fickle.

75

What word is used to describe these men's emotion toward Saul in verse 27? Circle your answer.

Jealous   Despise

Apathetic   Cruel

Despise is a very strong word. What makes someone despise another person?

Saul is going to have trouble on his hands if his subjects are not behind him being their king. God had been rejected, but we are going to clearly see that He was not going to leave Saul high and dry. God had led Samuel to Saul. Proverbs 16:9 declares: "In his heart a man plans his course, but the LORD determines his steps." God was faithful to orchestrate the perfect scenario to prove to everyone that the lot cast told no lie. Saul was the man for the job.

The Ammonites were a long-standing enemy of Israel. These annoying neighbors lived to the southeast of the people of Jabesh Gilead, a city belonging to the tribe of Gad. This city had the unenviable position in a time of crisis, along with the tribes of Reuben and Manasseh, of being isolated from the rest of Israel by the Jordan River. The Ammonites beseiged Jabesh Gilead. So a council of men from the city were sent to the king of the Ammonites to understand the terms of surrender that Jabesh Gilead would be required to make to live in peace. *The New International Bible Commentary* makes a careful distinction between a surrender and a treaty.[3] The Israelites wanted a treaty which would allow them to live in peace with Nahash, the Ammonite ruler. There was just one little problem:

What was Nahash's reaction to Israel's desire for a treaty rather than a full surrender to the Ammonites in 1 Samuel 11:2?

What request did the elders of Jabesh make of Nahash and where were the messengers sent according to verse 3?

The tribe of Gad had seven days to plead with their fellow Israelites to come help them. Amazingly, Nahash held off the eye-gouging ceremony to honor his word to his would-be conquered neighbors of Israel.

Let's see what insight Proverbs 21:1 reveals as the reason for this unreasonable compliance by King Nahash:

God knew that an earthly king was about to take a throne in His beloved Israel. He also knew how unbelievably important it was going to be for Saul to have united subjects under him. Girlfriends, I become more and more convinced of one thing: our God is the ultimate Multi-tasker. He does it beautifully and never becomes frazzled one iota over the threats of puny human beings. Nahash was unaware of what God had done in Saul since he had left his father's home to go look for some donkeys. He was about to find out that he had picked the wrong fight.

What was Saul's reaction to the plight of Jabesh Gilead in 1 Samuel 11:6? Circle the best response.

Burned with anger   Hid in the luggage

Rode away on a donkey   Apathetic

There are times when we can become angry about the right things. Righteous anger is a powerful head turner and heart changer because those who observe the one who is angry but does not sin can see the truth that may have been hidden before. Righteous anger can infuse everyone with courage because the anger is used to correct something morally wrong.

✳ What changed the man who had hidden in the luggage and what did he threaten according to verses 6-7? What change happened in others as a result?

WEEK THREE • PORTRAITS OF A KING

Our God is the ultimate Multi-tasker.

There is nothing like the fear of God to motivate even the most reluctant heart to change! Anger of man does not bring about the righteous life that God desires (James 1:12), but Psalm 4:4 tells us that it is possible to be angry and not sin. The Spirit of God produced anger in Saul which was the fuel that ignited a divided kingdom. Saul was furious about the right thing. It ultimately saved a part of the kingdom of Israel.

Every life has some shining moments. We might have to go back to someone's childhood to find out what made a person veer off the right path, but God gives everyone an opportunity to be redeemed. Are you at a crossroads today? Can you hear Him whispering to you? Do you have a choice to make. We fool ourselves into thinking that choices are "little" things. Nothing could be further from the truth. Pride, unfortunately is an equal opportunity deceiver and is willing to rear its ugly head at any time. We think that our arrogance is not detestable to God. How foolish we are!

All sounds well, but amidst the clamor of victory there would be one more test for Saul (see 1 Samuel 11:12-13). Saul shows great wisdom here. It is human nature to want to beat down those who have rejected us in the past, especially when we feel justified and have others telling us that we are justified. What did Saul choose to do against the advice of the crowd?

If we could only see the truth that God exalts those who are humble, we would be far less likely to make a wrong choice at crucial moments. Saul's actions are humble here in the last part of chapter 11. I don't know what his reason was for not becoming proud. I would like to think that he was still in awe of what had happened to him. We all feel a little more generous when life is going well. It is when our character is tested in a real crisis that who we really are comes to the surface. Saul had won the hearts of his subjects. That was enough for him—for now. But life is a fight. Saul fought the enemy this time and was granted a smashing victory, but he would not always be so valiant. An invisible enemy was crouching in the wings waiting to reveal itself—the enemy of his soul.

It is when our character is tested in a real crisis that who we really are comes to the surface.

Day Five: A Royal Reaffirmation and a Somber Warning

Your eyes saw my unformed body.
All the days ordained for me
were written in your book
before one of them came to be.

How precious to me are your thoughts, O God!
How vast is the sum of them!   *Psalm 139:16-17*

I'd like us to start out today's lesson with the above truth from God's Word that has been a great comfort to me in uncertain times. I don't know about you, but there have been seasons of life in which it seems I cannot find God in my situation. It seems as though He has forgotten me because I cannot think of any other reason why life could be so hard.

The telephone rang only once, causing both my mother and me to spring up out of bed from a sound sleep. I glanced at the clock which read 1:45 a.m. What good news comes at that hour of the morning? An icy dagger of fear pierced by heart as I heard my mother's voice confirm this was bad news. Our worst fears has been realized: My father had been involved in a life-threatening automobile accident. Dad was eighty-five hundred miles away in Congo with some of his cousins who were there to put the roof on the newly constructed Bible school Building at Nkara-Ewa, the mission station where I had grown up.

In a matter of seconds, our plans for the immediate future had changed. We were about to embark on a new sense of normal, which none of us could have foreseen. My father had suffered a closed head injury and was now lying in a filthy, incompetent African hospital. I had often daydreamed about wishing I could fly through the sky as a young girl. I sat helpless to do anything for my father with an ocean and many hours of travel as obstacles preventing me from getting to him.

The thought that God may be asking me to relinquish my father to death was unthinkable to me. As I sat in the cramped airline seat on my way to Congo several days later, I struggled with the seeming injustice of the frightening possibility that my father would not survive for me to see him alive one last time.

According to Psalm 139:16, what were written in God's book and when were they written?

 What has been known by God before I even took my first breath? Circle all that you can gather from these verses:

My birthdate   All the days of my life

The date of my death   All of these

The confusion and terror my family had to grapple with the night we learned about my father's accident was no surprise to my God. Although we were stunned with the news, God had not suddenly turned His back for a moment as the accident occurred. He was not caught off guard but knew every detail of that frightening situation. I am forever grateful that the Lord performed a miraculous act of healing in my father's life so that one would not know today how close to death he had come.

God is unchangeable. There is a part of me that takes great comfort in that. Another part of me trembles. One part of me laughs in the freedom that that brings. Another part of me humbly begs God to help me through those things that are ordained which may cause me or those I love great pain.

Today's lesson is going to hinge on that truth. Let's read all of 1 Samuel 12. While reading, carefully consider who is leaving the scene and what his attitude is about the decision that God has ordained for him. Note any phrases or words that give insight into the character of this person in the margin.

We are going to summarize the 1 Samuel 12 in sections.

Verses 1-5
What does Samuel point out to the people in these verses for the reasons he is not stepping down from his position?

What is the people's response to Samuel in verse 4?

> God is unchangeable. There is a part of me that takes great comfort in that. Another part of me trembles.

Verses 6-11
What does Samuel give for the reason of his confrontation of the people in verse 7?

Why did God sell them into the hands of their enemies according to verse 9?

How was God merciful to the Israelites according to verses 10-11?

Verses 12-18

Scripture is a masterpiece of a story. Looking back at 1 Samuel 8:5-6, we can see that the Israelites gave an entirely different reason for wanting Samuel to step down than what is revealed in 1 Samuel 12:12. What were the reasons given in both instances?

I cannot say it enough—God will not share His glory with anyone else. The Israelites had committed a grievous sin; however, I suspect that many did not realize the extent of this sin at the time. Note the people's response to the miracle Samuel performed in verses 16-18. Sometimes we do not realize just what we have done. I'll give you some examples of how this could play out and then I want you to think about your own life example.

- That flirtatious relationship with someone not our spouse that led to an emotional and/or physical affair.

- The choice to quit going to church and the great gulf that resulted between you and God.

- Not forgiving when I should have, resulting in a friendship forever altered.

- Marrying outside of the will of God.

Your turn:

✳ What does Proverbs 16:2 say about how we can be deceived in what we ask for?

According to 1 Samuel 12:19, did the people agree with the Lord's weighing of their motives? What did they ask Samuel to do for them because of their realization?

Samuel was a man who had been trained in righteousness. When God revealed the reason for Samuel's rejection, Samuel chose to believe Him and not hold it against Saul or the Israelites. Wow. What a big person. Samuel had the God-given ability to see past the rejection to what it really was—rebellion against God. But don't you and I take so many things personally? There have been too many times that I have failed to see the real reason behind someone's rejection of me. I have taken it personally. And in the end, I am the loser for that attitude.

> Girlfriends, I cannot say it enough—God will not share His glory with anyone else.

What happens when we rise above what others do to us? When we ask God for spiritual eyes and He enables us to have wisdom far beyond what the situation seems to be, we become a beacon of hope for others—maybe to the very ones who have hurt us the most. If we have been unjustly accused or suddenly removed against our will, Samuel's response is one we should strive to have in our pain.

After assuring them that they should still serve the Lord with all their hearts, what incredible conclusion did Samuel come to after wrestling with personal rejection in verse 23? Write the verse out here:

Now that, sweet sisters, is an example of someone who has wrestled with God and has overcome. Samuel had a choice to be bitter and withdraw. He could have said, "Whatever you people have coming to you is what you deserve." Instead, he actually sees how failing to pray for those who had hurt him the most would be just as sinful in God's eyes. Why? Because Samuel would have been rebelling in his own way against the One who had ordained this time of rejection. I wonder how powerful Samuel's teaching was to those who took him up on his offer to show them the way that was good and right. I would imagine those lessons were very impacting on those who had ears to hear because of the example of Samuel walking away from his rightful leadership position without bitterness.

I believe that one of Satan's biggest lies to us is that God will leave us in the mess we have made. Perhaps we don't come to change our ways sooner because we see ourselves as the rejected one—the one beyond God's forgiveness. Samuel assured them that although they had rebelled, God would not withhold Himself from them. They could start again and obey. Who of us needs to hear that in our own lives? Yes, we may have made an absolute mess of our lives, but He is the Redeemer of wrongs. We don't have to stay stuck in our mess; we can choose to serve Him in our mess and He miraculously works His salvation of us in the middle of it.

My beloved sister, our God can change our circumstances in a blink of an eye. He is the Way Maker. He is the Ruler of the universe. Nothing is impossible with Him. So why doesn't He just snap His fingers and make everything better the first time we beg Him to? I believe the answer to that question is found in 2 Thessalonians 1:3-5:

> *We ought always to thank God for you, brothers, and rightly so, because your faith is growing more and more, and the love every one of you has for each other is increasing. Therefore, among God's churches we boast about your perseverance and faith in all the persecutions and trials you are enduring. All this is evidence that God's judgment is right, and as a result you will be counted worthy of the kingdom of God, for which you are suffering.*

> I believe that one of Satan's biggest lies to us is that God will leave us in the mess we have made.

You and I are being counted worthy of the kingdom of God as a direct result of what we are suffering if we are suffering for something that will bring Him glory. Walking away from the bitterness of rejection, without retaliation, is of great worth in the sight of our God. Hold on, my darling friend, hold on. The One who has ordained every day of our lives and has written them in His book is fully aware of the painful rejections we have experienced. When He says the trial is over, you and I are going to be given something that cannot be bought—the assurance that we have been counted worthy of the One whose kingdom will never end.

The Ugly Turn of Disobedience

When we have convinced ourselves that we are more important than others, we can be sure the ground on which we are making that false assumption is going to give way at some point. This week we are going to see what Saul was willing to do to look good in front of other people. Instead of being zealous for God's glory, Saul was jealous for his own name. That destructive choice would ravage those close to him and tear away what he held onto so tightly.

Although I can promise that almost all of us will be shocked at Saul's actions this week, we must remember that none of us are above wanting the praise of others. We have all committed acts we wish we could take back because those acts hurt someone dear to us. A truth I want us to keep in mind this week is found in the book of Proverbs:

The fear of human opinion disables; trusting in God protects you from that.
Proverbs 29:25 (The Message)

Now that truth is one to write on our hearts by memorization!

✸ **Day One:** Revealing What's Inside

I have sporadic childhood memories that stand out in my mind between the ages of four and eight. I can vaguely remember singing with my dad and sister in front of our church congregation during a Sunday night church service. I remember making snowflakes in kindergarten and how much I adored my teacher, Mrs. Henderson. I remember watching television most afternoons for an hour at my buddies' house across the street during first grade. I also remember running all the way home crying after being frightened by neighbors I did not know well who had asked me to come see their dog. My mother had just told me not to talk to strangers; I was convinced that they had evil intentions to kidnap me.

Because those years seem to be a blur in my mind, I might be tempted to say that the period of my life between ages four to eight did not really matter. Our lives, however, are shaped by our pasts, even if we do not remember each day individually. Watching my children make choices from the ages of two to eight has allowed me to conclude, fairly accurately, how each one would react in a given situation. We are the sum of our experiences, even if we don't remember clearly the individual days that got us to where we are as individuals.

Sometimes, there is a gap in the Biblical narrative of an individual. God, in His wisdom, abruptly throws us forward an undisclosed number of years in the narrative of an individual's life. Scripture remains silent during a period of Saul's life lived out from the end of the previous chapter we studied yesterday to where his story continues today.

I would like us to read all of 1 Samuel 13, but before we start our lesson today, I have to try to help clear up any confusion over 1 Samuel 13:1. Some translations say that Saul was thirty years old when he became the king. Others say he reigned one year. Some translations omit this verse altogether. This is what the ***Believer's Bible Commentary*** has to say about 1 Samuel 13:1:

"The most likely explanation for this confusion is that some letters were dropped out of the Hebrew text by careless copyists in later centuries. We do know that Saul was a mature man when he came to power because his son Jonathan was old enough to go to war." [1]

Please read 1 Samuel 13:1-23.

By the time we come to 1 Samuel 13:2, some significant amount of time has passed since the resignation of Samuel and Saul being the ruler of a united kingdom. To get an idea of how many years may have passed, we are suddenly introduced to a new character we will come to know in the life of Saul—Jonathan, eldest son of Saul and rightful heir to the throne of Israel.

There are some passages in Scripture that give very specific details and other passages that are frustratingly lacking in detail for someone like me who wants to know. We can only guess at Jonathan's actual age because Scripture never does tell us, but it does give us a clue that will help us to make more of an educated guess.

Let's turn to Numbers 1:2-3. What age did an Israelite man have to be to be able to serve in the army?

fifteen   twenty   twenty-seven

thirty   thirty-five

If we use this verse as a guideline, Jonathan had to be at least twenty years old. What did Saul have Jonathan do in 1 Samuel 13:2? Choose one.

Carry his armor   Command one thousand men

Ride in front of him

I seriously doubt that Saul would have had enough confidence to put Jonathan in charge of a third of his soldiers during Jonathan's first, second, or even third year as a warrior. I would expect that perhaps Jonathan had as much as ten years' experience by the time he experienced the battle in 1 Samuel 14. Although this study focuses on the life of Saul, you and I will come to realize how God can choose great men and women to come from homes with parents that do not honor Him.

> Although this study focuses on the life of Saul, you and I will come to realize how God can choose great men and women to come from homes with parents that do not honor Him.

What thoughts come to your mind when you hear the words, "he lived in the shadow of another?" Are these generally positive thoughts or negative thoughts and why?

Why do you think that we want to be recognized by others? Circle all that apply:

To feel loved   To feel important   To feel needed

To be noticed

Let's meet Jonathan through the pages of 1 Samuel. We are going to be reading quite a bit today, but I think it is so important that we get a grasp of the kind of person Jonathan was.

After glancing over 1 Samuel 13:1-7, answer the following questions:

Who did Saul put in charge of one-third of his soldiers in the battle?

What word would you use to describe Jonathan in verse three?

Timid   Fearful

Courageous   Spiteful

What was the result of Jonathan's actions in verse three?

In contrast to Jonathan, what was the emotional state of Saul's men according to verse 7?

Let's pick up in verse 16 and read through 1 Samuel 14:14. This scene describes a battle between Israel and the Philistines, but the war between the two nations had already gone on for centuries. The conflict would long outlast Saul's reign. This was a dreaded enemy that had inflicted damage on the Israelites for many years. Saul needed his courageous son to lead the army. Fathers and sons need to have common interests to bond. Saul and Jonathan's bond came through trying to defeat Israel's enemy. As we will see later, father and son shared little else in common.

> Saul and Jonathan's bond came through trying to defeat Israel's enemy.

I want us to focus on Jonathan's character in 1 Samuel 13:16-14:14. List every clue that shows Jonathan as fit to be Saul's right-hand man as a soldier on the battlefield:

❋ To whom does Jonathan give credit in verse 6 and verse 12 for giving him the victory even though he does not know what the outcome of his decision will be?

Let's now read 1 Samuel 13:7-15. What was Saul guilty of in this passage?

What was the consequence of Saul's actions?

This is perhaps one of the most sobering passages in Scripture. We live in a disposable world. We like text-messaging, email, overnight delivery, and disposable dinner plates. Our lives are incredibly fast-paced. Hurrying is the rule of the day. We want everything yesterday. Saul could not bear to wait a minute longer for Samuel, the prophet of God who was the only one able to give the sacrifice. With an army quaking in fear and no God in sight that he could see, Saul decided to hurry things up a bit. The consequences were devastating.

How do you think reacting out of panic from not waiting on the Lord could set us up for jealous feelings toward someone else?

God does not make us wait to see us squirm, grovel, or to withhold something from us just because He can.

What distressing news did Saul receive in verses 13-14 for not waiting on Samuel as he should have? Check the correct answer:

He would lose his life.   His kingdom would be torn away.

Israel would be humiliated.

How do you think Samuel's words to Saul in verse 14 could have laid the foundation for Saul's jealousy toward the one who was to succeed him?

Saul chose to hide in caves, thickets, and cisterns and allow fear to dictate his actions (verse 6). When our mind is chaotic with fear, we can make very poor decisions. Saul did not have faith enough to wait on the Lord, as he had been instructed to do. In contrast to his father's foolishness, Jonathan had the faith to know that any victory he and his armor-bearer might see that day was not due to his skill as a warrior, but to the Lord. His faith in God's power to save him against a fearful enemy infused not only Jonathan with courage, but also the man who carried his armor.

Do we understand that waiting and God's glory being revealed are intricately connected? I despise waiting, especially if I feel I can help the situation move along. There is nothing sinister or cruel about God's nature. He does not make us wait to see us squirm, grovel, or to withhold something from us just because He can. God does not abuse His power like human beings do. As we wait, we are forced to relinquish our will, thus making room for His glory to be shown in our lives. The purpose of the wait is for God to

bring more glory to Himself. If He has said no to a heart's desire of yours, my dear sister, it is because there is much glory at stake if you and I are willing to wait for His will to be done in our lives.

I believe that God also has us wait to see if our hearts want the glory to go to Him or to ourselves. Saul usurped God's right to set the conditions for the slaughter of the Amalekites. Sometimes God asks us to do something that seems utterly foolish to us. Like Saul, we can be tempted to believe we know better than He does what is best. By refusing to wait for Samuel to offer the sacrifice, Saul's heart was exposed. Saul's glory was more important to Saul than God's glory being shown to the many people in Saul's sphere of influence.

As we wait, we are forced to relinquish our will, thus making room for God's glory to be shown in our lives. When we refuse to wait for the Lord, we allow traps to be set for us by the enemy. David hasn't even come onto the scene yet, but Satan has carefully laid a net of jealousy that Saul will walk right into when he realizes that David will be his successor. Saul's not waiting on the Lord also affected Jonathan's life. Saul's jealousy would rob Jonathan of the throne of Israel because Saul's sin caused the kingship to pass to David. The amazing thing that we will see is that Jonathan never let ownership of the throne come between him and David.

We may not have specific examples of the choices that Saul made during the years in which Scripture is silent on the life of Saul. That does not matter because what we have seen of his character reveals much about the choices he made during the years about which the Bible is silent. The character we have seen displayed in Saul today reveals the fact that Jonathan was head and shoulders above his father in maturity. We will see just how great the gap between father and son was about to become in tomorrow's lesson.

Day Two: Jealous For His Name

The goal of this Bible study is to expose the many faces of jealousy. I have prayed continually that the Lord would give us insight into this heart problem that deceitfully hides its presence in our lives. Before this study, I generally believed that jealousy was something I had to wrestle with over a material possession that someone else had or a character trait or ability for which I envied them. I had never asked myself, however, if I was jealous of something that had been mine since the day of my birth—my name.

During my adolescence, I spent a year and a half trying to reclaim my name which had been stolen from me through the slander of others. That painful situation seemed to cost the perpetrators of the untruths nothing, but resulted in isolation and suspicion from my peers for me. There was nothing I could do except wait the awful ordeal out and let time prove the lies were unfounded. Crushed in spirit, I spent hours alone in my room sobbing over my pain. Without the wisdom of Scripture, I was unable to analyze why I was so traumatized.

Why are our names so precious to us? I would like to suggest that our name is our identity. When others carelessly or viciously throw our name around, they are being careless and vicious to us. We take those words personally because we place high value on our names. May I even say that we are jealous for others to represent our names justly and with kind consideration. If anyone dares to smear our good name, we will try to find every way we can to clean up the damage—possibly at any cost.

There is nothing wrong or sinful about the desire to protect our name when we have done nothing wrong. What does Psalm 138:2 reveal about God and His name?

To start today's lesson, we have to refresh our memory of yesterday's text from 1 Samuel 13. The Israelites were facing sure destruction as an army before their enemies the Philistines. Jonathan quietly slipped away from the rest of the men and asked his armor bearer to climb a treacherous hill, asking for God's protection, as the two of them killed about twenty enemy soldiers. God came to their rescue and sent an earthquake to cause massive confusion among the Philistines. Saul and his men witnessed the Philistines killing each other as the battle moved on to another location in Beth Aven.

Let's resume our study as we read 1 Samuel 14:24-29. What did Saul call down on the man who ate before the evening of the battle day?

a curse   a blessing   a reward

> When others carelessly or viciously throw our name around, they are being careless and vicious to us.

Do you see an element of pride in Saul in verse 24?
If yes, what allows you to come to that conclusion?

We have a classic case of a self-absorbed commander who wants the glory of the battle to belong only to him, not to the Lord. Saul did not think it worthy to consider the cost to those fighting alongside him. We do ourselves great harm when our inflated ego fuels our jealousy for our name. Saul did what I have done so often. I have manipulated a situation so that I come out looking great to others. What is worse than Saul's self-centeredness is the fact that he bound all of his men under oath to obey him so that his name could be exalted in front of everyone watching or hearing about the battle's outcome. Wanting to claim the glory of victory for himself, Saul forced his men to take an oath against their wills.

How have you been a similar victim of someone else's selfish decision?

Who had not been aware of the oath (verse 27) and what did he do that was in direct violation to what had been ordered?

What was Jonathan's explanation for eating before evening?

Let's continue by reading 1 Samuel 14:31-46. What was the result of Saul's foolish pride in verses 31-32? Circle one.

The men ate raw meat.   The army revolted.

The men were slaughtered by the enemy.

More than being unappetizing, the men eating raw meat was a sin against the Lord. The Israelites were forbidden to eat any animal whose blood had not been drained from its body (Leviticus 19:26). Saul's jealous eye, fixated on bringing glory to his name through winning this battle, caused his whole army to sin against the Lord. We cannot downplay how serious this is. I want us to think a minute about how our jealous motives have possibly caused someone else to violate a command of God. Maybe we got someone to agree to let us cheat off a paper in class, wanting the "A" with no thought of the violation it was to the other person. Maybe we encouraged someone to do something that we knew was wrong because we hoped the person would be exposed, making us look better. Maybe our jealousy for power or to feel loved led us to use someone to make another person jealous in a dating relationship or in our marriage.

Saul's jealous eye, fixated on bringing glory to his name through winning this battle, caused his whole army to sin against the Lord.

What did Saul do in verse 35?

Do you find this a little odd? I have heard a girlfriend tell me that it is easier for her to apologize afterwards to her husband for doing something than to ask his permission before. Do you think maybe this is what was going through Saul's mind? He wanted God's favor, but he should have known that placing his men under an involuntary oath was foolishness that led to the men's sinful behavior.

How did God respond to Saul in verse 37? Choose one.

He forgave him.   He was angry.

He required more sacrifices.   He was silent.

Silence is terrifying, isn't it? I would rather have the lash of anger than the cold, unsettling silence from someone I have offended, how about you? I can at least have a plan to resolve the problem when I know the person's feelings. But silence… now that is truly frightening.

I have pondered the motive behind Saul's oath and rashness. I think it was sheer panic on Saul's part. Saul knew how impossibly ill-equipped his army was to conquer the Philistines, so he wanted God's blessing. But girls, did Saul want God Himself? How often I do the same thing! *"Oh, Lord, please bless me, but don't make me give up this behavior that brings dishonor to your Name!"* Have I ever prayed those words? *Never!* I would smugly think. But have I lived as though I have? Absolutely! How about you? Now we see one of the most unbelievable disconnects between a father and his son ever recorded in Scripture.

✳ Do you see Saul passing the blame on to someone else here in verses 38-42? What do you believe he should have done as commander before God and his men?

Before we allow the gasps of horror to escape from our mouths over Saul's rashness, we need to examine our own hearts. We may have never threatened physical death to someone in outrage over the disgrace they have brought to our name, but have we done any of the following?

• Exposed an individual's private offense to outsiders with the intent of slandering and bringing shame to the one who, in our minds, dared to make us look foolish.

• Exposed the individual through the sharing of information under the guise of a prayer request, knowing that our motive for sharing was to reveal what she did to us.

92

- Made life miserable for that person by exclusion and trying to get others to side with us.

Ouch, ouch, ouch! Sometimes the medicine for the wound stings more than the gash itself, but when the wound comes from the Word of God, we can expect healing after the medicine has been applied. What happens when we believe our name has been smeared in front of others? Like Saul, we can panic.

What does Proverbs 27: 4 reveal about the power of jealousy?

That is an amazing statement! Even anger in all of its cruelty and fury in its passion is easier to withstand than a jealous heart. Jealousy is a monster. Unbridled jealousy has the potential to kill its victim (literally or figuratively) with no thought beforehand of the harm it will do. It is a raging beast, knowing no limits to the depravity to which it can stoop to. We can't stand before jealousy—even our own! And so we commit cruel, shortsighted sins against others under envy's terrible weight. We shame them out of spite and the obsessive need to clear our name. Jonathan made Saul look bad in front of his men. Saul could not bear the thought of the possible fallout that would be the result, so he determined to do away with his own son.

How do you think Saul's statement in 1 Samuel 14:44 affected his relationship to his son?

Who were the rational ones in verse 45 and what did they prevent Saul from doing?

My darling sisters, I was blessed beyond measure to grow up in a loving home, but I have heard enough heartbreaking stories from others to know that a nurturing environment is not always the norm for other families. Have you been hurt as deeply by a parent as Jonathan was? I could weep over the devastation that has happened in the lives of you who are taking this study. I cannot say anything to erase the pain you continue to carry to this day from the cutting comments that came from the lips of your mother or father. I want you to know that you have a daddy that loves you so very much in your heavenly Father. He knew the devastation that happened in your soul because He was there! He has bottled your tears, my precious one (Psalm 56:8). For reasons He alone knows, He allowed the agony you suffered at the hands of

Sometimes the medicine for the wound stings more than the gash itself, but when the wound comes from the Word of God, we can expect healing after the medicine has been applied.

your parent to glorify Him. He wants to transform the ashes into beauty and bind up your broken heart. But you have to give Him permission to do that. You will carry your scars everyday, but they don't have to hurt and taunt you anymore.

How does Revelation 5:6 describe Jesus?

The apostle John saw the risen Jesus in heaven still bearing His scars. Dear friend, I believe the scars we allow our Jesus to heal will be heaven's glory! There is no shame in your scars. They will be your crown for all eternity because your Redeemer proved that by His scars you were healed. What do you want to tell your Abba, (the Aramaic word for *daddy*) your heavenly Father today? I pray that you feel His arms around you as you crawl into His lap and safely pour out your broken heart to Him.

✳ **Day Three:** Throwing It All Away

My son, Chase, continually amazes me with the depth of his thinking. He is twelve going on twenty-five. Yesterday as I was bringing him home from school, he suddenly piped up,

"Mom, if I were given three wishes, I would wish that I had $500,000 (okay—that one wasn't so deep), that I could fly like a bird, and that I owned a time machine."

"Really, Chase? If you had a time machine, what would you use it for?" I asked.

Chase and I share an insatiable love of history. I was sure that he would want the time machine to take him back to the days of the Roman Empire or maybe the Civil War battle of Gettysburg.

"I would use the time machine to go back and unsay every bad thing I have ever said to anyone. I would try to undo the hurt I caused in their life," he replied.

I sat there stunned at the maturity of his answer. How many times have I wished the same thing! I knew I was a blessed mama at that moment.

Girlfriends, we all have rash moments where we have said things we wish we could take back. Imagine that you are Saul.

What two situations have you seen Saul involved in that have struck you as containing the most regrettable words or actions he has said or done thus far:

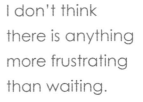

I don't think there is anything more frustrating than waiting.

We have seen some shocking—may I say, appalling—situations in which Saul has dug himself into a pit. But today we are going to see his character revealed like we never have before. I am praying right now as I write this that God's Spirit would be able to reveal a huge disconnect that some of us may never have seen until now. I cannot do that, but His Holy Spirit will reveal sin to an open and repentant heart. I am praying that this will be our attitude as we study 1 Samuel 15 today.

We are going to have to go back to something we may have completely overlooked in Week Two of the study. What did Samuel command Saul to do in 1 Samuel 10:8?

I don't think there is anything more frustrating than waiting. I know a poem that sums up the danger of not learning to wait. Its lines leave me convicted every time I read it:

"First I was dying to finish high school and start college.
And then I was dying to finish college and start working.
Then I was dying to marry and have children.
And then I was dying for my children to grow old enough so I could
go back to work. But then I was dying to retire.
And now, I am dying ... And suddenly I realized I forgot to live."

– Anonymous

Have you ever been so discontented with life that you have forgotten to live while waiting for the next stage of life to happen? Please share here if you can relate:

We can stew and mope while having to wait and regret later that we forgot to live in the process. We are going to see how dearly Saul's decision to not wait cost him.

Please read all of 1 Samuel 15 and let's ponder some of the following questions together:

Who sent Samuel to Saul and what explicit instructions did Samuel give Saul in verses 1-3?

Do you think that obedience would be any easier if you had a prophet from God come to you and tell you exactly what you were to do? Why or why not?

What does Luke 16:27-31 reveal about the heart of someone who refuses to take God seriously?

We are desperately wicked to the very core of us. Without giving Jesus Lordship over our lives, we are hopelessly lost and are guaranteed to make mistakes full of destructive consequences. Yes, He can redeem any situation, but we may live with the ramifications of our rebellion and disobedience long after we disobey.

At what point did Saul make a life-altering decision in
1 Samuel 15:4-9?

Saul did not see how his disobedience in not waiting for Samuel would be the catalyst for throwing away the blessing of God on his life. Without the Word of God illuminating our sin, we can be as blind to the consequences of disobedience as Saul was. Let me give you some examples of how I think this could be played out in our lives as believers. Have any of us been involved in any of the following acts of disobedience without considering the cost of these acts to our spiritual health?

• Allowing pornography or wickedness through various forms of media
  to invade our minds.

• Being part of keeping a slanderous rumor alive.

• Cherishing secret sins (e.g. premarital sex, emotional and/or physical
  adultery with someone outside our or their marriage, binge eating or
  drinking in secret, an arrogant or unteachable heart that cannot accept
  rebuke from godly people, an obsessive love of money and lust for power,
  etc...).

What emotion did Samuel pour out to the LORD in
1 Samuel 15:11 over Saul?

disgust   anger   grief   impatience

What was the purpose of the monument Saul erected in Carmel
according to 1 Samuel 15:12? Choose one:

To honor God   To honor the town   To honor himself

According to 1 John 4:17-19, what is the problem with fear
being the motivator for obedience? Who loved us first?

Without the Word of
God illuminating our
sin, we can be as blind
to the consequences
of disobedience as
Saul was.

What motivates you more to obey—fear of punishment or the
fear of grieving God's heart? Please be honest and remember
that there is no condemnation for those of us who are in Christ
Jesus (Romans 8:1).

The one who had been handed the kingship by God Himself, whose bravery had united the kingdom, and had even been part of a company of prophets as they praised, had a fatal flaw—prideful rebellion. Saul allowed himself to believe his modification of God's plan was better than obeying God, causing him to set himself up for a fall from which he would never recover.

❋ What did Samuel point to as the fatal flaw in 1 Samuel 15:17 and what did it lead Saul to do in verse 19?

Saul made himself the judge here and pushed God out of His authority over him. He rationalized this behavior by telling himself that he was saving the "best" for God for sacrifice. I have done the same thing! I have fooled myself into thinking that God would want me to have the best, so it was all right for me to become obsessed with the desire of my jealousy, even though He had clearly said to destroy that thing in my life. I have thought, I can always ask for forgiveness later.

Have you ever kept the "best" for yourself when God clearly forbade it (e.g. a dating relationship, getting into debt you couldn't repay, continuing to hold a grudge)?

List all the blessings Saul's disobedience cost him in 1 Samuel 15:23-29, 35:

The character of a man or woman is not shown until he or she is faced with a deserved, godly rebuke. What do you gather was the reason for Saul admitting his sin in verse 30?

brokenness   fear of God

fear of being dishonored in front of others

The stern words of rebuke from Samuel's lips come back to me:

> *"For rebellion is like the sin of divination,*
> *and arrogance like the evil of idolatry.*
> *Because you have rejected the word of the LORD,*
> *he has rejected you as king." 1 Samuel 15:23*

Another name for *divination* is witchcraft. How serious is it to God when we act out of a rebellious spirit fueled by pride? He takes it personally and cannot bless us! Rebelliousness is what cast Satan out of heaven. He wanted to be the judge instead of God. God rejected him and cast him out of His presence (see Isaiah 14:11-17). Satan knows that the blessing of God and our ability to find our God-purposed destiny will be denied us if we do not take obedience to God seriously.

The true colors of our flawed subject have been displayed. At any moment do we see Saul wanting to repent? Instead of being grieved over his sin, he is in distress over how he would look if Samuel didn't attend the sacrifice with him in front of the people. We have seen Jonathan recognize God's ability to help him in the fight against the Philistines. Sadly, his father's cry to God for help against the enemy is absent in this portion of Scripture.

The kingdom has been torn away and Saul has failed to recognize that, "the wounds from a friend [Samuel] can be trusted" (Proverbs 27:6). Samuel and Saul never saw each other again while Samuel was alive, although Samuel continued to pray for Saul. Saul had lost his authority by refusing to be under authority. The slippery descent into the pit of destruction, caused by Saul's rebellion, had begun.

Saul had lost his authority by refusing to be under authority.

Day Four: The Boy Who Would Be King

Growing up in Congo with no electricity, moonless nights were a sea of almost impenetrable blackness. Our diesel generator was located about 400 feet from our house. My dad would occasionally ask me to go down and turn the generator off. I knew that I must grab a flashlight before I left to shine a light for my feet or getting back to the house could be dangerous. With the knowledge that black mamba snakes sometimes make the trees around our house their home, the blackness of my path could mean death to me.

God's Word is living, breathing, and illuminating. It shines a spotlight on the lives of those on its anointed pages. If we do not read and really study that illuminated path, our life's journey on this planet will be walked in dangerous darkness.

Our text for today is going to shine the light on a new person for a time. What had Samuel told Saul in 1 Samuel 13:13-14?

Israel should mourn.   Saul's kingdom would last forever.

Saul's throne was being given to someone else.

Please read 1 Samuel 16:1-2. Have you ever known someone who grieved to his or her own detriment? I know of someone who lost her husband while her boys were in elementary school. I don't know if she ever grieved properly. To talk to her, I would have thought that the event had just happened within the last several years. I came to know her when she was approaching seventy years old, decades after her husband had passed away. Please do not misunderstand me. I am not saying that the void that a loved one's passing does not leave a scar that is carried forever on our souls, but I believe we can grieve ourselves into a state of being paralyzed.

Samuel, the judge of God over Israel for so many decades, was broken over what Saul had become. He mourned for him as though he were dead. According to 1 Samuel 15:36, Samuel lived the rest of his days as though Saul were dead. Samuel had one more anointing to carry out for God. Unfortunately for Samuel, God was going to require him to carry this out at the risk of his own life.

Let's read 1 Samuel 16:1-10 and answer the following questions:

What did the Lord ask Samuel to do and why did Samuel at first protest to that request in 1 Samuel 16:1?

What does Samuel's fear tell us about what Saul was capable of doing (verse 2)?

Grief is an all-consuming thing. It is a fire that smolders long after it has ravaged us. Grief can paralyze us and make us live like those long dead. It can keep us from the next chapter of the plan that God has for us. It can make us miss out on the beauty that God promises can come from the ashes of the fire of our grief. It kills our hope. Without hope, we cannot believe that there is a tomorrow worth living.

How much would God be able to work through us if others saw our primary priority being a life of sacrifice to Him? Samuel was in a tight spot because Saul wore the crown. If word got around to Saul about the mission God gave Samuel, Saul might have taken the old prophet's life. Because Samuel trusted that God would keep him safe, the fears of the people to whom he had come were quieted. Samuel sought to glorify God first with a sacrifice. There is nothing more powerful than people united in worship to prepare the way for the Word of the Lord to accomplish what it was sent to do.

What was the response of the elders of Israel to Samuel's coming to Bethlehem and who did Samuel specifically invite to the sacrifice (verses 4-5)?

> Grief can paralyze us and make us live like those long dead.

❋ There are some lessons, girlfriends, that we may never learn. One of those lessons is judging someone by what we see on the outside. Which brother appeared to be the one worthy of anointing and who made that judgment (verse 6)?

Contrast how a human being judges someone's qualifications for a position of honor with how God determines someone's worthiness for the same position in verse 7.

I could get on my soapbox for an hour and discuss this point. We live in a society that is obsessed with power, beauty, and sex appeal. Unfortunately, I believe that this obsession can and does infiltrate our churches. Sometimes the deacon and elder board of the church looks like a who's who of prominent business men. There is absolutely nothing wrong in electing a successful business man to a leadership position in a church. We should examine our hearts to see if we are giving him that position and denying leadership to the spiritual man who is a factory worker because he doesn't "fit" our image. Let me say this loud and clear: God is not interested in how good we look as a congregation to ourselves. Many times we make decisions not based on the heart of God, but on how those decisions will make us look to others. Give me a poorer man any day who has been trained by God to hear His Holy Spirit over someone who works for a Fortune 500 company and is not Spirit-filled. The quickest way to kill a church's power and effectiveness is to elect leaders solely because of their outward appearance or affluence.

Righteous Samuel was tempted to believe he had found the next king based solely on the outward appearance of Jesse's eldest son. If a truly spiritual man like Samuel could have been tempted to fall into this trap, who am I to think that I could not make the same mistake?

Share a time when you made a judgment based on someone's outer appearance or behavior that you realized later you were dead wrong about:

Counting Eliab, how many brothers were refused by Samuel before the one he was to anoint was sent for (verse 10)?

Where was the one whom God had chosen and what was his birth order in Jesse's family?

Glance back at verse five. Samuel invited Jesse and his sons to the feast. Yet this passage of Scripture tells us that the youngest son had to be sent for from the fields. In Congo, the youngest and least-likely-to-succeed child is chosen to care for the family's livestock. Most commentators believe that the shepherd boy's father was so certain that Samuel would not be interested in his youngest son that Jesse believed the whole family was represented in the seven sons he brought with him to the sacrifice. What Jesse did not realize was that he had left the son God had chosen with the sheep.

I don't think that there is a pain like the pain of rejection by family members. There is something that becomes broken inside our souls when those who should love us most don't value us. Some people never recover from curses that were said over them as children like:

"You are a good-for-nothing. I wish you had never been born."

"You are… lazy, stupid, fat, or ignorant; you will never amount to anything."

"No man is ever going to love you. You don't deserve any better!"

"You better work at being smart because your face will never get you anywhere."

My heart is broken for the little girls turned women who are walking around with these lies in their heads—lies which have robbed them of their dignity and hope. Maybe that is you, sweet sister. Can I tell you the truth about how our God, who only looks at your heart, sees you?

Let's turn to Isaiah 49:14-23. What does your broken heart need to see as the truth in these verses over the rejection you have faced in your life from family members?

With Jesus, we can be rebuilt. We are empowered by His Holy Spirit to not pass on those deep wounds to our own children in our mothering (hallelujah for that! Somebody needs to praise Him right now!). Though we may feel bereaved and barren in our souls, our God can heal those broken places. Our disappointment over the way life has treated us can be replaced by hope that will never be disappointed because He is GOD, not a human being!

If you grew up in Sunday school, I know that you know the name of this handsome young man God found worthy of anointing. But what if 1 Samuel 16 was our only frame of reference for this boy's name? Look at verses again. After looking for his name do you and I realize that we wouldn't know it? It is not mentioned. I am so excited, I can hardly type this out! Maybe you feel as though you have lived in the shadows all your life, even in your own family.

What balm does Isaiah 49:1-4 provide for the ache that this produces in our lives?

I want us to take these verses so personally. The "I" in these verses is you, sweet friend!

At this point of the story, the shepherd boy who would be king remains nameless to the rest of the world. No one could have known the significance of that anointing oil on the least significant one in his father's eyes. This boy's heavenly Father trumped the faulty way humans judged him and pointed to the future destiny of the obscure shepherd boy spoken in the words of rebuke to Saul, "The LORD has torn the kingdom of Israel from you today and has given it to one of your neighbors—to one better than you." (1 Samuel 15:28)

We are empowered by His Holy Spirit to not pass on those deep wounds to our own children in our mothering.

The man to sit rightfully on the throne had been called, although no one knew his name at this time except an old man who had been rejected himself and the God of the universe. My sweet sister, do you need to know that you have been called to an extraordinary life, no matter how obscure and forgotten you have felt? Let's glory in the Glorious One who is able to make all things new!

"Can a mother forget the infant at her breast,
    walk away from the baby she bore?
But even if mothers forget,
    I'd never forget you—never.
Look, I've written your names on the backs of my hands.
    The walls you're rebuilding are never out of my sight.
Your builders are faster than your wreckers.
    The demolition crews are gone for good.
Look up, look around, look well!
    See them all gathering, coming to you?
As sure as I am the living God"—God's Decree—
    "you're going to put them on like so much jewelry,
    you're going to use them to dress up like a bride.
                           Isaiah 49:15-18 (The Message)

My sweet sister, do you need to know that you have been called to an extraordinary life, no matter how obscure and forgotten you have felt?

Day Five: The Appointed Time

Pride has been one of the most heartbreaking sins in my life. You see, I was a "good" girl on the outside. I had mastered the role of what I thought everyone wanted me to be. Unfortunately, the abundant life Christ had promised me through His Word, and which I saw in others, remained as elusive to me as ever. As I look back on my childhood and young adult years, I realize that the main reason I obeyed the rules was fear of disappointing others, not necessarily because I wanted to do the right thing. I never thought I was attractive or talented or particularly smart. I had a driving need to feel significant, but I felt I possessed nothing that was honored by my culture to make me feel I was worthy. I did, however, have my reputation. That was the area in which I was admired and fawned over by others. I was the responsible one, the mature one—I was even called the spiritual one. I strove with all my might to be what others said I was. This standard became my personal criteria to being accepted by others. After making some destructive decisions in a dating relationship in my college years, I realized I had failed to meet my own standard of what it meant to be a "good" Christian girl. The result was crushing guilt that extinguished my joy. Worse than that, I believed the lie that I had disappointed God beyond hope of His forgiveness or redemption.

What have you latched onto in your life as a direct result of your need for acceptance or attention? Has this been something that has proven to be constructive or destructive to your relationship with God, yourself, and others?

Until I was confronted with my own inability to be "good," I was extremely prideful of that false goodness. Pride is first on the list of detestable sins that God hates in Proverbs 6:16-19. I truly didn't see my pride as sinful. I was my own judge and jury when it came to my righteousness before God.

What does 1 Corinthians 4:4-5 have to say about the danger of judging ourselves?

We have witnessed jaw-dropping moments lived out in the life of an insecure ruler in our study thus far. If we grew up in the church, King Saul was never held up as a person to emulate, but maybe we have never realized why that was so. Girls, no one reacts the way he or she does without reason. There is always a history behind someone's actions. Scripture is silent on the years before Saul's momentous encounter as a donkey wrangler with Samuel. Maybe Saul felt rejected by his father. After all, couldn't the servant have gone to look for the donkeys by himself? Why would a man of standing send his son to do a servant's task? We can't know for sure.

> Pride has been one of the most heartbreaking sins in my life. You see, I was a "good" girl on the outside.

✳ Let's go back to 1 Samuel 16 and read verses 14-23. What are we told was the reason that the evil spirit was allowed to torment Saul in verse 14? Check one.

He oppressed his people.   The Lord had left him.

He had lied to Jonathan.

Cancer is a horrible disease that can lie dormant in our bodies for months or years before we discover its presence. We can feel fine and then suddenly be informed that we are suffering from a disease that could kill us. Saul had been warned by Samuel about the deadly disease of his arrogance, but Saul cared more about his ego than the spiritual death his arrogance could produce. Sin never announces itself. It is stealthy and subtle. We are going to take an introspective look at how Saul's torment might have begun and use the living and active Word of God to see where the trouble might have started long before the disease of torment was full-blown in Saul. Proverbs is the book of wisdom. My sweet sisters, if any time called for wisdom, it is now. We must seek wisdom like treasure and get it at any cost (see Proverbs 4:7). We do not want to be fools.

My sweet sisters, if any time called for wisdom, it is now. We must seek wisdom like treasure and get it at any cost (see Proverbs 4:7).

Match the Scripture reference with its corresponding verse below:

The way of a fool seems right to him, a wise man listens to advice.	*Proverbs 26:24 but*
A rebuke impresses a man of discernment more than a hundred lashes a fool.	*Proverbs 26:12*
Do you see a man wise in his own eyes? There is more hope for a fool than for him.	*Proverbs 12:15*
Do you see a man who speaks in haste? There is more hope for a fool than for him.	*Proverbs 17:10*
A malicious man disguises himself with his lips, but in his heart he harbors deceit.	*Proverbs 29:20*

Briefly summarize each passage below and use the above Scriptures as the possible explanation for Saul's actions. You can use each Scripture passage more than one time. This is somewhat subjective so know that there are no wrong or right answers.

<u>1 Samuel 13:7-15</u>
Brief summary:

Applicable Scripture from Proverbs:

<u>1 Samuel 14:38-45</u>
Brief summary:

Applicable Scripture from Proverbs:

<u>1 Samuel 15:12-16</u>
Brief summary:

Applicable Scripture from Proverbs:

<u>1 Samuel 15:17-26</u>
Brief summary:

Applicable Scripture from Proverbs:

<u>1 Samuel 15:24-31</u>
Brief summary:

Applicable Scriptures from Proverbs:

What is the cost of disobedience? A price that we cannot possibly calculate during the trembling moment of testing. Had Saul been able to see himself as a man oppressed by Satan, if not possessed by him, he **still** may not have decided any differently in the choices he was making. Does that sound harsh? Maybe. But Saul was given crucial opportunities when he could have sought God's face and repented. Not in any of the above scenarios do I see one inkling that Saul was sorry for his sin. He was only sorry for getting caught in that sin. I fail to see humility in Saul. Instead, I see fear of not looking good in front of others driving him to make decisions that would ultimately seal his doom. I see someone so afraid of his name being forgotten that he didn't care that he was defaming the Name above all names.

How did Saul get to this place, girls? Not in a day. He chose to spurn repentance and the forgiveness that could have been his to continue living in his rebellion. If we are to live victorious lives through Jesus Christ, obedience is never an accident. We have made a deliberate choice to obey Him in the "little" things. That act of the will may have cost us dearly in the area of how we look to others. We may be mocked as fools. Jesus said that any one who wanted to be His disciple would need to deny herself and pick up her cross daily and follow Him (Luke 9:23). I believe that cross of denial is for putting our reputations and our names to death so that the name of Jesus Christ's can be exalted above our own. The process of starving our sinful nature is heart-wrenching, agonizing work, but through that death to ourselves we can begin to really live!

> *If we deliberately keep on sinning after we have received the knowledge of the truth, no sacrifice for sins is left, but only a fearful expectation of judgment and of raging fire that will consume the enemies of God.*   Hebrews 10:26-27

Beloved sisters, we are desperately wicked at our cores. That is not an appealing truth for those who only want to hear what tickles their ears. Is it possible that we may be trying to apply grace where there is none available anymore because we have so grieved the heart of God? Our God is slow to become angry, abounding in love and mercy, but there is also a part of Him that is just. I love this quote from the famous British preacher Charles Spurgeon:

> *"No Christian [wo]man is all that [s]he thinks [s]he is; our purest gold is alloyed. We have none of us so much faith as we impute to ourselves, nor so much patience, or humility, or meekness, or love to God, or love to men…*
>
> *Child, it is needful for thee to feel the weight of thy Father's hand, or thou wilt never behave thyself as a man. Thou must see his face veiled with frowns, and hear his voice in harshness chiding thee for thy transgressions, otherwise thou wilt always retain the follies of childhood. Our chastisements are our promotions. They are privileges more precious than the rights of princes."* [2]

If we are to live victorious lives through Jesus Christ, obedience is never an accident. We have made a deliberate choice to obey Him in the "little" things.

Our God does not want us to feel the weight of His frown because He is cruel or has a giant ego. He wants us to examine our lives because we are His beloved children—the apple of His eye—and He wants to keep us from destroying ourselves. We must stop playing the fool! Repentance of our rebellion toward Him is the first step toward our healing.

Look back at 1 Samuel 16:23. Who was the only one who could calm Saul's demonic-induced fits?

Saul's son Jonathan   Jesse's youngest son, David

Saul's father Kish

The music birthed out of the purity of the heart that beat inside the chest of a lowly shepherd boy named David was the only salve for a maniacal king. The Spirit of the living God was evident in its power through the life of the overlooked son of Jesse. David is not yet a threat. The appointed time for the revealing of Saul's heart was just around the corner, which would be clearly seen to the embarrassment and jeopardy of those closest to the king of Israel. The road ahead is going to become treacherous from this point forward.

Under His Jealous Eye

God sometimes asks us to do what we do not understand. When we refuse to obey Him, our decision will always prove to be detrimental to our well-being. Rebellion may seem to be in our best interest at first, but what we do not realize is that our disobedience sets us up for defeat by the enemy of our souls.

This week we will see Saul and the nation of Israel triumph over a familiar enemy through the bravery of an obscure shepherd boy. Ever wanting the praise of others for himself, Saul will be driven into the pit of jealousy over the victory won by David and the resultant admiration of others toward the boy who would be king one day.

Watch closely, sweet friend. Does the praise of the crowd for another cause us to turn a jealous eye toward the person in the limelight? May we have the courage to see how the praise of men affects our motives and actions toward others. A question we need to ask ourselves is how well we are following Scripture's command found in the apostle Paul's letter to the Philippians:

Do nothing out of selfish ambition or vain conceit, but in humility consider others better than yourselves.   *Philippians 2:3*

Day One: Same Enemy, Different Day

My obsession with food started before I left elementary school. By the time I was in fourth grade, I resigned myself to the fact that my love of food outweighed my desire to be thin. The fact that I was a picky eater just meant that I gorged myself on foods I loved while we lived in the United States. One could say I was chubby at ten years old. My grandma told me, "You are just right," when I asked her if I was fat. Her answer pacified me at that age and gave me comfort as I continued the pattern of overeating. I honestly did not care all that much about my reflection in the mirror at that age.

I was ten years old when we moved to the Democratic Republic of Congo as missionaries. My food choices changed dramatically as resources were impossibly scarce.

Our bland diet in Congo stripped me of most of the foods I loved. I lost about fifteen pounds in the first year after we had arrived, which brought me back to a healthy weight.

When I moved back to the United States at age fourteen, I went crazy with food. After being deprived of so many of my favorite choices for almost four years, I packed on almost twenty pounds by the end of the summer. I had not given a thought to how my appearance was changing or to the fact that the clothing I had bought in May looked two sizes too snug on me four months later. As I entered my freshman year of high school, my love-hate relationship with food started to cause me to view food as my enemy. I believed that my lack of will power in this area was an enemy simply too strong for me to overcome. As a result, I lived with constant defeat in my battle with the scale.

> I lived with constant defeat in my battle with the scale.

What do the following passages say about how we can feel fighting an enemy we believe is too strong for us? Write down the key idea in each passage:

Psalm 13:2

Psalm 13:4

Psalm 42:9

Psalm 55:2-3

Psalm 143:3

Proverbs 27:6

 What in your life experience has made you feel as though you are fighting an enemy and consistently losing? Which of the above verses can you most closely identify with in that situation and why?

My freshman year of high school was not the last time I had to face the enemy of overeating. After a brief regaining of control of my weight during my junior and senior year of high school and my first year of college, I was looking my old enemy square in the face and cowering again. Like my on-again, off-again struggle with my weight, we are going to read about an enemy of Israel who had raised its head a long time throughout Israel's history.

We are going to study the events of 1 Samuel 17 over the next five days. There are too many discoveries than we can adequately discuss in one session. I am asking the Lord to give us great insight into ourselves as we study this chapter today and tomorrow. We have seen jealousy in Saul before this time, but this is the chapter in Scripture that points to the beginning of the change in Saul toward his new courtier, David. We are going to go over this chapter thoroughly because, as we will come to see over the course of this Bible study, it contains the defining moment in the relationship of King Saul and David, although David would not know that reality until much later.

Let's read 1 Samuel 17:1-11 and complete the following from your observations:

Draw a simple picture in the margin depicting the scene in verses 1-3. After drawing the two camps, use the words *tents of Philistines, tents of Israel,* and *valley of Elah.* Draw a battle line between the two camps.

In whose land was the battle to be fought—the land of the Philistines or the land of the Israelites?

The enemy of Israel, the Philistines, had invaded Judah, one of the tribes of Israel. Before Saul was established as the first king of Israel, the nation was ruled by men who were called judges. This was not the first time that Israel had faced their enemy, the Philistines, on their home turf. There were at least two earlier battles during the lifetime of the judge Samuel in which the Philistines had fought Israel in their homeland. Where was each one fought and what was the outcome of these battles?

1 Samuel 4:1-2, 10-11
Location of the battle   Battle outcome

1 Samuel 7:7-13
Location of the battle   Battle outcome

The first battle happened when the former leader of Israel, Samuel, was very young. Eli, the high priest of Israel, and his wicked sons, Hophni and Phineas, were terrified before the Philistines. Although they were supposed to be the righteous leaders of Israel, they did not have the moral courage to stand in the day of battle. The Israelites got the tar knocked out of them. Thirty thousand men were lost in one day. Compare this loss to the number of casualties the United States has experienced in our current conflict in the Middle East since 2001. We have yet to lose even a fifth of that number of men and women in our eight year struggle. Can you imagine how demoralizing losing 30,000 troops in one day must have been for Israel? Their losses did not end there. Israel lost both its high priest, Eli, and the ark of the covenant, representing God's presence, was captured by the Philistines.

Looking at the second battle in 1 Samuel 7:7-13, did you notice that the enemy who was defeated in the second battle during Samuel's time as judge over Israel was the same one who had attacked and killed 30,000 of Israel's soldiers in the first battle? The only difference between the first battle and the second was whether the Israelites looked to God as their help. Samuel stepped forward with a heart that God listened to because he presented acceptable sacrifices for the nation.

The righteous man, Samuel, did not take an ounce of credit for what had happened. He was merely the liaison between the nation and God.

What did Samuel erect as a memorial to the deliverance God gave them that day according to verse 12?

An altar   A monument   A stone   A building

Who is our enemy according to 1 Peter 5:8?

Satan is absolutely heartless. As much as his interest is in doing us physical harm, he is really after the destruction of our heart, spirit, and, ultimately, our soul. His goal is to steal, kill, and destroy (John 10:10). Saul had heard the whisper of the enemy until the whisper became deafening shouts luring Saul to disobey.

What did Saul do to commemorate the victory in 1 Samuel 15:12?

A monument to himself   An altar of praise

Another prophesy session

Satan is absolutely heartless.

Saul wanted to steal part of God's glory. When our God does not get the glory He deserves for winning the battle over our enemy, our pride will allow the enemy to invade again and again. If we dare to set up a monument to ourselves, we will have to look to ourselves to win the successive battles alone. Oh, girlfriends, our egos are such a burden, such a horrible and disgusting thing in the sight of a holy God.

I saw an amazing parallel between the Ebenezer stone that Samuel set up and Luke 20:17-18. What did Jesus say would happen to two different sets of people in these verses? Fill in the blanks:

"The one that _____ on the stone would be _____ to pieces, but the one on whom it _____ would be _____."

Oh, sisters, let me fall and get my ego broken to pieces in the process, but may I not be crushed by the Stone as I fall from my self-erected monument set up to glorify myself through my pride! A badly broken bone is difficult enough to heal from, but a crushed bone—well, it may never be right or useful again—not without extensive surgeries and painful rehabilitation. You, Jesus are the only One deserving glory.

Let's return to 1 Samuel 17. You know what I see as one of the most tragic realities in this battle scene? The Israelites had been given victory against this very enemy, but they had forgotten Who had saved them. But now, Saul's disobedience in not carrying out God's instructions concerning the destruction of the Amalekites (see 1 Samuel 1) had affected his ability to rule as a righteous leader. Saul had thought he knew better than God in that situation and used his position for what his bottomless ego could get from it. A humble heart did not beat in the chest of the man who wore the crown. Because of this, there was no one to step forward and remind the Israelites what God had done in the past for them—at least no one they could yet see. The result was a feeling of terror and defeat before the enemy.

Has God put you in a position of facing the enemy yet again over the same thing you battled him over before? What is the plan of victory for the same battle, different day? The strategy is found in 1 Samuel 7:8-13:

Step 1 Cry out for help! Admit that we do not have the strength to face the enemy alone (verse 8).

Step 2 Sacrifice what needs to be sacrificed. Girlfriend, a broken and contrite heart is one our God will not despise. If we can't do it for ourselves, we need to share the burden with a godly person who will stand in the gap to help us learn how to do this (verse 9).

Step 3 Watch for our God to come rescue us, no matter how long it takes. Sometimes that deliverance is immediate (verses 10-11). Most of the time, however, it is not. It is a battle, remember?

Step 4 Give all glory to God that He alone will win the battle. Tear down any monument to yourself or your pride that you have erected in this area (verse 12).

Step 5 After following steps 1-4, praise God that His favor is with you in the heat of the battle. Stand in that belief the next time the enemy tries to invade you in the same place (verse 13). One of my favorite sayings is, "When fear comes knocking, send faith to answer the door and no one will be there!"

Sweet friend, the above strategy is not easily carried out. Life with Jesus is a marathon, not a sprint. God's timing is hardly ever our own, but, rest assured, it is always perfect.

However, what if we have followed these steps and the battle still rages on? The apostle Paul cried out to God to deliver him from the enemy and the Lord said no three different times to Paul's request. Write the answer in 2 Corinthians 12:7 here:

A broken and contrite heart is one our God will not despise.

Could it be that you need the enemy to keep you close to the only One who can save you? Does the battle keep you on your face and desperate before Jesus because you know you don't have the strength to handle its fierceness by yourself? Have you learned to depend on Him more because of the fight for holiness in this area? As crazy as it sounds, thank Him for the battle because you are in the safest place you can be. You are learning to trust Him through the storm.

I would like to close our day of study with some encouragement from Scripture as we wrestle through the battle we are currently involved in. I would encourage you to pick one of the following verses and write its truth on a 3x5 card today. Carry the card with you wherever you go this week and let the living Word of God bring comfort to your heart whenever you need it— even a hundred times a day, if necessary.

I am still confident of this: I will see the goodness of the LORD in the land of the living. Wait for the LORD; be strong and take heart and wait for the LORD. Psalm 27:13-14

But as for me, I watch in hope for the LORD, I wait for God my Savior; my God will hear me. Do not gloat over me, my enemy! Though I have fallen, I will rise. Though I sit in darkness, the LORD will be my light. Micah 7:7-8

Who is among you who [reverently] fears the Lord, who obeys the voice of His Servant, yet who walks in darkness and deep trouble and has no shining splendor [in his heart]? Let him rely on, trust in, and be confident in the name of the Lord, and let him lean upon and be supported by his God. Isaiah 50:10 (Amplified Bible)

☀ **Day Two:** Who Is This Enemy?

My in-laws' former house had a breathtaking living room ceiling which soared above the floor. The huge distance between the ceiling and floor gave the entire room a sense of being much larger than it was. If, however, the ceiling was brought down to a normal height, the room would not have looked as spacious.

There is something about height that fools our minds into thinking something is bigger than it is, just like my in-laws' living room. In this lesson, we are going to take a look at the enemy facing Saul and his men across the valley of Elah on Israel's home turf. It is my prayer that we will see the enemy in a whole new light.

Let's read 1 Samuel 17:4-11 for our text today. What is the height of the tallest person you personally know?

My high school principal was six feet, eight inches tall. Goliath of Gath would have made Mr. Holmer look short in comparison. The giant was like a walking tree! To get an idea of how big this hulk of a man was, let's look at how much his coat of armor and spear shaft weighed.

Bronze coat of armor: _____ shekels

Iron spear shaft: _____ shekels

I think that the word shekel can hinder us in realizing how heavy these weapons were. Biblegateway.com says that his coat of armor was about 125 pounds and the iron point of his spear shaft was 15 pounds![1]

What reaction did this cause the Israelites to have toward the giant and the Philistine army behind him (verse 11)?

Courage and patriotism   Terror and dismay

Anger and indignation

Contrast this reaction with what God had promised his covenant people Israel would be their enemies' reaction if they obeyed him in Deuteronomy 33:29?

What happens to us, girlfriends, when our pride and name become more important in our eyes than pleasing God? We cower in terror when the enemy of our souls comes threatening us. Our ego denies us the grace that would be ours because we cling to the worthless idol of our self-absorption (see Jonah 2:8). We can't remember the victories that God has given us in the past over the same enemy because our eyes have become so used to watching out for

> Our ego denies us the grace that would be ours because we cling to the worthless idol of our self-absorption.

our fragile egos. We don't see when the enemy broke through and invaded our territory until he is looming over us. Even if we have fooled most of the people around us about our character, we never fool the King of the universe.

Look back at what had happened to Saul's mind by the time of this battle in 1 Samuel 16:14. Our lives can become overtaken by paranoia, just like Saul's. We can become full of what Romans 1:21 in the King James Version says:

"Because that, when they knew God, they glorified him not as God, neither were thankful; but became vain in their imaginations, and their foolish heart was darkened."

Being ungrateful and refusing to glorify God alters our minds, girlfriends! Our minds can start down a slippery slope of neurotic behavior, the end of which no one—including ourselves—can know. Saul was ill-prepared for spiritual conflict. The real enemy came and he was terrified in Goliath's presence.

What were Goliath's terms of victory according to 1 Samuel 17:8-9?

After pondering the reaction of the Israelites in verse 11, do you think he was willing to honor his promise when he spoke those words?

I never feel more unsafe than when I have reason to believe that someone in power over me is telling me a falsehood that I cannot refute. God absolutely detests a lying tongue. Let's look at some of the reasons why we cannot make lying a habit.

Match the following Scriptures with the correct reference:

A lying tongue hates those it hurts.	Proverbs 26:28
You, however, smear me with lies.	Job 13:4
You destroy those who tell lies.	Psalm 5:6
I long to redeem them, but they speak lies against me.	Hosea 7:13
In my dismay I said, "All men are liars."	Psalm 116:10-11
The tongue... is itself set on fire by hell.	James 3:6

What incredible destruction is found in a lying tongue! The most sedentary person in the world has an extremely fit-from-use muscle lying between his or her bottom teeth! The Lord is continually healing me from trust issues from my past. I don't know of anything more frightening in the world to me than someone who I believe means me harm, trying to make a deal with me! Similarly, a promise in the mouth of an enemy became the inspiration of terror among many strong men in the army of King Saul.

Did you see who was among the terrified in 1 Samuel 17:11? What had happened to the mighty warrior of 1 Samuel 11 who inspired 330,000 men to fight as one man against the Ammonites and had won the victory soon after he became king?

I believe the hidden answer can be found in what came out of Saul's mouth in 1 Samuel 15:30. After writing out the verse here, underline the phrase that leads you to conclude what might have happened to the once-mighty warrior:

Saul had been rejected by the Lord for not obeying His command to completely destroy the Amalekites, but Saul had done the rejecting first. "Go back with me so that I might worship the Lord your God," Saul requested of Samuel. The real enemy had come and Saul was terrified and powerless in Goliath's presence.

If we have been promised that we are more than conquerors through the blood of Jesus Christ, why do we still cower before the same enemy, sweet sisters? Could it be that we have disobeyed and failed to do what God has asked us to do in the past? We feel as though He has rejected us, but is the truth that we are actually the ones who did the rejecting? We live in an age of grace. But I fear that we have a warped, twisted view of spiritual warfare. We think that we are fighting the devil, but could it be we are fighting conviction? Could it be that we are not really fighting an enemy at all from the outside, but are cowering in terror over the sure judgment of not toppling the idol of ego in our lives? When we do this, we can be guilty of abusing grace and treating it as cheap.

Do we examine our lives only when our kingdom is being threatened or taken away from us? Is our quick confession coming from a heart that is broken over our sin or from a desire to unload a guilty conscience with no real intention of turning away from the sin?

Saul had faced the enemy before and had won. In his quest for fame and recognition, the real enemy he should have been fighting was set aside to fight for his ego.

I don't hear it very much anymore, but the truth of the matter is that God will not contend with us forever (Genesis 6:3). He tells us to seek Him while He may be found. That must mean that there is a day when He may not be able to be found so easily. We can quench that still, small voice of the Holy Spirit with our rebellion, sisters. We can make our lives a living hell because we are convinced that everyone is out to get us when that could not be farther from the truth. We can think we are seeing a devil behind every bush. The devil doesn't have to be there! We are like the cat chasing her own tail, trying to bite our own skin and never realizing the pain is coming from our own teeth.

Do we examine our lives only when our kingdom is being threatened or taken away from us?

✳ What did the apostle Paul warn Timothy, his son in the faith, about this matter in 1 Timothy 1:18-19?

I wrote the following lines about jealousy's poison. Apply them to your own life's experience:

O jealousy, what bitter fruit! What poison to my soul you bring. You steal the joy that once was mine and make me poor indeed.

Who is the enemy we are fighting? The answer to this question may come when we determine what is more dominant in our lives. I think we can discern what is dominant by two huge signposts in our lives:

1) active faith instead of paranoia or irrational fear ruling us and

2) a good conscience that is at peace, not because we are perfect, but because we are not afraid to submit to the authority of God and do whatever needs to be done according to His Word to have that good conscience instead of a guilty conscience.

David wrote a beautiful word of instruction for us in Psalm 4:3-5:

3 Know that the LORD has set apart the godly for himself;
the LORD will hear when I call to him.
4 In your anger do not sin;
when you are on your beds,
search your hearts and be silent.
Selah
5 Offer right sacrifices
and trust in the LORD.

> We must be diligent to keep short accounts between ourselves and the Lord. We then can fight the good fight with the true enemies of God.

If we are offering the right sacrifice of a humble heart after we have searched and confessed any hidden sin in prayer on our beds and are willing to do what God asks us to do, then we can have confidence that the Lord will hear us when we call to Him. We must be diligent to keep short accounts between ourselves and the Lord. We then can fight the good fight with the true enemies of God. Even if that enemy is over nine feet tall, our response need not be one of terror and dismay. We will be able to trust God at His Word that His weapons will triumph over whatever sort of spear head or armor the enemy has in his possession. Why? Because the Lord assures us that, "… we are more than conquerors through Him who loved us." (Romans 8:27)

Day Three: Between Brothers

Ah, the complexity of family relationships! There is something we all have in common: we are all part of families. We had no choice in the matter to whom we were born or whether we had any siblings. The greatest encouragement and the greatest discouragement can come from people with whom we have shared a great part of our lives living out our very formative years.

Take an assessment of your family relationships right now. How would you rate your intimacy level in the following relationships on a scale from one to five (with one being extremely distant and five being extremely satisfying)?

Your parents _____ Your siblings _____ Your husband _____

Your children _____

I once ripped open a scab on my knee as a young girl playing on the playground. I had gotten the original wound through a traumatic and unusual fall. The wound was deep and took several days to form a protective scab. Although I had never been particularly aware of my knee before, the thought of protecting my open wound was never far from my mind after my injury. I did all I could to avoid falling and re-injuring myself. I purposely did not involve myself in certain games because I was afraid to see the blood and feel the pain again. A couple weeks passed by and I was not being as careful as I had been. Unexpectedly, I fell as I was running. The impact of the fall was taken on the hurt knee I had been so carefully protecting all that time. The pain and fear were instantly relived as I experienced fresh pain on my old wound.

I believe that we can be protecting an old wound, sweet sisters, that we have forgotten about when it comes to family relationships. Today's text of Scripture is going to let us look through a window into the family of David. We may catch a reflection of ourselves as we stare.

Let's read through 1 Samuel 17:12-31. Pay careful attention to the dialogue exchanged between the two brothers and write your observations in the margin.

My parents were in their mid-twenties when I was born. My father was thirty-seven when his last child was born. What does 1 Samuel 17:12 tell us about David's father?

He was very old.   He was a skilled hunter.

He was deceased.

121

How do you think this affected his relationship with his youngest son? My sister-in-law, Karen, was pregnant with her third child at age thirty-six. Another sister-in-law, Molly, had her third child when she was twenty-nine years old.

How do you think the age of a parent affects his or her parenting?

I could imagine that the father Eliab knew as a young boy was much different than the one that David could recall growing up. Eliab might have indeed seen Jesse as a strong, virile man in his prime. David's first memory of his father was one of a man who was aging noticeably every year.

What is your birth order and who can you relate to more in your memory of your father—Eliab or David?

I am the eldest of four children. My youngest brother, Jack, was born when I was eleven. When he started first grade, I was a freshman in college. He was into matchbox cars; I was into my college syllabus. He was not allowed to cross the street. I was five hundred miles away in another state completely on my own. His television choices were cartoons. Mine were drama shows. We did not have anything in common other than the same parents. It is only in the last five years that Jack and I have developed a relationship with common bonds.

Can you relate? Do you have a sibling much younger or older than yourself that you could not/cannot relate to very well? Has that changed over time and why?

Eliab and the other two brothers were men at this point in Scripture, maybe with children of their own, while David was still a boy. The older three had left home to fight in Saul's army against the Philistines.

What were David's two responsibilities according to 1 Samuel 17:15?

This is where I believe we have our first clue for the reason the encounter between the oldest brother and the youngest had a nasty tone about it. The kid brother was in the king's service. Now nothing grates on an older sibling more than when the younger one seems to have unmerited favor on him or her. After all, the youngest hasn't had to pave the way, pay his dues, or be responsible like the oldest one has had to! We have already seen that David did not necessarily have the respect of his father or his brothers from the day Samuel secretly anointed him as the new king of Israel. When asked to bring all of his sons to Samuel, Jesse had left David in the fields!

But David had already made a name for himself. All those hours of solitude allowed him the ability to practice on his harp, preparing him, unbeknownst to David, for his service to Saul. David did not waste the lonely hours. He communed with Jehovah. Isn't ironic that the only way to keep the evil spirit that tormented Saul at bay was have the forgotten brother play for him? God never wastes anything in our lives, my sweet sister. We will be summoned to high places from the solitude we spent in communion with our God.

What task did Jesse give David in verses 17-20?

Verse 18 in the NIV reads like this: "… See how your brothers are and bring back some assurance from them."
This is how verse 18 reads in the New Living Translation:

"… See how your brothers are getting along, and bring me back a letter from them."

The King James translates "getting along" as "welfare."

According to Strong's Concordance, welfare in the Hebrew means: completeness, soundness, welfare, peace
1a)   completeness (in number)
1b)   safety, soundness (in body)
1c)   welfare, health, prosperity
1d)   peace, quiet, tranquillity, contentment
1e)   peace, friendship
1e1) of human relationships
1e2) with God especially in covenant relationship[1]

The part of the word meaning "peace in human relationships" tells me that it was not all harmonious inside the household of Jesse. There were nine men, after all, under one roof at some time in David's life. Three big brothers had left home to make a name for themselves as the bravest soldier of all. Just a little competition and the stage was set for hotheaded emotions to boil over between the three. Could it be that daddy Jesse was telling David to do a little spying on his big brothers? And Jesse wanted David to bring back some assurance from the three that all was well. I wonder how that request went over with the big boys.

God never wastes anything in our lives, my sweet sister. We will be summoned to high places from the solitude we spent in communion with our God.

What was the response of some other older brothers to a similar mission their father had sent the youngest on? Let's look at Genesis 37:12-20 for the answer.

Mocking   Murderous intentions   Hiding from him

David arrived at the campsite just in time to hear the blasphemous threats of the Philistine giant across the valley of Elah. Contrast the Israelite army's reaction to Goliath (1 Samuel 17:24) with David's reaction in verse 26.

Sometimes, girlfriends, we do not have to do anything to provoke the ugly green monster of jealousy to arise and stun us with its cruelty.

I don't read that the only men who did not run away from Goliath were the brothers of David. I read that all the men ran, which leads me to conclude that Eliab was among those who had run every day for forty days. Then Eliab's eyes fell on David talking with Eliab's fellow soldiers.

Look at Eliab's words to David in verse 28. There was no, "Hey, little brother! I am so happy that you came to see me." Instead, Eliab cut him down in front of the other men ("With whom did you leave those *few* sheep in the desert?") and accused David of being wicked and conceited. He also accused him of impure motives.

The Bible not only gives us the blueprint for living abundant lives, but it makes us wiser than our enemies (Psalm 119:98). Through the breathing Word of God, we can put together pieces of a puzzle that those without this knowledge cannot figure out. Jealousy is so ugly, so detrimental, and so self-centered; its partner in crime is anger. Anger is always a symptom of a deeper problem. I would like to suggest that there was a whole lot of dysfunction in the household of Jesse which caused unhealed wounds so many years after the hurt happened. Both Eliab and David were wounded. We all are. David's motives for visiting his brothers were completely misunderstood by Eliab. David probably could not have known that his visit had torn off the scab that Eliab had unsuccessfully tried to protect.

Sometimes, we do not have to do anything to provoke the ugly green monster of jealousy to arise and stun us with its cruelty. David's mere presence was a reminder to Eliab of how unfair life can be. Eliab was passed over when Samuel brought the anointing oil and was witness to the obvious favor of God that rested on David's head that day. Eliab was a grown man; David was still a boy. Eliab was a warrior; David was only a shepherd boy. Yet, it was David who had been summoned into the presence of Saul to play his harp and calm the king. Eliab was wrestling with a problem much larger than his baby brother showing up unannounced. Eliab was struggling with a heart that believed the lie that God had given David more than he had Eliab. Unfortunately, don't we all empathize all too well with Eliab's broken heart?

Listen to what Matthew Henry says about Eliab's behavior in this situation:

"See the folly, absurdity, and wickedness, of a proud and envious passion; how groundless its jealousies are, how unjust its censures, how unfair its representations, how bitter its invectives, and how indecent its language. God, by his grace, keep us from such a spirit!" [2]

I believe David, in response to Eliab's wrong judgments about him, did what he had done many times before: he walked away because he knew it was useless to argue with his brother. The matter between them remained unresolved.

What are we told in 1 Samuel 17:31 about David? Choose one:

Eliab forced him to leave.   King Saul summoned him.

David retaliated against Eliab.

While his big brother, Eliab, misjudged the shepherd boy, God did not. David was summoned before King Saul for the words spoken by his mouth that revealed his brave heart. Remember, sweet friend, our God always judges our hearts. He is never swayed by others' opinions of us. He knows the truth. May we live lives worthy of being summoned by the King, unburdened by the misjudgments of others and full of grace toward them when they do—especially when those misjudgments are made by those who should be closest to us.

> While his big brother, Eliab, misjudged the shepherd boy, God did not.

125

Day Four: A "Foolish" Plan and a Resounding Victory

Jesus is the most controversial figure in the history of mankind. We all have a sinful nature that does not allow us to see the wisdom in His teachings. We need to be made new; we need to be given new eyes for answers to those familiar patterns in us that lead us down a path of destruction.

Jesus spent much of His ministry teaching radical new ideas. Ideas that seem, well… downright unbelievable because they are so contrary to what our culture says is the way to live life. On a windy mountainside, Jesus proclaimed what would become known as the Beatitudes—eight pathways of death to our fleshly desires that would bring us the abundant life He promised to those who love Him. These eight are listed in the Gospel of Matthew.

What does Matthew 5:8 say?

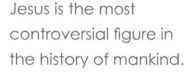

Jesus is the most controversial figure in the history of mankind.

Girlfriends, a pure heart is a heart that is not haughty. Pride and arrogance will prevent us from seeing God and knowing His will. Scripture is very clear on this.

What insight does Isaiah 29:18-19 give to the relationship between blindness and humility?

We left yesterday's lesson with David's intentions being misjudged by his older brother Eliab. David had been summoned by Saul for his righteous indignation over Goliath's relentless tirade against the armies of the living God. We must ask this question about Saul: why had Goliath been able to terrorize the army of Israel for over a month, twice a day? Saul was no longer the fearless warrior who we saw the Spirit of the Lord come upon and route the Ammonites soon after he was anointed. Saul had rejected the living God and now was left to cower along with his men. Does it strike you as odd, as it does me, that an adolescent boy was summoned as the possible hope of Israel when an able-bodied man sat on the throne?

Let's pick up the story and read 1 Samuel 17:32-40.

Based on what we read as the condition for seeing God in Isaiah 28:18-19, what word of self-description by David to Saul denotes humility?

Our American culture worships independence. We can struggle with submitting to anyone. David did not come into the king's presence with swaggering bravado. Instead he first encouraged Saul's heart and then told Saul that he was his servant. What would happen if we would first encourage someone else and then tell him or her that we would serve by fighting a worthy enemy instead of offering answers out of pride? For example, instead of joining in the bashing of a friend's husband as the cause of her marriage being under crisis, what would happen if we encouraged our friend by telling her we would fight alongside her in prayer for that marriage to be restored?

My husband loves to root for the underdog. It doesn't matter how impressive a college team's record for wins is, Rob always cheers for the little team facing the giant. There is something in all of us that loves an unexplainable victory. But part of the reason the victory is so sweet is because of the many discouraging voices that rang in the ears of the victor before the trophy was won.

How did Saul react to David's bravery in verse 33?

Saul accepted David's offer.　　　　He discouraged David.

Saul realized his own duty to fight.

What did David say in response to Saul's lack of belief in his ability to fight in verses 34-37?

> Many private battles have to be fought before God allows such a public display of His power in the life of an individual.

I want to ask all of us a question. Where do you get the strength to fight the battle of life? Is it in your education, your intelligence, your financial resources? David had experienced victory in battles with the lion and the bear that threatened his father's sheep. David had come face to face with the vicious, murderous face of the lion before this day in front of Saul. He had no illusions about who had let him escape from those jaws before. David had already experienced the strength that the Lord his God gave him before the eyes of the enemy army watching. No one saw those amazing feats of courage and victory. Many private battles have to be fought before God allows such a public display of His power in the life of an individual. I believe that it would be far too easy to credit ourselves with the glory that He alone is due if we do not learn His might in the privacy of our own lives first. The battle is won on our knees in obscurity before the God who sees everything.

Why do you think Saul reacted the way he did to David's argument in verse 37?

Could it be that the madman was having a lucid moment? Possibly. Or perhaps Saul was showing the cowardly side of his character by sending an adolescent out to do the job that should have been his as the king of Israel. Regardless of Saul's motives, David was dressed by him in a coat of armor and a bronze helmet.

What was the problem with Saul's armor in verse 40?

Have you ever had to attend an event wearing clothes that did not fit you well? I had a close relative who would buy me clothes that never fit me well. She loved what she had picked out. I despised the article of clothing because it was not made for my size. I think David realized that the best armor in the world would not help him, but endanger his life on the battlefield. So he went in his own skin with the weapons that had brought him victory before, even though this enemy loomed over nine feet tall. We run into problems when we try to be someone else. I like formulas. I like trying a tested method that works rather than stepping out in faith believing that what God has equipped me with is adequate for the job. It is Satan's ploy to get us to fear that God has not equipped us with everything we need through His Word to cause him to run.

Have you ever tried to win a battle dressed like someone you were not? Please share here.

After refusing the armor offered by the king, David decided on the most foolish battle plan of all. What weapons did David have with him as he approached the giant?
Fill in the blanks from verse 40:

"Then he took his _____ in his hand, chose _____ _____ _____ from the stream, put them in his shepherd's bag, and with his _____ in his _____, _____ the giant."

What was Goliath's reaction in seeing David approach him (verses 42-44)?

What explanation did David give Goliath for fighting him (verses 45-46)? Pick one:

____ David was avenging God's holy Name.

____ David would strike him down and cut off his head.

____ The whole world would know that there was a God in Israel, to whom the battle belonged.

____ All of the above.

I can guarantee the top military academies in our nation would never recommend that kind of arsenal. What did David know that neither of the two enemy armies knew in Isaiah 32:17?

What is the reward of an ordinary life lived out in communion with God? Righteousness that calms our hearts when everyone else is in chaos. Our souls will be blessed with quietness and confidence to face a challenge that would undo those who look for peace elsewhere (Isaiah 30:15). God then takes that ordinary life that is yielded to Him and does extraordinary, logic-defying feats with that life.

Not only did David kill the giant with Goliath's own sword, but the terrified army of Israel regained their courage through the "foolish" battle plan of a young boy who knew that God was behind him. The Philistines were chased back into their own land, allowing the Israelites to plunder the enemy who had threatened them twice a day for forty days. Oh, sweet sisters, do we realize that this is the reason God chooses to use us? Not so we can puff ourselves up, but so that the body of Christ is encouraged and the enemy of our souls is plundered in the very place where he used to terrify us!

As we close today, we need to make note of where Saul's head was at this time. What did Saul ask his commander as David was going out to meet the giant 1 Samuel 17:55?

> God then takes that ordinary life that is yielded to Him and does extraordinary, logic-defying feats with that life.

How bizarre! How could Saul have not recognized the only one whose playing could bring him relief from his mental torment? He acted as though he had never seen David before. Disobedience and rebellion have so many tentacles. We are blinded to the presence of help and comfort in the confusion of our souls when we are in that desert place. In the days and years to come, I wonder if David wished Saul would have been as forgetful of who David was as Saul had been on the day of the undeniable victory when Goliath of Gath fell before all Israel.

Day Five: A Jealous Eye On Him

The story of King Saul allows us to take another look at the multi-faced ugliness of jealousy. Today we will explore the slippery slope of a heart unrestrained in its rashness. We will stand with our mouths open as we see what jealousy led Saul to think, believe, and, tragically, do and say. May we learn from his example and not have to learn from this one from experience. Let's refresh our memories about a passage from yesterday's lesson.

To establish how a temptation becomes death to us, let's examine James 1:13-16.

How are we tempted?_____

Where is desire conceived in us?_____

Left unattended, an evil desire gives birth to what?_____

Sin leads to what?_____

James is clear that God never tempts us to sin. To be enticed and dragged away down a destructive path, a wrong desire conceived in our thought life has had to go through three steps before it leads to a spiritual death. Do you see that our sinful nature plus an act of our own will is involved in each of the three steps? If we are facing spiritual death, we are the guilty party involved, not God.

We are going to observe the downward spiral Saul took as his jealous desires led to behavior that can only be described as rash. *Rash* is defined as, "acting or tending to act too hastily or without due consideration."[3]

Please turn to 1 Samuel 18:6-11 and record your observations in the margin:

I think that it is important that we establish when the first evil thought towards David started to entice and drag Saul away from a sense of morality. Verse six of the passage tells us from what battle the men of Israel were returning home.

Who had been defeated?_____

How was David praised?_____

Nothing stings on the back of pride like the whip of humiliation, and Saul surely felt his pride take a beating with that refrain. Do you see the mental jump he made in his mind from the humiliation he felt over the women's praise of David to the judgment he made about David's intentions? Don't let the words, he thought, in verse eight escape your attention. We are led to believe that Saul did not speak a word about his feelings to anyone, but the change in his attitude toward David could not have been more drastic.

> Nothing stings on the back of pride like the whip of humiliation.

To emphasize Saul's drastic change of heart toward David, please go back to 1 Samuel 16:17-22. How did Saul perceive David when David first entered his service (verses 22-23)

Saul, because he felt diminished in the eyes of his subjects, let the words of others rob him of his fondness for David. Saul's affection and admiration for David were replaced with murderous thoughts.

Have you, like me, let praise directed toward another person rob you of the desire to see that person succeed, killing the chance for a possible relationship between you and the object of your jealousy? If yes, write the name of the person here.

Saul, tempted by jealous thoughts, was enticed and dragged away from the warm feelings he once had for David. Instead of rejecting those jealous thoughts, Saul allowed them to fester and grow until he rashly made a false judgment about David's intentions. Now he was convinced that not only was David outdoing him in popularity with the women, but that David was looking to take away his throne! Instead of glorying in the magnificent victory the Lord accomplished through David, Saul chose to believe David had an ulterior motive for killing the giant. Saul was following Satan's plan exactly to step into the hidden net laid in front of him.

Romans 3:23 reveals to us that the wages of sin is death. In this case, Saul ceased to be able to think clearly about David. Looking back at our text, what did Saul try to do to David the day following his humiliation over the women's refrain (1 Samuel 18:10-11)?

David has just slain the giant, Goliath, and, as a reward, has been taken into Saul's household. Glance back over at 1 Samuel 18:5-9 and summarize according to the following columns:

David's accomplishment   Saul's reaction

✳ Oh, girlfriends, this is HUGE! What made David fall out of favor with Saul (verse 8)?

Did you see how Saul's perception of the possible future implications hidden in the women's praise of David was a threat to Saul's own glory? What did this perception cause in Saul (verse 9)?

Oh, how quickly a favored person can become the object of our rage and jealousy when we perceive him or her to be a threat to our own glory or standing with others. How easy it is to love those who pose no threat of appearing better than we are. Give me someone I perceive can show me up, and it is much more difficult to not feel threatened within myself. I remember a situation involving a roommate whom I felt was trying to move in on my boyfriend. I angrily told my boyfriend that if I ever saw him even talking to her, I would end the relationship. Why did I do that? I was threatened that he may see something he admired more in her than me. I couldn't handle that fear and gave him an ultimatum (can you believe it—he ended up marrying me).

> How easy it is to love those who pose no threat of appearing better than we are.

After not being able to pin David to the wall with his spear, Saul became afraid of David. What was the reason for Saul's fear of David (verses 12-16)?

What's more of a torment—a fear that you can rationalize is valid only in your imagination or one that you know is not going to go away because it contains truth? The scariest movies to me growing up were not the ones in which inanimate objects could talk. I knew that was not reality. The scariest situations were those that really could happen because they were within the realm of possibility.

Saul's actions toward David became truly bizarre from this point on. After reading verses 17-19, record Saul's plan of being rid of David.

It didn't work, and like the spider who cunningly spins a web, Saul weaved his wickedness with deceit with the addition of a lie in verse 22. Contrast this with his real intent in verse 25:

After having failed to kill David on his own and not being able to rid himself of David through a battle with a fierce enemy, Saul slipped into madness. Instead of concentrating on his God-appointed responsibilities in leading his country against the Philistines, Saul convinced himself that his enemy was David. Instead of ridding Israel of the threat of a pagan nation, Saul squandered his time and energy trying to extinguish a threat that never existed except in his own mind.

The battle is always in our minds, sweet sisters. We daily have a choice to be conformed to our own thoughts or the thoughts of Jesus Christ (see Romans 12:1-2). Saul continued to be a rebel, which Samuel likened to witchcraft (1 Samuel 15). Rebellion is a very serious sin and one we must be absolutely aggressive about rooting out. I want us to look at a sobering passage which we need to keep in the forefront of our minds when we see the spirit of rebellion raising its ugly head in us.

What does Deuteronomy 28:15 say will happen? List some of those in verses 28-29:

I am not against using antidepressants. I know someone who struggles with a mental illness. She has chosen not to go the route of drugs, but the effects are very debilitating on her and her family. Please hear me loud and clear! My sweet friend is walking with God daily and still struggles with depression. It is very real illness. But I believe that there is a huge difference between a brain that cannot produce enough serotonin and one that is tormented by sin. Scripture gives a window on Saul's life. He never wrestled with tormenting evil spirits or murderous thoughts until after he had deliberately disobeyed God. The Word of God does not indicate Saul ever being sorry for the right reasons. Instead, he jeopardized his family relationships, lost his spiritual mentor (Samuel), and, as a result, was chasing the wrong enemy. My dear sister, is that us? Has sin and rebellion caused us to grope around blindly in the dark, tormented in our souls, without knowledge of how to get out of the mess that life has tragically become?

Minimizing sin's destructiveness in our lives is just what the enemy wants us to do. He does not doubt, as we may at times, in Christ's power to set us free. If Satan can make us think that we are justified in our jealous thoughts, he has won! He is the real enemy, not the person we are jealous of! Until we come to believe this is the truth, we will never know the abundant life that Jesus Christ died to give us. We will live and die having missed His purpose for us. We cannot afford to conform to the way this world thinks! Our mental health may be at stake for the costly decision we make to not repent and beg God to help us change.

God knew that all this would happen in Saul's life. He knew that the Israelites would reject Him as their King and ask for someone like the nations around them had.

> Rebellion is a very serious sin and one we must be absolutely aggressive about rooting out.

Let's read Deuteronomy 17:14-20. What did God instruct the king to do in verse 18? Choose one:

Go to the temple often.   Provide large sacrifices.

Write for himself a copy of the law.

The purpose of being immersed in the law of the Lord was to keep Saul from a rebellious heart and arrogance toward others. This was the antidote for Saul's problem in 1 Samuel 17. He didn't take God up on it. How do I know that? Because individuals who know truly follow after God cannot go on sinning without changing their sinful behaviors (1 John 3:6). I have heard this phrase and believe it to be so true based on my own experience:

"Dusty Bibles give us dirty lives."

May Saul's life show us the truth of that statement and cause us to turn away from a rebellious heart and its arrogance. May we realize the truth of this Scripture:

"If your law had not been my delight, I would have perished in my affliction."
Psalm 119:92

Fugitive of a Hardened Heart

It has been my prayer throughout the writing of this study that we would come to see jealousy as a symptom of a broken heart. Somewhere, dear sisters, we have come to believe the lie that our God is not trustworthy in His justice towards us. The fallout of that untruth is that we cannot believe that God loves us because our idea of His goodness has been skewed by life's difficult and inexplicable circumstances.

The following Scripture gives us the reason for our blindness in seeing the glory of God in our own lives:

Make every effort to live in peace with all men and to be holy; without holiness no one will see the Lord. See to it that no one misses the grace of God and that no bitter root grows up to cause trouble and defile many.
Hebrews 12:14-15

We can make the false assumption that the secret sin of jealousy is contained to our thoughts, hidden away from others. Scripture assures us that this is not the case. The moment we detect the bitterness of jealousy entering our thoughts, we must take those thoughts captive and make them obedient to Christ. If we do not, we are in danger of not seeing the Lord. This week we are going to see the heartbreaking consequences of Saul's sin and its effect on those he should have loved the most.

I want us to ask ourselves this question as we participate in our homework this week: How has jealousy made us a fugitive, either as its perpetrator or its victim? We must intently examine our thought lives, my dear sister, to ensure there is no place for a bitter root to grow.

✳ **Day One:** Victims of a Father's Jealousy

As I have thought through jealousy as a Bible study topic, I have come to realize that its complexity is best compared to a spider's web. We can be the fly caught in someone else's web of envy as well as being the spider waiting for our prey in the web we have spun ourselves. Jealousy is so insidious because we can be both its victim and its perpetrator simultaneously.

Let's turn to 1 Samuel 18:30 and read through 1 Samuel 19:7. Whose allegiance did Saul demand in this passage?

Briefly look over 1 Samuel 18:20-26. How did Saul use another family member in a deadly plot against David?

> Jealousy is so insidious because we can be both its victim and its perpetrator simultaneously.

Jonathan had every reason to cooperate with Saul's plot to get rid of David. His father's power as king would have been an easy cover up for the jealousy Jonathan should have had toward the shepherd boy turned darling of Israel. List some of the reasons Jonathan would have had, from a human perspective, to hate David:

What amazes you the most about how Jonathan felt toward David in 1 Samuel 18:1?

Girls, we can't forget for a minute that Jonathan was the heir to the throne of Israel. David suddenly burst on the scene out of nowhere and took the lion's share of attention of Jonathan's future subjects. David was handsome, the object of adoration from the females, a mighty warrior, and God's favor rested on him in an obvious way to all around him. Jonathan should have hated David as much as Saul did. Instead, Jonathan found himself in the middle of an impossible situation with having to choose who would have his loyalty—his father or his dearest friend.

What steps did Jonathan take to try to achieve peace between the two men in 1 Samuel 19:2-7?

It's easy to love when relationships are pleasant and neat, but it is easy to want to bail out when the going gets tough. Have you ever felt caught between two people you love that cannot get along? I have. The anguish was indescribable because I loved both equally and felt like I had to choose between them.

Have you ever known a parent's jealousy toward someone to affect his or her child? Share how here:

Rewrite Hebrews 12:14-15 in your own words:

The bitter root between two people never stays between the two. Ever. Its poison seeps into all areas, causing trouble and defiling many. Bitterness prevents families from being together and forgiving each other. It makes us have to carefully guard our conversations to protect ourselves from appearing as though we are taking sides, loving one party more than the other. Dissension among us is detestable to God.

✳ What was the cause of the bitter root in Saul toward David according to 1 Samuel 18:29?

Say it isn't so! Yet my heart slinks back in shame because I have envied someone who seemed to have God's blessing on her life in an area I felt I didn't have that same favor. I have disliked someone simply because I thought God was blessing her more than He should.

Have you ever been jealous of someone because of God's blessing on her life? Share here:

Dissension among us is detestable to God.

Now we are going to see who else was caught in the web of Saul's jealousy. Let's continue by reading 1 Samuel 19:8-17. What event occurred in verse 8?

Jealousy is like a sleeping bear. The victim of the jealous person can be fooled into thinking that all is well with the who has decided the victim is the enemy. What was David doing in verse 9 when Saul tried to kill him in verse 10?

Glance back at 1 Samuel 18:10-11. Do you think David had a serious case of deja-vu as he played the harp now in Saul's presence? Saul had tried to kill him not once, not twice, but three times. My question is: why was David back in Saul's presence?

Before I share with you my thoughts for David's return, please share why you think David chose again to be with the man who had tried to kill him three times?

I think that David did not want to believe what he knew was the truth. What does Titus 1:15 say about the pure?

Saul could not believe any motive by David was pure. Saul had allowed his mind to become corrupt long before. The consequence of that corruption was a conscience that could not even recognize the sin he was committing against David. I believe Saul truly felt he was justified in killing David, the enemy of his corrupted mind and conscience.

Where did David run to after he dodged the javelin in Saul's hand (1 Sam. 19:10)?

To Jonathan   To Michal

To Jesse   To his sheep

How was this person was related to both David and to Saul?

Saul had promised his older daughter, Merab, in marriage to the Israelite brave enough to kill Goliath. Although David accomplished this feat, he did not, at that particular time, feel worthy of becoming the son-in-law of the king and refused to marry Merab. Slaying the giant and routing the enemy army of the Philistines made David a superstar in the minds of every Israelite young lady including Michal, the younger daughter of King Saul.

Glance back at 1 Samuel 18:20-28.

What was the reason for Saul's pleasure in verse 21?

How did Saul use this knowledge to his advantage in verses 22, 25?

What happened in Saul's heart towards David when Saul's plot failed in verses 27-29?

Have you ever hidden a jealous agenda behind false flattery of another to help you obtain what you wanted?

Michal was terrified for her husband's life (the man that won her hand by the killing of 200 Philistines) as she saw the soldiers surrounding their home. As the night progressed, Michal came up with a plan to help David escape through a window and then put an idol with some goats' hair in their bed to fool the soldiers when they came to arrest him the next morning. The soldiers felt a duty to respect the king's daughter when Michal deceived them by saying David was sick.

Who had no sympathy for David's condition when he heard the soldier's reason for not raiding David's home in 1 Samuel 19:14-15? What did he ask the soldier's to do in verse 15?

Listen to what the prophet Isaiah says:

Their feet rush into sin;
*   they are swift to shed innocent blood.*
*   Their thoughts are evil thoughts;*
*   ruin and destruction mark their ways.*
The way of peace they do not know;
*   there is no justice in their paths.*
*   They have turned them into crooked roads;*
*   no one who walks in them will know peace.*   *Isaiah 59:7-8*

How far will jealousy take us? Let's ask Cain (Genesis 4). He killed his innocent brother because of his jealousy. Let's ask Achan who, because of his envious desires, stole the forbidden, devoted riches of Jericho, which resulted in the stoning and burning of his entire family (Joshua 7). Let's ask wicked King Ahab of Israel who had his wife, Jezebel, kill a man named Naboth because Ahab coveted a vineyard that Naboth refused to give to him (1 Kings 21). These may be radical examples, but we see in them the truth of how far the sin of jealousy can take us. Jealousy will never give us peace. That which is just and true will not be able to be seen through the blind eyes of envy. Our paths will become crooked and perilous to both us and to those we love.

Saul turned his full wrath on his daughter. I think Michal's lie to her father in verse 17 was the result of a little girl who had watched her father rule the house according to his own idea of righteousness, not God's idea. Perhaps Michal had been the indirect victim of Saul's jealous rages before this.

Let's finish our reading today with 1 Samuel 19:18-23. Saul tried twice to have David captured from the place of safety he had in Naioth with Samuel. On the third time, even though it had initially been beneath Saul's dignity, he came to get David himself, so intent was he on killing him.

What happened instead of Saul's original plot against David in verses 23-24?

What does Matthew 7:21-23 give as a possible explanation for Saul's behavior?

What sobering words! May Jesus never say these words to you and me. Saul's heart was about as far away from the will of God as we have ever seen it to be. David was God's choice of a king for Israel. Saul's jealousy had put him in the position of trying to thwart what God had already decided would happen. In His incredible mercy, God allowed Saul to be overcome by the praise of others, even when Saul's own heart was filled with evil plans. In trying to deceive others, Saul was the one who was the most greatly deceived. As painful as the process may prove to be, let's allow God to tear off the mask of deceit, sweet friend, and transform the deception of our lives into the truth!

Saul's jealousy had put him in the position of trying to thwart what God had already decided would happen.

140

✳ Day Two: An Impossible Choice

Today we are going to look at Scripture through the eyes of Jonathan. Jonathan was placed in a terrible predicament as both the son of King Saul and the soul friend of David. Whoever said the Bible was irrelevant to life could not have been familiar with the story of Jonathan. In a day when we live such complicated lives of pain, there is hardly a better example of how complex one's life story can be than that of Jonathan.

James 3:16 warns us about the boundless depravity a human being can stoop to when envy is involved. Disorder and every sort of evil practice can be the outcome. Saul's plan to use his children to rid his life of David horrifies me more than anything else. We are going to look at this in more depth now. *Rash, rush to judgment, and impulsive* are words which seem almost inadequate when we try to describe King Saul's next actions. Unfortunately, we will have to use them again to describe the next scene of our story.

To help us see how far jealousy can twist one's judgment, we are now going to look at a tragic exchange between Saul and his son, Jonathan, regarding Jonathan's loyalty to David. Please read all of 1 Samuel 20 paying careful attention to Jonathan's role in these verses.

What gave David reason to question Saul's motives in 1 Samuel 20:3 (Hint: Look back at 1 Samuel 19:2)?

Do you believe Jonathan really believed that David had no cause to fear for his life? Why or why not?

Have you ever assured someone positively of another's feelings toward her even when you both had reason to believe the worst? How did that make you feel?

What did Jonathan vow to do for David and what did he discover in 1 Samuel 20:12-16?

What motivated Jonathan to make a covenant with David? Choose one:

deceptive motives   jealous intentions   immense love

competitiveness

In a day when we live such complicated lives of pain, there is hardly a better example of how complex one's life story can be than that of Jonathan.

What did Jonathan find out about his father and what did it almost cost Jonathan?

Have you ever been ashamed of your parent's behavior? Use three words to describe how you felt:

Saul's bitter root of jealousy cost David and Jonathan daily companionship. Maybe you and I have been forced to make a similar choice. The truth we see is no one wins.

After checking your heart, is the Lord reminding you of a friendship that is no more because of your own bitter root of jealousy? Whose choice was it to end the friendship?

We are completely out of God's will and out from under the umbrella of His blessing when we do not do everything in our power to be at peace with everyone. No, not just the people we like or who like us. Enemies are also included.

What kind of harvest does James 3:18 promise if we are willing to do this?

envy   bitterness   peace   sorrow   guilt

I want that kind of harvest, don't you? There have been seasons in my life in which I have allowed all my relationships to be in total chaos. If I look back on those times, my goal was not to sow peace; it was lived out of complete self-centeredness. I can pinpoint a bitter root every time in those seasons that reaped a harvest of trouble that defiled everyone involved in my life. I daily fight allowing the bitter root to be planted, my friend. Daily, I have to choose to claim the power of Christ to enable me to not allow its poison to take over my mind, heart, and soul. I cannot free myself. Scripture assures me that I will one day be accountable for those relationships that I have been involved in—both the relationships that I have let Christ rule and those that I have not. I want life to be as joyful as it possibly can be here in this life. Where there is no peace, there is no joy. But I am sold as a slave to sin (Romans 7:14). I cannot pluck up the bitter root. Jealousy is like a weed that is killed in one part of my yard, but springs up the next week in another section. There is only one cure for this.

Who must do the pulling up or pruning according to
John 15:1-2?

❋ Jonathan had made a vow to his friend, David, to inform
him of Saul's true intentions. How did Saul's reaction to
David's absence reveal the true motives of his heart to
Jonathan in 1 Samuel 20:30-31?

The question we must ask ourselves is are we *peacemakers* or *peacekeepers?* Jesus
said that those who were *peacemakers* would be blessed according to Matthew
5:9. I have often confused my role as a peacekeeper for a peacemaker; I
have come to see there is a huge difference between the two. The harvest
of a peacekeeper is that no one has peace because the quick fix of putting
a bandage on a bleeding wound is more appealing than cleaning up the
infection required to heal the wound. A peacekeeper wants quiet—not true
peace—at all costs, ignoring the source of the problem. The peacemaker
realizes that the bandage itself may become an obstacle to peace and decides
to delve into the core issues of the conflict to build a sound foundation for
future peace. A peacemaker refuses the quick fix for the goal of lasting peace,
which may require him or her to make very difficult decisions between doing
what people want and what God requires him or her to do. Jonathan was a
peacemaker when he chose to stand with David against Saul's jealous plot.
A peacemaker, unlike a peacekeeper, does not attempt to make everyone
happy. Most importantly, a peacemaker realizes no one comes out unscathed
by the battle and still decides to engage in the fight.

The question we must
ask ourselves is are
we peacemakers or
peacekeepers?

🔍 Do you tend to be a peacemaker or a peacekeeper?
How is that working for you?

How far had Saul's malevolent desires taken him in his actions
toward Jonathan in 1 Samuel 20:33? Choose one:

Saul turned his wrath on Jonathan.   Saul tried to kill Jonathan.

Both are true.

All Saul could taste at that table was a desire for David's blood. When Jonathan
stood in the way of that evil plan, not even Saul's own flesh and blood was not
safe. Saul's jealousy had killed—but not its intended victim. Saul lost far more
that day than he could have ever imagined. He lost his son's respect and made
Jonathan choose loyalty to God over loyalty to his father. May we never put
anyone in such a horrible position!

God's Word reveals not only how people act wickedly, but also why they act wickedly. Please read this passage from Romans 1:20-22 from the Amplified Bible and apply its truths to Saul's rashness toward his son, Jonathan:

20 For ever since the creation of the world His invisible nature and attributes, that is, His eternal power and divinity, have been made intelligible and clearly discernible in and through the things that have been made (His handiworks). So [men] are without excuse [altogether without any defense or justification],

21 Because when they knew and recognized Him as God, they did not honor and glorify Him as God or give Him thanks. But instead they became futile and godless in their thinking [with vain imaginings, foolish reasoning, and stupid speculations] and their senseless minds were darkened.

22 Claiming to be wise, they became fools [professing to be smart, they made simpletons of themselves]. (Amplified Bible)

What were the causes of Saul's vain imaginings, foolish reasoning, and stupid speculations according to this insight from Romans 1:21?

What had happened to his mind (verse 22)?

> We may think that we have the right to complain and be ungrateful about our circumstances, but when we refuse to honor, glorify, and praise God with thanksgiving in our hearts, our minds become darkened.

We may think that we have the right to complain and be ungrateful about our circumstances, but when we refuse to honor, glorify, and praise God with thanksgiving in our hearts, our minds become darkened! We then develop minds full of godless thoughts and, eventually, become fools. Praise helps us to guard our hearts and minds from this devastating mental process occurring in us (Philippians 4:6-7).

Jonathan's love for David forced Jonathan to make an almost impossible choice between two people he dearly loved. Girls, we also have an almost impossible choice to make in our lives. Are we going to give Christ full reign over our lives? Tearing out the bitter root of jealousy is painful because it is not possible without the Holy Spirit's help. We have to stop living in denial and plead for our heavenly Father's empowerment. The peace we so desperately want in our lives will only be ours when we allow Him to give us new hearts.

I will sprinkle clean water on you, and you will be clean; I will cleanse you from all your impurities and from all your idols. I will give you a new heart and put a new spirit in you; I will remove from you your heart of stone and give you a heart of flesh. And I will put my Spirit in you and move you to follow my decrees and be careful to keep my laws. **Ezekiel 36:25-27**

What is our choice going to be today?

✺ **Day Three:** Jealousy's Plunder

My father was involved in a nearly fatal car accident twenty years ago. The event was so cataclysmic in the life of my family, that we refer to the years before 1989 as "before-the-accident" years and those after as "after-the-accident" years. The events we are going to look at today in 1 Samuel 21 mark the before and after chapter of David and Saul's relationship. Until this time, David still continued to have some kind of relationship with Saul. We found him almost losing his head by the point of the javelin in Saul's hand not once, but three times.

Have you ever had a relationship in your life that had so much at stake that you did all you could to make it work long after it had stopped working? Please share here.

As a result of the fury of Saul's madness, David lost several things he held as precious to him. Let's remind ourselves of what those are by looking up the following Scriptures:

1 Samuel 16:21:

1 Samuel 17:28-29:

1 Samuel 19:11:

1 Samuel 20:41-42:

> There are some days when I falter under the cost of desperately pursuing Jesus and His will for me.

There are some days when I falter under the cost of desperately pursuing Jesus and His will for me. Thoughts like, *Is this what I signed up for,* can bring despair to my heart and soul. Never do we feel the weight of the cross which Christ said we must take up daily, after denying ourselves to follow Him, than when the cross requires of us what we hold most dear. There is nothing quite like the despair that comes as a result of being tested over what we love the most.

⬤ Have you ever lost anything/one precious to you and how
  did that affect your sense of well-being?

We have known David as a shepherd, David as a courtier of King Saul, and David as the soul friend of Jonathan, but David's identity is about to change. From this point forward, David will now be known as the fugitive—the fugitive of a hardened heart. Life will never be the same for David as long as King Saul remains on the throne.

Turn to 1 Samuel 21 and read the entire chapter.

I want us to pay careful attention to anything that David does or says in this chapter that strikes you as out of character for him. Please make mental notes of these occurrences. One of my greatest interests in life is trying to analyze why people do what they do. Scripture remains silent on details that I wish I knew about. The importance of reading the entire Bible is that other parts of God's inspired Word can help us fill in missing information in a story line. Please put a bookmark in 1 Samuel 21 so that you can easily come back to the chapter because we are going to read between the lines of our story today with other Scripture.

Right away, we come to some thought-provoking verses in 1 Samuel 21:1-3. I need to give some background information about Nob. The ark of the covenant, symbolizing God's presence had been removed from Shiloh, the place where it had been for many years. The tabernacle and the ark were usually in the same place. However, in this case, the ark of the covenant was in Kireath Jearim while the tabernacle was pitched in Nob with Ahimelech the high priest serving Israel. After David fled from his home, he sought refuge with Ahimelech, perhaps hoping to find encouragement from the Lord there.

What was Ahimelech's reaction when he saw David and what did he ask David?

Sin that is not dealt with in our lives goes before and behind us.

We are a celebrity-crazed society. David was a celebrity in the kingdom of Saul. His hopes of blending in with everyone else were remote to none. He was the hero of Israel, the giant killer. And where a famous person goes, so does the whole entourage of body guards, managers, and personal assistants with him or her. Just to go to a grocery store is a major undertaking for someone in the limelight. The strangeness of David showing up solo to Ahimelech would be as bizarre as one of today's highest paid stars suddenly showing up at our door with no one else. I believe that there was another reason for Ahimelech's hesitant welcome.

Let's read Proverbs 28:15. With the realization that Ahimelech was subject to King Saul, what insight does this verse give?

Sin that is not dealt with in our lives goes before and behind us. It becomes the lens through which others see their relationship to us. Saul's wicked behavior might have been confined within the palace walls, but his sin found its way out into the open.

What did David do in 1 Samuel 21:2 that showed his fear in the moment? Choose one:

Fell down and cried   Lied to Ahimelech

Told the priest to offer a sacrifice for him

David panicked in the moment and lied to Ahimelech about his reason for coming to the town of Nob. A lie is a lie, regardless of our justification for telling it. 2 Timothy 3:16 tells us that all Scripture is useful to us for teaching, rebuking, correcting, and training us in righteousness. I believe that God includes parts of the story that we are to take away to learn what not to do in a given situation. That being said, haven't all of us done things under stress that we have immediately regretted? I wonder if Ahimelech's hesitancy and alarm at seeing David made David react the way he did. David was a hunted man, unsafe everywhere. That had to affect his judgment in withholding the truth from the priest. David's lie is not excusable, but, I certainly can empathize with the way he handled the situation.

We need to tuck away a fact that will become important to recall in a later day of study. Who had witnessed this conversation between Ahimelech and David according to 1 Samuel 21:7? What was this person's profession?

After securing five loaves of bread for himself, what did David ask of Ahimelech in verse 8?

A coat   A sword or spear   A donkey   A scroll

Have you ever had a stark reminder of a past victory God had given you middle of a fearful situation? What was it?

I believe that although David had no job, was estranged from his family, had lost the comfort of his best friend and Michal, his wife, God was fully acquainted with the situation. He knew that David needed to be remember the defeat of the giant that had loomed before him. He needed to remember the courage that God had given him, symbolized by the sword hidden behind the ephod. I firmly believe that when our hearts are breaking, God's is breaking, too. Not over the fearfulness of our situation which He is able to change in the twinkling of an eye, but over the distress His children experience because we cannot see where He is in the middle of our terror.

I firmly believe that when our hearts are breaking, God's is breaking, too. Not over the fearfulness of our situation, which He is able to change in the twinkling of an eye, but over the distress His children experience because we cannot see where He is in the middle of our terror.

✻ How does Isaiah 63:9 portray God's reaction to our distress over a troubling situation in our lives?

I believe that the angel of God's presence was made real to David when his eyes fell on the sword that had cut off the head of Israel's ferocious enemy, Goliath. David had no friend in the world he could go to at that moment, but he was reminded, in a very tangible way, that the Lord his God was with him.

David's lie to Ahimelech had him between a rock and a hard place. He had to leave Nob. The only place he felt he could go is shocking to me. Where is the city of Gath according to Joshua 13:3?

How was David recognized by the servants of the king of Gath (1 Samuel 21:11)?

It's a desperate situation when a person would rather go into enemy territory than face death at home. Life is a puzzle. The very fame that gave David his job, his best friend, and his wife, now was haunting him. We all long to be known, but, I believe we would despise the burden of losing our anonymity. Ahimelech had been concerned that the "star" of the Israelite victory over Goliath had shown up by himself. In the house of the enemy, before the king of Gath, David's fame revealed itself to be a curse.

There are some parts of the Bible that are just downright hilarious to me. Maybe I have a very bizarre sense of humor. But it just tickles my funny-bone to read how David slipped out from the grasp of those who would have loved to have the fame of killing Israel's superstar. Desperate times call for desperate measures. David became a slobbering fool in their eyes. I can just see the saliva dripping off his beard as he made marks on the city's gates and behaved as though he had lost his mind. Although I am sure that David was not laughing at the time, Achish's response to David's plan for escape just makes me laugh out loud.

I can almost hear the disgust in Achish's voice in verses 14-15. What did he say to his servants about David?

Thirty-five hundred years later, we are able to empathize with Achish's question to his men. There is no shortage of madmen in this world. The massacres at Columbine High School and Virginia Tech are stark examples to us of the ravages of unrestrained evil passions. The more things change, the more they stay the same. I started out this lesson by noting that this chapter was a watershed moment in the life of David. Never again would David feel safe in the presence of the madman named Saul. For his own protection, David would never again allow Saul to have knowledge of his whereabouts. I am sure that there were moments in David's life when David's reflection of all that had happened between him and his father-in-law pained him as he sat in the cold darkness of the situation. But both David and we have a great Savior, Jesus Christ, who is more than able to bring us hope in the darkness of our fear and shield us from those who would want to do us evil. And although the earth give way and the mountains fall into the heart of the sea (Psalm 46:2), by God's grace and power, we will not be moved. Hallelujah, amen!

Day Four: Hard Won Wisdom

We're going to dive right into our passage in 1 Samuel 22, but we are not going to stay here long except to get an understanding of where David is.

Let's read 1 Samuel 22:1-5. We have a brief glimpse into how far-reaching Saul's fury at David is. Who joined him at Adullam according to verses 1-2?

David had become a sort of Robin Hood. The unwanted conflict with Saul forced David to seek safety for his parents with the king of Moab—another great enemy of Israel. It is in verse 4 that we first are introduced to Gad the prophet who told David to leave the cave and go where?

We have discussed the vital importance of other passages of Scripture being able to fill in parts of a story-line that seem to be missing. If I had to pick a book of the Bible which is utterly transparent in its longings for unanswered questions to life, it would have to be the Psalms. David is believed to be the man behind the pen of over seventy-five of the one hundred fifty psalms written. Some of the psalms are David's personal journal over struggles he was facing in life. We are going to look at two of those "entries" in the Psalms today.

Psalm 34 is believed to have been written by David following his experience in the presence of Achish of Gath. Let's read verses 1-22, keeping in mind the traumatic events that David experienced in the last several chapters of 1 Samuel that we have studied.

What did David find was the only thing that brought him relief in Psalm 34:4?

How do you think fear and shame are connected in verse five?

What were some actual ways that David experienced the angel of the Lord delivering him from Saul's vain imaginations in verse seven? List as many as you can think of from memory.

How had David been a victim of Saul's lies (verse 13)?

What was David's emotional state in verse 18?

Angry   Depressed

Brokenhearted   Apathetic

What strikes me as so amazing about this psalm is the amount of confidence that David had in God's ability to protect both his physical person and his reputation. Even in the depths of despair, David believed that God had the power to redeem all that had been stolen from him. The last verse of this psalm was written before the victory had come. What would happen, if, when our natural eyes failed us in seeing Who is really in control, our eyes of faith were opened, allowing us to see the truth?

When Jesus was asked by someone what were the two greatest commandments, He told those who were listening that they were to love God with all their soul, mind, and strength and to love their neighbor as themselves. Somehow, my ears latch onto the first part of what Jesus said, but not the part about loving others like I love myself. When we allow jealousy to rule over us, we are not loving God the way He commands us to. A jealous heart is in love with nothing other than its own agenda. In its self-absorption, it does not care what its venom is doing to the other person.

I have said it before, but it bears repeating: Jealousy is a sin in which we can be both the victim and the perpetrator at the same time. I want to make this very personal to us so that we can recognize the danger of not surrendering those perilous desires to Christ.

Let's read all seven verses of Psalm 142 and thoughtfully answer the following questions:

Have you ever begged God for mercy in a situation where you have been the object of someone's envy?

Who do you think would have reason to do the same because of your jealousy towards him/her?

What would happen if, when our natural eyes failed us in seeing Who is really in control, our eyes of faith be opened, allowing us to see the truth?

151

To whom have you poured out your complaint when you have been:

1) jealousy's victim :

2) jealousy's perpetrator:

Do you think you honored God in both of those situations? Why or why not?

What snares has jealousy hidden for you as both its victim and its perpetrator?

How does jealousy make us feel abandoned as:

1) its victim:

2) its perpetrator:

How would believing that God is our portion relieve the burden of jealousy?

Verse 6 is a cry for deliverance against the overwhelming power of the enemy. The horrible lie that we believe as both the victim and the perpetrator of jealousy is that the enemy is the other person. The true enemy is Satan, who is telling us lies that we are believing above the Word of God. What lies has he told you in justifying your actions toward the other person?

How has jealousy imprisoned you as:

1) its victim:

2) its perpetrator:

Which answers came more easily—those in which you saw yourself as jealousy's victim or jealousy's perpetrator? Underline one:

Seeing myself as the victim

Seeing myself as the perpetrator

I have a much easier time seeing myself as jealousy's victim. I have lived long enough to have known myself as a perpetrator as well. It is a painful exercise to recognize the same cesspool of jealousy in my own heart that I have seen in someone else. My natural tendency is to give myself a break and justify the sin of my jealousy. But the truth, sweet friend, is that my justification is a great barrier between the abundant life Jesus has for me and the place of self-absorbed arrogance in which I may find myself to be.

WEEK SIX • FUGITIVE OF A HARDENED HEART

My natural tendency is to give myself a break and justify the sin of my jealousy.

❋ What is the stunning truth we are told in 1 John 4:20 about the danger of allowing jealousy to conquer part of our heart?

Why did God allow David to experience such pain? Although David may not have known it then, he would be the ancestor of "the Man of sorrows"—Jesus Christ, the Savior of the world. David was God's mouthpiece through the Psalms. It was this period in David's life which was the training ground for some of the most heart-wrenching words penned in Scripture which have comforted Christians throughout the ages. He was the one who had been wronged, yet he was on the run! David's son, Solomon, penned these words years after David ran from Saul:

"Wisdom is supreme; therefore get wisdom. Though it cost all you have, get understanding."
Proverbs 4:7

The wisdom that is supreme, which will protect our feet from walking down a path of destruction, will cost us all we have in our natural desires. Our God never allows a trial to come to us that does not have the possibility to refine us into someone more like Him (1 Peter 1:6-7). David would need to learn hard-won wisdom that could not be learned any other way than as a fugitive from Saul. Could his natural eyes allow him to see his deliverance in the cave? Absolutely not. But his eyes of faith, supported by his belief in God's sovereignty, enabled him to see the deliverance that was his to claim before he had cried out to One who saved him.

Could we do that, sweet friends? Could we dare to believe that God has His own perfect and just reasons for having us exactly where we are in life (in the house in which we live, in the family situation we are living in, in our current stage and position of life, with those who seem to be against us) for our benefit? Wisdom that trusts when faith is the only foothold on which to stand is wisdom that is supreme. Its benefits are worth the cost they exact to lead us to godly understanding.

Acts 13:22 shares this astounding insight:

"After removing Saul, [the Lord] made David their king. He testified concerning him: 'I have found David son of Jesse a man after my own heart; he will do everything I want him to do.'"

David had to learn wisdom's lessons through the fiery trials. What is God's purpose in the trial we are agonizing through at this moment: to give us a heart after God's own, dear friend? God uses those fires to refine us into women more like His Son, Jesus Christ. You and I will struggle to believe that God is for us if we believe the lie that God has changed His methods for teaching us wisdom. David did not understand God's methods, but he trusted His heart. He praised the Source of wisdom and found relief from his terror. If Saul had only learned the same lessons, he would have found relief from the burden of envy. One of the main goals of this lesson was to support the fact that we can be both jealousy's victim and perpetrator. We have—everyone one of us—been in each position. Being on either side of jealousy is a prison to us, making us captive in our minds. Those prison doors that have been locked shut against us will swing open as we praise the One who holds the key.

The wisdom that is supreme, which will protect our feet from walking down a path of destruction, will cost us all we have in our natural desires.

154

Day Five: Like a Rabid Dog

One of my favorite Disney movies from my childhood was **Old Yeller**. We had many cats and dogs growing up, so the story line of the movie was captivating to my animal lover heart. I have watched the movie no less than twenty times, but I always cry at the transformation that happens between the young boy of the movie and the yellow mutt. And by the time the credits roll, I am sobbing into my tissue over the sadness of Old Yeller's fate. Hopefully I am not spoiling the story line for anyone, but Old Yeller the dog turns rabid after an attack by an infected wolf and has to be put down for everyone's safety.

I see many parallels between King Saul and a rabid dog. Our text of Scripture is so barbaric and horrible that we will gasp in shock over the evil that is involved in today's lesson. Let's begin by reading all of 1 Samuel 22 and then carefully make some observations as we see how obsessive and full of vain imaginations Saul's jealous mind has become.

What had Saul been apprised of in 1 Samuel 22:6? Choose one:

David's location   The existence of David's army

David's reunion with Michal

Three kinds of men made up four hundred who had joined David in the cave at Adullam. How are they described according to 1 Samuel 22:2?

> The jealous mind is blind to its own treacherous acts and is obsessed with its own self-absorption.

Kind of a motley crew, wouldn't you say? Still, beggars can't be choosers. David needed protection from the maniacal mind of King Saul. We can't go into any depth here what kind of men these distressed, debt-ridden, and discontented soldiers were except to briefly look at 1 Chronicles 11:15-19.

What amazing act of loyalty did some of these men carry out for their leader David in this passage?

Word had gotten back to Saul that David had surrounded himself with soldiers. The jealous mind is blind to its own treacherous acts and is obsessed with its own self-absorption. When we look back at David's life as a courtier, commander of Saul's army, and member of Saul's family, there is not even a hint of traitorous behavior from David towards Saul. It is all imagined in the seared conscience of the deluded mind of Saul.

What does Proverbs 29:12 say about a ruler who listens to lies? Choose one:

All his men become lazy   All his men become wicked

All his men steal

I grew up in Congo while an oppressive dictator was in power named Mobutu Sese Seko. It is estimated that during his thirty-two year iron grip over the country, he pocketed over four billion dollars in aid that poured into the country.[1] The result of his stealing from his country for his own personal profit was a government rampant with corruption. Bribes were a normal part of business. Much fraud happened under the table. Decent men turned to vile behavior.

We have already seen Saul in a demented state. He was not above attempted murder to get what he wanted. Both David and his own son, Jonathan, were the would-be targets of his spear. At the beginning of Saul's reign, we saw that God's Spirit had come over the timid man he once was so mightily that he had been able to unite his kingdom as one man against the Philistines. After Saul's rebellious disobedience towards God regarding the Amalekites, an evil spirit started to torment his mind.

There are times when jealousy is so subtle that we mistake its presence for something else.

What is Satan called in John 8:44? The father of _____.

What is his native language? _____

There is no such thing as a half-truth. A half-truth is a whole lie. Satan is the master deceiver because of his ability to mix shades of truth with lies. Saul listened to the father of lies and, in so doing, all of his men became wicked in Saul's mind—even when there was no wickedness in them. Proverbs 29:12 helps to shed light on the following observations about jealousy.

A jealous heart perceives a threat.

How do we know that Saul felt threatened? Glance back at 1 Samuel 22:6. Saul had called this inquisition under the tamarisk tree with the threat of the spear in his hand. There are times when jealousy is so subtle that we mistake its presence for something else. But when jealousy perceives a threat, the ugly mask of envy can be revealed in all its furor. David had raised up an army for his protection from Saul, not for the destruction of Saul. Saul was, in effect, saying to his men, "I will remain king of Israel even if I have to kill every one of my officials to maintain that position."

Did you perceive a threat which resulted in your jealousy toward someone else? Was that threat real or imagined?

A jealous heart appeals to the envy in others.

What was Saul inferring when he asked his men if David would give all of them fields and vineyards? Saul desired to set his men against the son of Jesse. He argued the thought that David would take away their positions of honor if Saul was ousted from power. Saul tried to goad his men into betraying David through envious thoughts.

Have you ever appealed to the envious nature of anyone else trying to protect your own interests (e.g. in a dating relationship, in a friendship, with a coworker, etc.)?

A jealous heart is an unrestrained heart.

Who besides David was mentioned by Saul as a conspirator in 1 Samuel 22:8?

A jealous heart knows no bounds in its treachery. Twice we have seen how little value Saul placed on his son's life. Jealousy can cause those who are closest to us to become our enemies. Jealousy causes families to be split apart. Jealousy demands that objective persons take sides. No one's actions are innocent in the mind of the jealous person because she or he cannot believe in the innocence of others. Jonathan's friendship with David was pure, but Saul could not see it for what it was. Jonathan for David meant Jonathan against Saul in Saul's deluded mind.

Do you have an example of jealousy wreaking havoc on family relationships?

A jealous heart cannot distinguish between good and evil.

Who shared information with Saul in verses 9-10?

We only briefly mentioned this person in yesterday's lesson. What reason does the Bible give for this person being at Nob with Ahimelech in 1 Samuel 21:7?

Doeg was detained before the Lord for some reason. Matthew Henry states in his commentary that Doeg was a foreigner (an Edomite) who used the Jewish religion as a means to promoting himself in the court of Saul. Scripture does not tell us what he was doing, but we shall soon see that his detainment before the Lord did not restrain the evil he did toward David and Ahimelech.

There was someone else who used false pretenses of spirituality to serve his own interests mentioned in Acts 1:15-17. What was his name? Choose one:

Simon the sorcerer   Judas, one of the twelve disciples
Ananias

Doeg capitalized on Saul's jealous rage. I believe he saw an opportunity for his own advancement and implicated Ahimelech as a player in a conspiracy against Saul. Doeg was an evil man with impure motives, but jealousy had blinded Saul to that fact.

How have you seen jealousy blind yourself or others to evil?

A jealous heart positions itself as both the judge and jury of others.

How do we know that Saul considered Ahimelech guilty before he sent for him (1 Samuel 22:11-13)?

Ahimelech was a very brave man. I do not see one hint of Ahimelech trying to place the blame on David to defend himself. Remember David's lie to Ahimelech in yesterday's lesson? Ahimelech trembled in fear when he saw David alone. I have to believe that the scenario he now finds himself in was the cause of his terror because he knew what a madman Saul was when David came to him. Ahimelech had to know that his life was on the line, but he relied on his integrity rather than further implicate David. A jealous heart also wants someone else to do its dirty work to avoid direct implication. Notice that Saul was too cowardly to carry out the murder of the house of Ahimelech himself.

What command in Deuteronomy 17:6 did Saul violate with Ahimelech's death?

A jealous heart is an arrogant heart (see Psalm 5:5 and Isaiah 42:8).

The quickest way to shut out the presence of God in our lives is to become arrogant. 1 Samuel 15:23 likens arrogance to idolatry. When we become arrogant, we exalt ourselves above others and remove the blessing of God from our lives. The jealous heart worships the false god of selfish ambition. God will not give the glory due Him to us. How are we to treat those in spiritual positions of leadership over us according to Psalm 105:15?

Ahimelech was God's voice to Israel. He was the conduit for those seeking spiritual answers from God. Saul's depraved mind committed what, I believe, was a satanically inspired massacre.

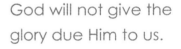 What can happen when envy and selfish ambition motivate an individual according to James 3:16?

How does this truth come to life in 1 Samuel 22:17-19?

Did you notice that Saul, through Doeg the Edomite, killed every living person and animal in Nob? These actions were supposed to be carried out on the Amalekites in 1 Samuel 15, but Saul disobeyed God in an act of rebellion. **Anger is cruel and fury is overwhelming, but against jealousy who can stand (Proverbs 27:4)?** Jealousy can make us out-of-control murderers of its victim. Whether the murder is physical or emotional is all the same to God (see 1 John 3:15).

If we are involved in these behaviors, we are fools running straight toward our own slaughter. We can say we are sorry as often as we please and still not have the heart that grieves appropriately over our sin, enabling us to repent and turn away from our certain destruction. We will never change until we become jealous for what we really need—our repentance and healing through the blood of Jesus Christ.

God will not give the glory due Him to us.

In Enemy Territory

My children's favorite game on a rainy afternoon is to play hide-and-seek. Several games ago, I found a hiding place that they still have not discovered. I burrowed down in the darkness and held my breath as they came within inches of my hideout.

There is something about hiding from someone else that causes the adrenaline to start flowing and the heart to race. I have never been forced to hide out of fear for my life, but this week we will see David's choice to hide in enemy territory rather than be tracked down by maniacal King Saul.

Has someone else's jealousy caused us to do something against our better judgment? Most sobering of all to consider is how has our jealousy toward someone else caused our victim to run into enemy territory? Survival is a basic instinct with all of us, no matter how spiritually mature we may be. Although we will see David making poor choices because of his fear this week, which one of us has not done the same?

Listen to how the God of the Old Testament revealed Himself to Moses:

"And the LORD said, "I will cause all my goodness to pass in front of you, and I will proclaim my name, the LORD, in your presence. I will have mercy on whom I will have mercy, and I will have compassion on whom I will have compassion."   *Exodus 33:19*

We are going to see the mercy of God to David, in spite of David's lapses of judgment. I pray that we might remember when God's mercy has triumphed over His judgment concerning our own foolishness. I praise His Name that when He sees a heart fully committed to Him, He works supernaturally within our mistakes and hides us in the shadow of His wings.

✳ Day One: Two Kinds of Betrayal

We left week six of our study as onlookers of the smashing defeat of the Philistines by David and his motley crew of soldiers. David's bravery at that moment was unmatched. His character was stellar. God was undeniably with David.

Let's refresh our memories about how this brave act was interpreted by Saul by reading 1 Samuel 23:7-13.

What was Saul's reaction to hearing about the routing of the Philistines by David in Keilah? Choose one:

Repentance   Gratefulness

Resolve to cause David harm

We already discussed that jealousy forces others to take sides. The Bible does not give us specific details, but being familiar with human nature, how do you think David learned that Saul had not given up the hunt for him in verse 9?

I would love to see your answers. Sin forces the best of us to be traitors at times. A deadly trap of jealousy is paranoia, resulting in the belief that nobody else is trustworthy. There were traitors surrounding David, willing to sell information to the highest bidder. Proverbs has much to say about the result of unchecked anger that I believe will give us insight about the information being given to Saul about David's whereabouts. Remember that cell phones and email were not available to help aid a treacherous person to relay information. Technology wasn't needed. The muscle that lies between the bottom teeth was all that was necessary to aid in the spreading of destructive words regarding David to Saul.

Let's look up the following Scriptures about the effect of Saul's anger and jealousy on others:

Proverbs 20:2

Proverbs 22:24-25

Proverbs 29:22

161

Have you ever known a person who was easily angered? In thinking about your own experiences, how did someone else's anger influence your actions toward the object of their fury? If you believed your own neck would be on the line, did you defend yourself or the target of the anger?

My dearest sisters, our rage is incalculable in its influence on others (Hebrews 12:15). We may have deceived ourselves into thinking we have our unconfessed anger hidden and are fooling everyone else. We need to ask ourselves some really hard questions. Are we doing what God detests by causing dissension among others because of our anger issues (see Proverbs 6:16-19)?

Saul had surrounded himself with "yes" me—the kind that said what he wanted hear and did not force him to be accountable for his actions. Did you notice that we have never heard anyone from Saul's camp discourage him in his madness or try to reason with him about David's innocence? Saul had shown himself to be capable of the worst sort of treachery imaginable when he had killed God's servants without remorse. Surely, Saul's anger sounded like a lion's roar in their ears. And like many of us would do, they had decided they were not going to be his prey.

We are going to see something very disheartening about the people of Keilah. David had saved them from certain annihilation by the Philistines. Remember where Keilah was—in Judah, the very tribe where the golden boy who had slain the giant had been born and raised. I can imagine how proud Keilah would have been to claim David the day after Goliath's head had rolled off the end of the sword. But when the madness of Saul reigned and the once-fawned over celebrity became the hunted fugitive, all expected outcomes changed.

Do you think David had reason to expect that Keilah would have protected him from Saul's madness as David had protected Keilah from the Philistines?

We may have deceived ourselves into thinking we have our unconfessed anger hidden and are fooling everyone else.

✳ Instead, what distressing news did David learn after he had inquired of the Lord about with whom Keilah's loyalty really lay in 1 Samuel 23:9-13?

No one had risen to David's defense yet! The crushing truth was that Keilah was going to fold under the pressure of a maniacal king. David learned that from consulting the ephod through Abiathar the sole survivor of the priesthood. He did not rely on human sympathies. We walk into such horrible snares when we expect fallible, frightened human beings to display honor and courage in a difficult predicament. Every now and then, there will be someone who is willing to put her neck out on the line for us, but we must not count on people to always do what they should. What we can count on is the truth of Scripture and the answers God gives to us in fervent prayer over the situation. I love what the Psalmist says:

"Your commands make me wiser than my enemies, for they are ever with me."
Psalm 119:98

We are not left alone, sweet friend! We have the revealed Word of God that can help us to outsmart the enemy's snares. If David had relied on how his own people should have reacted to the knowledge that Saul was on his way, David likely would have paid with his life for that naivete. God's Word instructed him and kept him safe. It will do the same for us, too.

David decided to move on before Keilah had a chance to betray him. I want to make a point here. Did you notice that Keilah was left alone by Saul after he found out that David had left the city's gates? Keilah was spared the sin of carrying out an actual betrayal of her favorite son.

How have you been disappointed in your expectations regarding another's reaction to you? How have you disappointed others in their expectations of you?

Let's continue by reading 1 Samuel 23:14-29. How relentless was Saul's pursuit of David according to verse 14? Why was he not successful?

Can you imagine how distraught and discouraged David was? The desert was his place of refuge as he made his bed on the hard floors of caves. It would have become very easy for David to lose faith in everyone. His fear could have easily turned into paranoia.

In the middle of the chaos of his world, where did encouragement come from according to verse 16?

A reunion with Jesse   A reunion with Michal

A reunion with Jonathan

God knows specifically how we need to be encouraged. Look at the specific words Jonathan said to David and share how you think each one reflected David's struggles or fears in that area:

"Don't be afraid." _____

"My father will not lay a hand on you."

_____

"You will be king over Israel and I will be second to you."

_____

"Even my father knows this."

_____

To show His faithfulness to you, God will send encouragement from a source that only He could ordain.

Oh, my darling friend, are you discouraged today? Perhaps God's promises seem a distant memory. Don't you know that David had to wonder whether the anointing by Samuel all those years ago was not just a colossal joke? Do you see the incredible temptation David was faced with to doubt God's Word to him? Perhaps you have become weary in the waiting, too. Have faith in God! He will never fail you! And to show His faithfulness to you, He will send encouragement from a source that only He could ordain. If fear has come knocking on the door, send faith to answer it and no one and nothing will be on the other side! Jonathan's precious words must have been like a cool drink to David's parched soul. Oh, to be a friend like Jonathan to someone almost ready to give up! God knows that we are just dust and need times of refreshment and renewed hope. He sends Jonathans into our lives to help us find our strength in Him.

Who is your Jonathan? _____

But life is a fight; there is great evil in the world. As much as we love our Jonathans, real life is lived in a world filled with evil. I believe that there are two kinds of sin. There is sin that is premeditated and sin that is reactive. The first will get result in no mercy in a court of law. The other has consequences, but not the same kind of wickedness associated with it. Let's take for example a person who masterminds and plans down to the last detail another's murder. That person should get the severest sentence possible for the crime. Compare that with someone who kills an intruder in her home. This person reacted and took life. I believe that there is a big difference in the eyes of God. Keilah's would-be betrayal of David was reactive to the fury of Saul. Now, however, we are going to witness an intended betrayal of David that is nothing short of premeditated murder.

164

David was still in Judah. Ziph was a small town on the edge of the wilderness in the hill country of Judah. The Ziphites, like those who lived in Keilah, were fellow tribespeople of David. They should have protected David. What was their plan when they found out that David was living among them according to 1 Samuel 23:19-20?

Whom did Saul ask to bless the Ziphites for their allegiance to him (verse 21)?

Are you scratching your head over Saul's faulty mental processes? How in the world could Saul possibly dare to allow himself to believe that this cat and mouse game he was playing with David's life had anything to do with God?

What is the motivation of Saul here according to Psalm 10:2-4?

Matthew Henry said this of Saul's delusional thinking about the blessing of God:

"We must not think that one smiling providence either justifies an unrighteous cause or secures its success." [2]

Notice how Saul sends the Ziphites to do his dirty work. What did Saul imply about David's character to the Ziphites in 1 Samuel 23: 22-23?

The Ziphites must have thought there was something in it for them to act so traitorously to one of their own. What do you think they were seeking since no mention of reward is made by Saul?

I believe the Ziphites were hoping some of the glory of Saul's kingship would splash on them. Isn't it like human nature to want to have the acknowledgment and favor of someone in power? We must be very careful about associating with someone who is eager to rush into evil against someone else. Passion to do wrong against someone else should alert us that something sinister lurks beneath. That passion can quickly turn on us and tear us to pieces.

We leave our story today looking at two sides of the same mountain. If we didn't know that Saul was going to become distracted with the threat of his real enemy, David's hope for survival would look very bleak. The only thing that divided Saul from David was the mountain terrain itself. And here is where we need to realize something of utmost importance. Although to human eyes it appeared Saul had David in the cross-hairs of his deadly arrow or spear, Scripture assures us that nothing could have been farther from the truth (see Psalm 62:6-7). David had made the Lord his Rock. God was not going to allow David to be delivered into the wicked king's hands.

Saul's position was extremely dangerous because he was out from under the umbrella of God's blessing. It was only God's mercy that Saul did not hurtle to his death due to the wicked slipperiness of the path on which his feet were running. Girlfriends, what side of the mountain are you on today in your pursuit to get what you want? Are you going about it by consulting our God and living out Psalm 15 or are you pursuing your dream at the cost of someone else's integrity, livelihood, marriage, or call of God on their lives? Are we quick to betray another's trust to achieve our goals? Our peace will only come when we slow down enough to stop running and have God search our hearts. May we be brave enough to do what God requires of us.

Our peace will only come when we slow down enough to stop running and have God search our hearts.

Day Two: A Sparing by Humility

Modern psychology has a label for every kind of behavioral abnormality. While I believe that there are legitimate chemical imbalances that people struggle with, I also firmly believe in the existence of evil. No one wants to call sin by its rightful name anymore; we just slap a psychological syndrome on someone exhibiting deviant behavior and look for someone or something on which to put the blame for the sin in the person being evaluated by our human understanding.

Eventually, evil reveals its ugly face and we see it for what it really is. Unfortunately, there can be great collateral damage before we call evil by its real name. We are going to look at that collateral damage today in the last exchange of words between David and his would-be killer.

Let's read 1 Samuel 24 in its entirety and answer the following questions:

Whom did Saul take with him in pursuit of finding David in the Desert of En Gedi?

Warriors of Ziph   3000 of his choice soldiers

David's wife, Michal

Organizational skills are not part of my makeup. I am a big picture kind of person. I so admire people who can see the big picture and organize the details to make it come to life. I am lost without someone to help me be practical and realistic. Regardless of what Saul's specific role was in the process of selecting 3000 choice warriors to pursue David, there was planning involved in putting the group together. Remember how we talked about the difference between premeditated sin and reactive sin? Nothing could have been more premeditated than Saul's bringing together Israel's finest to seek out David to end his life.

How does Isaiah 57:20-21 explain Saul's relentless drive to hunt down and kill David?

Once Saul's sin-sick mind had determined that David was the enemy, that obsession drove him to leave the country of Israel vulnerable to the attack of the real enemy, the Philistines. He was willing to go to the desert! Can you imagine exposing yourself to the blistering sun to walk on hills with caves to search out one person? Saul was so intent on accomplishing the job that he took the best of Israel's military with him.

> Unfortunately, there can be great collateral damage before we call evil by its real name.

Sweet friend of mine, the arrogance of our sin leaves us and those we love vulnerable to great harm. Our pride, however, cannot let us see the danger. How did Saul, unknowingly, put himself in a potentially life-threatening situation in 1 Samuel 24:3-5?

What great temptation did David overcome in verse 4? Choose one:

Listening to his men   Throwing a spear at Saul

Setting the cave on fire

 Have you ever been encouraged by trusted friends to do something you knew you had a right to do in their eyes but was wrong in God's eyes? Did you give in? Why or why not?

Do you think David would have been justified, humanly speaking, for exacting vengeance on his enemy? Why or why not?

David's writings in the psalms are some of the most violent word pictures ever written. What is even more astounding is that these were kept by God for us to see. Let's not for one minute think that David did not wrestle with vengeful thoughts toward Saul. Write out his wish in each of the following Scripture references:

<u>David's prayer for his enemy</u>

Psalm 17:13:

Psalm 109:17-20:

Psalm 139:19:

How many of us would like someone praying those words over us? We can get so discouraged by mighty men and women portrayed in the Scriptures. We can fool ourselves into thinking that they were superhuman and utterly spiritual all the time—that somehow they always acted godly. Wrong! 1 John 1:8 assures you and me of the following:

"If we claim to be without sin, we deceive ourselves and the truth is not in us."

✳ David immediately regretted the cutting of Saul's robe. What pricked his conscience and had him restrain his men against killing Saul according to 1 Samuel 23:5-7?

In times of great distress or passion, we can forget that God is in control and move forward with our own plan. David did not back down because of Saul! He backed down because of his fear of God. We gravely sin against God when we plow ahead without His approval, even when we have human justification for our actions. David respected Saul because he was still God's anointed king of Israel. David bowed in submission to God's choice. Can you imagine the freedom we could walk in if we allowed our need for revenge to be God's deal toward someone who has so deeply wounded us? We are only going to be able to do that when we know Scripture's commands, after we have that hard-won wisdom that has cost us much in order to be obedient to our God. David was not perfect. Did he want revenge? Yes! But more than the desire for revenge, David wanted to bow in submission to the will of God. God had not deposed Saul. David would not, either. He made the choice to walk away from the temptation to run ahead of God in this situation. We can do the same thing!

I believe that one of the surest ways to figure out if we have an issue with pride is if we can bow in submission to the other person, even when we are just in our confrontation of them. Underline the actions or words of David to Saul in the following verses that speak to you about the humility of David's heart:

8 Then David went out of the cave and called out to Saul, "My lord the king!" When Saul looked behind him, David bowed down and prostrated himself with his face to the ground. 9 He said to Saul, "Why do you listen when men say, 'David is bent on harming you'? 10 This day you have seen with your own eyes how the LORD delivered you into my hands in the cave. Some urged me to kill you, but I spared you; I said, 'I will not lift my hand against my master, because he is the LORD's anointed.' 11 See, my father, look at this piece of your robe in my hand! I cut off the corner of your robe but did not kill you. Now understand and recognize that I am not guilty of wrongdoing or rebellion. I have not wronged you, but you are hunting me down to take my life. 1 Samuel 24:8-11

Can you imagine the freedom we could walk in if we allowed our need for revenge to be God's business toward someone who has so deeply wounded us?

Who did David call on in the presence of the king to judge between he and Saul in verse 12?

Jonathan   A court of law

The LORD   Abiathar the priest

What did David promise Saul in verse 13 that he would not do?

My sisters, like me, are you starting to see the jeopardy we put ourselves in when we allow bitter envy and hatred toward others rule over our hearts? We chase after the wrong enemy and we usurp God's authority in our lives. God has placed us in our homes, in our socioeconomic position, in our current professions for His divine purpose. When we cast a jealous eye toward something He has not given us, we are in danger of divine judgment. Our anger is misplaced on the object of our jealousy. We need to take up our hurt and anger with the Lord who can give us mercy in our unsatisfied longings, not on a human being who is powerless to do anything for us.

I would like to suggest that David took the most powerful position against his enemy that we humans can take. What did he request of the Lord in v. 15?

Vengeance is not ours to take, but we can expect our righteous Judge to be faithful to His promise to uphold our cause when we are being wrongfully sinned against by another. When God vindicates, girlfriend, He vindicates! And He does a much more thorough job than we ever could. We don't have to worry for one minute whether He sees. He knows everything and will rescue us *if we wait for Him to do it!*

What was the emotion with which Saul responded to David's words in v. 16?

He wept   He laughed

He became angry   He repented

Let's read the rest of Saul's response in verses 17-21. We have not come to the last of the many troubling questions Saul's life raises in our minds. Have you ever had someone appear genuinely sorry for a wrong done to you only to have that person stab you in the back again? How did their false apology affect your ability to believe their sincerity the next time you were apologized to? Share here.

What brings us to true repentance according to 2 Corinthians 7:10?

What had happened in 1 Samuel 16:14 to make godly sorrow impossible for Saul?

So what caused the tears? I don't think they came from a heart of repentance but from a heart confused by its own deceitfulness. I want to make a distinction here: I am addressing this particular issue toward the people with whom we are *not* in a covenant relationship. Marriage is a covenant relationship between two spouses and God. It is not to be broken. We have the responsibility, Biblically, to grant forgiveness when we are asked for it. Our responsibility is not to judge how sincere someone's apology is; we must leave that judgment with God alone. With that having been said, the Bible warns us to be as shrewd as snakes and as innocent as doves (Matthew 10:16). Girls, just because someone says that she is sorry doesn't mean she is! Unfortunately, talk is cheap. Our actions speak to the true condition of the heart. We believe someone when we see that what they have promised is what they do. Trust cannot be demanded. It must be earned. Saul's track record gives us every reason to doubt the sincerity of his tears at this moment. David was commanded not to take out vengeance on Saul, but not once did God ever command David to trust Saul. We must have great discernment not to take things at face value—especially an enemy's tears. We do not wish them ill, but we don't take them into our close circle, either.

What did David swear on oath to Saul in 1 Samuel 24:22?

Look carefully at the end of that verse:

"Then Saul returned home, but David and his men went up to the stronghold."

The collateral damage of jealousy, sweet friend, is the destruction of trust. We can so damage each other as we walk this planet that we may have to live apart. But you know the glad truth that awaits us as believers one day? Let's look at Revelation 21:25-27 to get a glimpse of heaven:

"On no day will its gates ever be shut, for there will be no night there. The glory and honor of the nations will be brought into it. Nothing impure will ever enter it, nor will anyone who does what is shameful or deceitful, but only those whose names are written in the Lamb's book of life."

Perfection awaits us in a place where we will hurt each other no more. Hallelujah!

The collateral damage of jealousy, sweet friend, is the destruction of trust.

Day Three: A Deadly Garment

We have so much to cover today. Before we even begin, I want you to know that I have begged God to make me smarter than I am. This lesson is going to speak to His ability to answer that prayer as we have to use other portions of Scripture to help us figure out why a person acts the way he or she does. I am asking for a special anointing of His Holy Spirit as I claim the promise of having the mind of Christ that the apostle Paul revealed is mine in 1 Corinthians 2:16. I come to you humbly, asking the Lord to guide this day of study.

We are going to do a comparison of 1 Samuel 24 and today's portion of Scripture of 1 Samuel 26. As you read both chapters, record any similarities that you see between the two in the margin.

Although these events happened separately, I can see disturbingly familiar themes in both chapters. I see obsession Saul's part to find David. Did you notice that David had an opportunity to kill Saul again and didn't? I again see David begging for Saul to stop this mad chase to take his life. I see Saul having a lucid moment after being confronted in his sin by David. I again see a lack of trust on David's part toward Saul as the two go their separate ways. And Saul's words again reveal his knowledge that David will triumph in the end.

So my question today, girlfriends, is how do we explain Saul's behavior? How did he get from the humble man who felt unworthy to become Israel's king to the paranoid and obsessive fool he had now become?

This is where the validity of 2 Timothy 3:16 becomes apparent. Turn there to fill in the blank:

"_____ Scripture is God-breathed and is useful for

_____, rebuking, correcting, and _____

in righteousness."

When the answers are not readily apparent, we must go to other Scripture for the counsel of God given elsewhere that will speak to our questions. David had never given Saul any reason to suggest that he was trying to overthrow Saul's throne. It was all in Saul's mind. The question I want to tackle today is how did Saul come to believe the lies in his mind as truth?

I am going to share a verse from a psalm that I must have read twenty times before, but I have seen its truth with new eyes with the goal of exposing the many faces of jealousy. As I have become immersed in the topic of jealousy's deadly consequences, I have started to see familiar Scripture in a different light. Through this Scripture we are going to see the how powerful a spotlight God's Word shines on judging the thoughts and attitudes of the heart.

> When the answers are not readily apparent, we must go to other Scripture for the counsel of God given elsewhere that will speak to our questions.

Listen to the following words:

"He wore cursing as his garment; it entered into his body like water, into his bones like oil."
                                                                    Psalm 109:18

I wanted to share the Hebrew root word and corollary words I found in *Strong's Concordance* for cursing with you because I think it is fascinating in lending insight into jealousy's thoughts and motives toward its victim. Pay particular attention to the definition of **curse** in the corollary words:

1) curse, vilification, execration

   Transliteration: qalal

   "be slight, be swift, be trifling, be of little account, be light"[1]

   (corollary words)

Saul's jealous eye cursed David's life as it made David the villain in Saul's eyes. Saul had put on the garment of jealousy the first time he heard the women's comparison of David's military exploits to his. The praise for David was greater than that of Saul. Saul let his ear hear those words of praise repeatedly, causing them to result in David being seen as his enemy. Everyday, Saul had a choice how his eyes would view David. Girlfriends, think about this! When jealousy first begins, we choose to look differently than we did before at the object of our envy. We choose to wear the garment of cursing toward that person. When we do not ask for God to help us rid our thoughts of envy, a bitter transformation starts to occur. Sin slowly starts to harden us. As the bitter root of jealousy finds a place to plant itself in our minds toward that individual, a subtle process starts to take place. The jealousy starts infecting every part of us.

Life-giving marrow is in the center of bones. Red blood cells are made in the bone marrow, allowing our body's cells to receive oxygen and nutrients which give us health. After nursing jealous thoughts enough, our whole bodies become infected with its poison as it enters our bones.

Look at this amazing verse in Proverbs 14:30:

"A heart at peace gives life to the body, but envy rots the bones."

A benchmark of a jealous heart is lack of peace. Saul was obsessed with killing David. Instead of concentrating his energies on the real enemy of Israel—the Philistines—Saul gave his life to the meaningless pursuit of someone who feared God too much to retaliate. We are deliberate in the putting on of jealousy in the beginning. What do I mean by that? When we are envious of someone, our thoughts toward her change. If we do not call out for God's deliverance, those thoughts begin to fester and actually change the way we view that person. We perceive her as a threat to our world. That threat left unattended by God's promises to us leads to the death of that relationship.

When jealousy first begins, we choose to look differently than we did before at the object of our envy.

Cancer of the bones is extremely serious. Cancer found in other tissues can be eradicated with the right medical treatment if caught in time. But when those deadly cells find their way into the life-producing marrow of our bones, the prognosis for survival is grim. By the time envy enters our bones, girlfriends, that garment of cursing found in jealous thoughts which we put on in the beginning towards another human being, has become part of us! And we never see when it happens! We run the dangerous risk of becoming blind to what has happened to us because jealousy has become so deeply entrenched with who we are. Instead of life being produced in our bones, jealousy invades and takes over, producing death in our relationships.

Let's look back on the definition for cursing. We are going to take the words given in the definition one by one and apply them to the behavior of Saul.

1) curse, vilification, execration
Transliteration: qalal
"be slight, be swift, be trifling, be of little account, be light"

To be swift

I believe the swiftness part of the definition has to do with how quickly we can dismiss the feelings of our victim. It also speaks to the lack of prayer we have covered our actions with toward others. We act before we bring the matter before God. Saul is never depicted in Scriptures as throwing himself before the counsel of God before he acted.

Be trifling

The trifling in David's affairs (asking for information on his hideouts, leaving the palace and Israel undefended in his pursuit, etc.), helps to explain Saul's obsession with harming David. He could not let it go.

Be of little account

The only accountability we have seen demanded of Saul was by Samuel and David in their confrontations of Saul's sin. A person not accountable to anyone else is a danger to herself and others. We cannot be our own mirror and not see a distorted reflection of ourselves. Listen once more to what the preacher, Charles Spurgeon, said about our distorted view of our arrogance in this area:

"No Christian man is all that he thinks he is; our purest gold is alloyed. We have none of us so much faith as we impute to ourselves, nor so much patience, or humility, or meekness, or love to God, or love to men. Spurious coin swells our apparent wealth." [2]
— From his sermon, Trial by the Word, Metropolitan Tabernacle Sermons

We cannot be our
own mirror and
not see a distorted
reflection of ourselves!

How do we know that we are submitting to the safety of accountability of godly people—if our attitude is the same as the writer of Psalm 141:5:

"Let a righteous man strike me—it is a kindness; let him rebuke me—it is oil on my head. My head will not refuse it... "

Saul had surrounded himself with men who would not dare to speak up to him in the face of great evil. Remember how not one man came forward to side with Ahimelech the priest, but watched at Saul's side as he allowed Doeg to be the instrument of his rage in the city of Nob's destruction? Girlfriends, have we filled our lives with people who are going to tell us what we want to hear? Have we rejected those who have dared to give us godly instruction and spurned the life-giving reproach that we have refused to take to heart?

To be light

The light part of the definition speaks to Saul's attitude toward David's life. Because David was not important to Saul, Saul could make light of David's situation. David was dehumanized in Saul's eyes, giving Saul the justification to make David's life the living nightmare of a fugitive. Saul's twisted thinking made him believe he was the victim, instead of seeing the grievous sin he had committed against David. Instead of standing in awe before the coming wrath of God over his continued attempts to take David's life without cause, Saul counted his actions to be a light matter in the eyes of the Righteous Judge.

What clothing are we wearing, my dear friend? Have we lived in the muck and mire of jealousy for so long that we do not see that its poison has entered our bones? Is our conversation about others full of grace or do we spew hatred from our broken hearts? We must not make light of our sin; we must show no mercy to our sin because wearing sin's garment comes with a price tag too costly to afford.

My reluctance at taking off the garment of my sin comes from the fear of knowing that my naked rebellion will be exposed before God—as if I could hide anything from Him! What I failed to realize for so many years is that my God is never into shaming me. He does not leave my naked heart exposed without giving me a different set of clothes. How does He want to dress me? Listen to this precious promise:

"I delight greatly in the LORD;
my soul rejoices in my God.
For he has clothed me with garments of salvation
and arrayed me in a robe of righteousness,
as a bridegroom adorns his head like a priest,
and as a bride adorns herself with her jewels."   Isaiah 61:10

Do you and I want to feel as beautiful on the inside of our soul as we long to be on the outside of our person? We have to change clothes, sweet friend! Let's allow our Jesus to remove the soiled garment of jealousy we have been wearing for so long and have Him clothe us in the robe of righteousness He has waiting for us when we bow our knee in repentance before Christ.

❋ **Day Four:** Despairing of His Deliverance

Have you ever had a paradigm shift—an experience where you saw the same set of circumstances through different eyes? This study has spent a great deal of time looking at jealousy's perpetrator. Today we are going to try to discover insights looking at jealousy's victims through Scripture. I pray that today's lesson will bring hope and a warning that we will not soon forget.

We have seen how Saul's rebellion and disobedience created vacuums in his soul which beckoned jealousy's poison to fill the cavernous holes those sins produced in his heart. The awful truth about sin is found in Hebrews 12:15.

What two things are produced from a bitter root allowed to grow in us in this verse?

Rage and hatred   Trouble and defilement of others

Laziness and complaining

We must always remember that sin in us never just affects us. Let's recall how have we seen the bitter root of jealousy in Saul cause trouble and/or defile the following people:

Jonathan (1 Samuel 20:30-35):

David (1 Samuel 19:18, 20:1, 21:10):

Michal (1 Samuel 19:11-17):

Ahimelech the priest and the people of Nob (1 Samuel 21:1, 22:16, 18-19):

So how does jealousy ravage its victim? Let's read 1 Samuel 27:1-12. Record any observations in the margin that strike you as unusual in David's choice of a refuge in this chapter or choices he made that are uncharacteristic in his behavior.

After the Persian Gulf war, a new term emerged in the medical field to help explain the shell-shocked behavior of returning veterans. Post-Traumatic Stress Syndrome[3] described the ravages of war on the minds that had been the target of the enemy. In this new warfare, the enemy wore civilian clothes. Ordered to provide security and to protect the public, our brave men and women in uniform had found themselves living in a foreign land in which the enemy was indistinguishable from those they were commanded to protect. The result of not being able to tell who the real enemy was caused the soldiers to live with constant distrust of everyone. They had been forced to run from enemy fire for a prolonged time. Depression, fear, and nightmares characterized many soldiers who suffered from the stress of being the target of the enemy over a prolonged time.

※ Even the bravest soul is not immune to fear. God had continually allowed David to escape from the clutches of the crazed king, but what did David believe according to 1 Samuel 27:1?

Twice, we have seen David reject the opportunity to kill Saul and not harm him. Both times, David has confronted Saul about his senseless pursuit of him. Saul had seemed to understand his sinful actions toward David in 1 Samuel 24 and 1 Samuel 26. David remained wary.

What action did David take in 1 Samuel 27:2-3 that could give evidence to the destruction of the trust between Saul and David?

The alarming truth is that our jealous behavior towards another person can make that person run into enemy territory.

We have seen Achish before. Gath was in enemy territory, remember? The real enemy that Israel faced were the Philistines. What must David had known Saul would do if he fled to the land of the enemy according to verse 4?

The alarming truth is that our jealous behavior towards another person can make that person run into enemy territory. By the time jealous thoughts have stopped being a garment that we can take off and have become who we are (it has entered the marrow of our bones), the result can be that our victim does not trust us anymore. Festering thoughts become cruel actions.

"but each one is tempted when, by his own evil desire, he is dragged away and enticed. Then, after desire has conceived, it gives birth to sin; and sin, when it is full-grown, gives birth to death."　　　*James 1:14-15*

Apply the above Scripture in the book of James to 1 Samuel 18:6-8. Identify the evil desire Saul was enticed by and the sin it produced in his life:

That full-grown sin led to the death of the relationship between Saul and David—the victim of his sin. Have you ever been the victim of someone's jealousy? Did they exhibit characteristics that we have seen in Saul? Please share here.

Has someone's jealousy toward you ever caused you to despair of hope? Has it destroyed your trust of that person? Please share here.

What was happening in the heart of David as he had to run for his very life from the madman named Saul? I think we need to look at his own words in the Psalms to find out.

In view of what you might have shared in the reflection question above, see if you can relate to any of these emotions as a victim of someone's jealousy toward you by matching these verses with their correct reference:

I've been forgotten by God.	*Psalm 142:3*
I've been abandoned by God.	*Psalm 116:11*
God does not hear me.	*Psalm 22:1*
Everyone is a liar.	*Psalm 55:2*
My spirit grows faint.	*Psalm 38:12*
A trap has been set for me.	*Psalm 69:20*
Scorn has broken my heart.	*Psalm 13:1*

Do we see how devastating jealousy is to its victim? Its venom can cause us to doubt the promises and faithfulness of our God. When our jealous actions toward another cause this doubt in our victim, the fight we are waging against him or her becomes God's fight and we may become His enemy (see 1 Samuel 28:16).

If we are jealousy's victim, we must believe by faith that God has not abandoned or forgotten us. He always hears us. We cannot believe the lie that everyone is a liar—that is why we need community. The Lord has promised that we will not become faint when we wait on Him. He also promises that the hole the enemy has dug us will be what he will eventually fall into. If our jealous behavior toward another person has caused them to go to God and beg for His retribution against us, heaven help us!

My son was bullied unmercifully in third grade. Tell me, girlfriends, what happens when you find out your child is being abused undeservedly? Does the knowledge make you want to jump up and down and do the happy dance? Or would you react like I did inside and want to go snatch the bully bald-headed? *My One Year Chronological Bible* is such a wonderful tool to give me a fuller sense of the story because the psalms that theologians believe David wrote during this time period are recorded alongside the stories of his desperate attempts to get away from Saul. David continually poured out his soul to God whom he believed was his refuge and strength and who would exact vengeance on his enemy eventually.

Unfortunately, a continual diet of weariness and discouragement will wear down the most faithful believer. Elijah the prophet stood up to one of the most wicked kings in Israel, but he became so discouraged as he hid from him and his wicked wife that he wanted the Lord to take his life (see 2 Kings 19:1-5). On the authority of God's Word, sisters, our God will only tolerate evil toward the righteous for a set amount of time. If you and I are the bullies, we had better fall on our knees before Him, because His vindication will surely come against us.

My youngest child always loved to remind me that God gave bigger spanks than I did after she and I had a hand-to-bottom session together. Amen to that! When He disciplines, He is unbelievably thorough. We want His mercy to fall on us, girlfriends, not His anger. If you and I, through our rebellion and arrogance, are letting jealousy get the best of us, we need to beg our God to forgive us through the blood of Jesus Christ. Included in that repentance may be participating in some hard conversations that include eating a lot of humble pie, but we have got to do that! We must ask for forgiveness of the Lord and the one whom we have hurt through our jealous behavior. Listen to His plea with us today from Psalm 95:

"Do not harden your hearts as you did at Meribah,
*   as you did that day at Massah in the desert,*
*   where your fathers tested and tried me,*
*   though they had seen what I did.*
For forty years I was angry with that generation;
*   I said, "They are a people whose hearts go astray,*
*   and they have not known my ways."*
So I declared on oath in my anger,
*   "They shall never enter my rest."*   *Psalm 95:8-11*

If we are jealousy's victim, we must believe by faith that God has not abandoned or forgotten us.

Jealousy is built on the foundation of a lie. There is no such thing as greener grass on the other side of anyone else's fence. We will never fill the core issues of a broken heart by hunting down and hurting others. God has sworn on oath that if we harden our hearts toward His Holy Spirit's conviction, we will never enter His rest. The abundant life that Jesus promised us in John 10:10 will continue to elude us as the thief steals, kills, and destroys our own lives lived out in jealousy toward others.

Before we leave this lesson, I want to encourage the woman who is trying to live righteously before God in this area. You are trying to let God avenge you and not taking it into your own hands. You have not gossiped or slandered, though you have had those things done to you. You have fought against the lies that the enemy has tried to get you to believe that you are all alone in the fight—that God has abandoned you. Oh, my sweet sister, listen to the Word of the Lord:

"Dear friends, never take revenge. Leave that to the righteous anger of God. For the Scriptures say, "I will take revenge; I will pay them back," says the Lord.

Don't let evil conquer you, but conquer evil by doing good."
Romans 12:19, 21 (NLT)

Your heavenly Father knows! He will repay all the wrong. In the wait, He encourages you not to become weary in well-doing because the harvest He has promised will be yours. Though you sow in tears, you will **doubtless** return carrying sheaves of joy with you (Psalm 126:5-6 KJV). You can take that to the spiritual bank.

Hold on, sister, hold on!

There is no such thing
as greener grass
on the other side of
anyone else's fence.

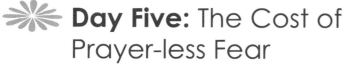

Day Five: The Cost of Prayer-less Fear

"He reached down from on high and took hold of me;
he drew me out of deep waters.
He rescued me from my powerful enemy,
from my foes, who were too strong for me.
They confronted me in the day of my disaster,
but the LORD was my support."   *2 Samuel 22:17-19 (NIV)*

Have you ever gotten yourself into an impossible situation where you were going to have to face awful consequences if you told the truth about what you had done? But you knew that if you continued to lie, it would mean disaster also? There is much hope for us in our study today because our God has declared Himself to be "the LORD, the compassionate and gracious God, slow to anger, abounding in love and faithfulness… " (Exodus 34:6) His mercies are new to us every morning.

What does 1 Corinthians 10:13 promise us when we are facing a temptation:

God will judge sin.   God sees everything.

God will provide a way of escape from the temptation.

Saul's bitter jealousy has forced David to run into the land of the Philistines, Israel's enemy. How had David established himself in Israel according to 1 Samuel 18:13-16, 30?

David's reputation was well-known with the Philistines also. He had humiliated them in battle many times before Saul ousted David from his position as a commander in the army. Although David was hoping for refuge in the land of his enemy, he certainly could not have hoped for anonymity. David's military victories were a thorn in the side of the officials of the king of Gath.

Let's pick up yesterday's lesson by reading 1 Samuel 29:1-5. Have you ever been in a situation where you felt bewildered and anxious because someone was there that should not have been there? I remember going to visit a friend in college on his campus when the guy I had broken up with a few months before suddenly appeared out of nowhere. He had not told my friend that he was coming to visit and had randomly picked the same day that I had to show up. As you might have guessed, all three of us spent an awkward few hours together. I could not wait to get in my car and get out of the miserable situation. My emotions were a mixture of confusion, disbelief, and sadness.

David, the killer of the Philistine giant, Goliath, was bringing up the rear of the Philistine army on a military expedition. The purpose of the expedition was to fight Israel in Israel's own territory (Joshua 19:30-31). Talk about awkward! Egos were ruffled and a complaint was issued to Achish about the absurdity of the situation.

How did Achish try to defend David in 1 Samuel 27:3?

What insight does 1 Samuel 27:12 give us why Achish might have wanted to keep David with him?

David had won Achish's trust, but through deception. David had been on some military expeditions of his own in which he killed every man, woman, and child who could have reported back to Achish of the battles. He let Achish believe that he was raiding his own country of Israel (1 Samuel 27:10), when, in actuality, he was killing other enemies of Israel outside of Philistine territory.

As carefully as David had covered his tracks to Achish, the impending battle against his own people could only spell disaster for him. He was caught between a rock and a hard place. If he told Achish the truth and reveal that he had not been trustworthy, he risked losing his life.

What problem was there with Israel seeing him fighting for the Philistines according to 1 Samuel 16:1?

How loyal would David's future Israelite subjects to their next anointed king if they realized he had become a warrior in the enemy's army? I don't think trust could have been rebuilt. Where was the last place God had told David to go through the prophet Gad according to 1 Samuel 22:5?

Judah   Gath   Ziklag   En Gedi

How did David get into such a mess? I believe the answer is found by contrasting 1 Samuel 23:9-11 with 1 Samuel 27:1-3. In both situations, David knew that Saul was hunting down his life. He was terribly afraid in both situations. In the first scenario, David went straight to God with his fear. God answered him. We do not see any indication that David consulted God through the ephod or Abiathar the priest before he chose to flee to the land of the Philistines. David's humanity prevailed, causing him to panic, which forced him to lie to cover up his deeds of the last sixteen months.

When have you failed to pray and panicked instead? What were the unforeseen consequences of your actions?

In 1978, my parents dropped a "bomb" on my maternal grandparents when they informed them that we were leaving the United States to become missionaries in Africa. My grandparents' alarm grew when they heard that we would be gone for three and a half years before returning to the United States. When they learned that our destination was the remote bush station, Nkara-Ewa, four hundred miles from the capital city of Kinshasa, visions of their grandchildren dying of some horrible tropical fever or from the venom of a poisonous snake bite filled their heads. My grandparents threatened, pleaded with, and cajoled my parents to give up such a preposterous and dangerous notion. My parents made the agonizing decision to not listen to the voice of man and to instead heed the call of God on their lives.

Can I just take a moment to testify to my great God's power? Not once did we ever meet up with a snake on our path. God always supplied our daily bread. We had medicine for the malaria we all had at various times. Even though the nearest hospital was only accessible by airplane or a six-hour car ride, no plane was ever flown in because of an emergency that happened within our family. God kept us safe. Yet, eight years later, my sister and I were in a very serious bus accident ten days after we had returned to the United States from Africa when I was eighteen. I came closer to death in the "safety" of America than I ever did in "God-forsaken" Africa. The safest place you and I can possibly be is in the center of God's will, though it go against all reason to stay there. No harm can possibly come to us if we make our God our refuge in times of trouble.

God had promised protection to David in Judah, not in enemy territory with Achish. David ran from God's refuge in the middle of Judah because of David's encounters with the town of Keilah and the Ziphites. One would have betrayed David; the other actively aided Saul in hunting David down. Instead of focusing on God's deliverance, David focused on the narrowness of his escapes at their hands. In his fear, David took matters into his own hands. The result was that he needed Someone to clean up the result of his flawed way of thinking.

How did God rescue David according to 1 Samuel 29:6-7?

How sincere do you think David's protest in verse 8 was and why?

> The safest place you and I can possibly be is in the center of God's will, though it go against all reason to stay there.

If it had been up to Samuel, Eliab, David's eldest brother, would have been anointed king that day long before in Bethlehem. But God never judges by outward appearances. He always judges the heart. And in His great mercy, He is quick to show compassion and graciousness to the fragile, sinful hearts of those He has made. David's lack of prayer could have cost him his head or his future. David made a foolish mistake, but God continued to see the heart that beat in the chest of that fallible man.

What does Psalm 103:10 tell us?

Strangely, Scripture does not record David being anxious over this situation. I wonder if he was blind to the danger he had put himself in until that walk home on the way back to Judah from Achish the following morning. It has sometimes taken me years to realize the horrible ramifications I could be experiencing today if God had not reached down and taken hold of me to draw me out of waters that could have taken my life or integrity in front of others.

How did Achish and David part according to 1 Samuel 29:9-10? Choose one:

Achish found David out.   Achish hated David. David was an "angel of God" to Achish.

We must never forget that our God is also our heavenly Father. He let David escape the situation with Achish's favor. You know what? He has done the same for me! My lying tongue has had me headed for certain doom; yet He has not treated me as my sins deserve, glory to His Name!

He has spared me from horrible humiliation and protected me from a trashed reputation. How about you?

After sixteen months in enemy territory, David is headed back to Ziklag. I am sure that his heart had to be heavy with dread as he left the enemy's territory. The thought of having to go back to the life of a fugitive caused by the vain imaginations of a mad king must have been disheartening. David had chosen his own means of rescue in a moment of faltering faith. It could have cost him his life had Jehovah not established his steps. Although David's terror may have caused him to doubt God's faithfulness to him, the truth that He is always at work for those He loves was about to be revealed in a way David could not have imagined. As we close today's lesson, I wonder if you are battle-worn and

> It has sometimes taken me years to realize the horrible ramifications I could be experiencing today if God had not reached down and taken hold of me to draw me out of waters that could have taken my life or integrity in front of others.

weary. Yes, God has not treated you as your sin has deserved, but the enemy is still persistent and has not yet been conquered. Dear one, listen to these words of comfort about the promise of Psalm 105:19 that we are soon going to gloriously witness in David's life:

Trial does not last for ever. Cheer up; the tide ebbs out, but the flood will return again. Note the word "until." He who counts the stars also numbers your sorrows, and if he ordains the number ten your trials will never be eleven. The text says, "until"; for the Lord appoints the bounds of the proud waters, and they shall no more go over your soul when they reach the boundary of the divine "until." [4]
    – Charles Haddon Spurgeon

Our "until" may be right around the corner! Our God is the God of hope, hallelujah! He is singing songs of deliverance over us and knows how to rescue His godly one. Take heart, dear friend! As we wait, let's make certain we are living in the place of safety and not in enemy territory.

"… the Lord knows how to rescue the godly from trials and to keep the unrighteous under punishment until the day of judgment."
                                    2 Peter 2:9 (HSCB)

God is singing songs of deliverance over us and knows how to rescue His beloved one.

A Bitter Ending

Do not be deceived: God cannot be mocked. A man reaps what he sows. The one who sows to please his sinful nature, from that nature will reap destruction; the one who sows to please the Spirit, from the Spirit will reap eternal life.   *Galatians 6:7-8*

Because Saul did not make any effort to live at peace with his unmet desires fueled by his jealousy, he faced the devastating reality of being out of fellowship with God. After chasing an enemy that only existed in his mind, he was completely unprepared when the true enemy faced him on a final battlefield.

We are going to see the results of the bitter root Saul never allowed God to eradicate from his broken heart. In trying to hold on to what he held most dear, he lost everything of importance to him.

No one wins when jealousy abounds. The final consequence of unchecked, unconfessed jealousy is a bitter ending in the relationship between the perpetrator and the victim, which we will witness this week among King Saul, his son Jonathan, and David the fugitive.

Oh, my beloved sisters, we cannot be deceived by jealousy's lies! We will reap what we are sowing in the soil of our hearts. If we are sowing destruction through our jealous actions and thoughts, we are going to face a bitter ending at some point.

Sin is tantalizing only for a season, but the wages of our sin is death according to Romans 3:23. We will ultimately be forced to drink a bitter cup because of our deception regarding sin's consequences. May Jesus show us how to be women who sow that which will allow us to reap the rewards of eternal life.

Day One: A Final Descent Into Darkness

When I was twenty years old, I sat for two weeks as a juror listening to evidence surrounding the murder of a man in his thirties. I was the youngest person on the jury by at least ten years. The prosecuting attorney wanted us to determine if the woman on trial was an accomplice in a murder. The man who pulled the trigger had already been convicted. The prosecuting attorney presented photographs, a history of the three persons involved, and the argument that the woman's motive for her involvement had been the murder of the victim. We listened carefully as the defense lawyer argued that the woman had been in the wrong place at the wrong time, innocent of premeditation in the killing.

After both lawyers had finished presenting their arguments, the twelve of us jurors were faced with the sobering responsibility of determining the woman's involvement in the crime and, thus, her fate. Although the woman had never touched the weapon that had snuffed out the victim's life, she faced long years in prison if convicted. In the eyes of the law, her crime, although it carried a lesser sentence, made her as guilty as if she had pulled the trigger. After a day and a half in the jury room, we unanimously agreed that overwhelming evidence had been presented indicating that the accused woman had known what the killer's intent had been before the crime was committed. Despite possessing that knowledge, the woman had not informed the victim or the police of the murderous plans that were to be carried out against the victim. I was shaken with the gravity of what we had determined when the jury was asked to deliver our verdict. The accused sat stone-faced with no emotion as her guilt was pronounced.

I was far too young at the time of the trial to be able to analyze why this woman might have chosen to be an accomplice in the wrongful death of another person. I have never seen her again, but I have come to understand the wickedness of our sinful nature more through the illumination of God's Word in the twenty-one years that have passed since the verdict was read.

What do the following Scriptures say about the condition of our hearts?

Psalm 14:1

Proverbs 16:2

Although our culture would argue that human beings are essentially good at the core of who we are, Scripture tells us that we are depraved and sinful from our births (Psalm 51:5). Beyond that, we are deceived as to the depth of our depravity. Sin can harden us to such an extent that we can justify our motives as we willingly participate in those things that are forbidden by God. Our pride will take us down a devastating path of no return when we do not remember that the Lord weighs our motives (e.g. living with the consequences of premarital sex, an extra-marital affair, bitterness or unforgiveness toward someone, jealousy, fits of rage or anger, gossiping, withholding love, etc.).

With those thoughts in mind, let's read 1 Samuel 28:3-24 and answer the following questions:

Why was Israel in mourning and what had Saul done according to verse 3?

Although our culture would argue that human beings are essentially good at the core of who we are, Scripture tells us that we are depraved and sinful from our births (Psalm 51:5).

We need to understand why Saul expelled these people from Israel. Match the warning God gave the Israelites with its reference in the following passages:

"I will set my face against the person who turns to mediums and spiritists to prostitute himself by following them, and I will cut him off from his people."	Leviticus 19:26
"Do not turn to mediums or seek out spiritists, for you will be defiled by them. I am the LORD your God."	Leviticus 19:31
"Do not practice divination or sorcery."	Leviticus 20:6

✳ What terrifying reality in 1 Samuel 28:5-6 caused Saul to sin in verse 7?

What explanation can be given for God's silence according to Hebrews 10:26-27?

The cost of a hardened heart is more than you and I can afford to pay. The blindness caused by our sin does not allow us to see the hidden net that Satan has so cunningly laid down in front of us. Without the resurrection power of confession and humility, we will die a slow, horrible death in our spiritual lives. God's purpose for our confession is never to shame us, but to save us! Saul deliberately kept on sinning and, eventually, found that God was silent when Saul tried to inquire of Him. Instead of finding grace, he found God's judgment was the consequence of Saul's refusal to repent of his sin.

After reading Deuteronomy 18:10-12, list the deliberate sins Saul committed in 1 Samuel 28:7-15:

What four facts did Samuel reveal to Saul in 1 Samuel 28:16-19? Fill in the blanks:

… the Lord has _____ away from you and _____ your _____.

The Lord has _____ the _____ out of your hands and _____ it to one of your _____ —to _____.

Because you did ____ _____ the Lord or carry out his fierce anger against the _____, the _____ has done this to _____ today.

The _____ will hand over both _____ and you to the Philistines, and tomorrow _____ and your _____ will be with me. The Lord will also hand over the _____ of _____ to the _____.

What was Saul's reaction in 1 Samuel 28:20-23?

The cost of a hardened heart is more than you and I can afford to pay.

Do we see that Saul was as guilty as the medium in disobeying God? Saul did not call up the dead, but participated in talking and listening to what he should not have. His deceitful heart believed that he was above the law of Moses! Saul had expelled the spiritists and mediums from the land and then deliberately sought one out when God would not answer him. He sought the medium in his desperate state, which was now void of the voice of God. Saul's repeated rebellion and refusal to wait on God and seek His face (as we saw first in 1 Samuel 15) was by now an established pattern and lifestyle which rendered Saul incapable of repentance. Instead of falling prostrate under conviction, Saul fell under the power of horror and fear as a result of his unconfessed pride.

I grew up in a country held in the clutches of demonism and witchcraft. Satan masquerades as an angel of light (2 Corinthians 11:14). If he can get us to believe that he is not as evil or powerful as he is (see Ephesians 2:2), we will be led like a lamb to our own slaughter. I have looked into the eyes of witch-doctors in Congo. Unlike here in America, evil is not as easily disguised as in that country. My grandparents came to the Bayanzi tribe at a time when they were prisoners to demons. Those precious people knew that they must atone for their sin, but they did not understand that Jesus Christ had paid the penalty for that sin on the cross two thousand years before. The demons had convinced them that they must sacrifice their own children as a means to find peace. Of course, Satan laughed his hideously evil laugh at their ignorance and the futility of their actions. When my grandfather, Laban Smith, told them that God had sent His beloved Son, Jesus Christ, to die for their sin, the Bayanzi were awakened to the hope and realization that their children no longer had to be sacrificed. In a period of five years, ten thousand Bayanzi had given their sin-sick hearts to Jesus Christ and had been baptized as a sign of the resurrection power that was now theirs through Christ.

We live in a culture that thumbs its nose at the power of Satan and the consequences of tangling with the spirit world. My dear sister, we cannot afford to be so ignorant or proud! We think those video games we or others in our household play, the movies we watch, our fascination with the paranormal and the occult, or the music we listen to that glorifies things which God detests somehow do not affect us. I believe we can fall into one of four camps:

1. We believe that God's commands are to be obeyed. Although we know that Jesus Christ's power is greater than Satan's, we respect the spiritual world we cannot see and flee from becoming defiled by our involvement in what God detests.

Read Proverbs 6:16-19 and list the seven things God detests in the margin.

2. We believe that God has covered us with His power and that we are immune from Satan's defilement. We believe demons exist, but we have never personally encountered them. Therefore, we believe our attendance at church each week, our involvement in acts of Christian service, and the fact that we can confess our sin at anytime gives us license to participate in activities that we know we shouldn't, but we participate in nonetheless.

What does Ephesians 6:11-12 say about Satan and the demons?

3. We do not believe in the spirit world. We cannot see it, so therefore, we believe that anything that is invisible does not exist.

What does 2 Peter 2:10-12 reveal about our ignorance?

4. We love a thrill. Although we know what we should do, we do not care about sin's consequences. Yes, we know we shouldn't be involved, but that knowledge doesn't have much effect on our actions when we are faced with the temptation to be rebellious.

What does 1 Samuel 15:22-23 reveal about the seriousness of this kind of attitude?

Now the hardest question of all—which camp describes you most accurately right now? Does the camp you fall in allow you to experience the fullness of joy God has promised can be yours?

If we involve ourselves in the things God detests, those wicked deeds cling to us, become a part of us, and will eventually destroy us.

I would be a liar if I said that I have not lived a great part of my life without recognizing my arrogance related to my sin. Rebellion and sin appear so tantalizing for a season, but they leave us feeling hopeless and helpless like Saul did after he had made his final descent into darkness. If we choose to tangle with powers we do not understand, we will be defiled and, ultimately, destroyed.

The judgment we rendered in the court trial I was involved in when I was twenty indicted the defendant based on her passive, but nevertheless, real part in the murder. Are you and I passively aiding Satan in destroying our lives and forfeiting our peace?

Write out what David promised to God in Psalm 101:3:

If we involve ourselves in the things God detests, those wicked deeds cling to us, become a part of us, and will destroy us. Our eyes and ears are the gateways for sin, just as they were for Saul and the woman I discussed at the beginning of this lesson. We give approval to sin through our ears and eyes, even if our hands remain uninvolved! The fleeting happiness of a rebellious act lasts only for a season. True joy, which we spend our lives desperately seeking, is only found through obedience and a refusal to be involved in those activities that God hates.

What will Jesus give us in exchange for the burden of the consequences of our sin according to Isaiah 61:1-4? What do you need the most?

Finally brothers, whatever is true, whatever is honorable, whatever is just, whatever is pure, whatever is lovely, whatever is commendable—if there is any moral excellence and if there is any praise—dwell on these things.
Philippians 4:8 (HCSB)

Following this standard will keep us from the descent into darkness. I pray that God would strengthen us as we flee from all things evil.

✳ Day Two: Rescue By Fire

What would life be like without hope? Yesterday's lesson was filled with despair and a sense of hopelessness. I shudder at the harvest Saul's actions reaped for him.

What can you and I cling to in life's darkest moments as believers in Christ according to Psalm 119:116?

When it looks as though we are standing on the very edge of the precipice of our circumstances, we have the promises of God to sustain us. Our hope will not be dashed, even when it seems that nothing can save us. Someone else besides me needed to be reminded of that today. Was it you? If yes, how?

Even in our sin, we always have hope through repentance! Always. That hope is based on a never-changing God whose Word will sustain us when we have the sense to do things His way. Sometimes, however, we have to face some serious consequences of our wrong choices before our soul can believe that the hope is available as God's Word has said it is. Let's rejoin David on his walk back to Ziklag with his men after his dismissal by Achish from the Philistine army.

What was significant about the city of Ziklag according to 1 Samuel 27:6? Choose one:

Achish had given it to David.   Goliath had lived there.

David had fled there from Saul.

How long had David and his men been living in enemy territory according to 1 Samuel 27:7?

> Even in our sin, we always have hope through repentance! Always.

The last place the Lord had told David to go was to Judah. David's decision to leave Judah was his own, a decision he had made sixteen months before he moved to enemy territory in Gath. We have already discussed how David's fear over Saul's ability to kill him there had overwhelmed him. David knew that God had anointed him king over Israel. But somewhere in the battle for his life, David had grown doubtful of God's sovereignty.

🔍 Can you relate to losing hope when the fight for something has worn you down? Share here.

195

What did Achish request of David in 1 Samuel 29:10-11 and where did David go as a result?

What does Joshua 15:20, 31-32 reveal about this city?

But something had happened to the city since the time of Caananite conquest by Joshua. Ziklag, a town on the southern border of Judah, had fallen into enemy hands. Achish, by bequeathing Ziklag to David, had returned to him what had been Israel's in the first place. Although verse 11 of 1 Samuel 29 says that David was going "back to the land of the Philistines," he was returning to his homeland of Israel and family tribe.

Let's now read all of 1 Samuel 30 and answer the following questions:

What had happened to Ziklag when David had been marching to battle against the Israelites with Achish and the Philistines?

Whom had David and his men left in Ziklag unprotected and what had happened to them?

We have seen the Amalekites before. They were some of Israel's fiercest enemies. Saul had lost the kingship for not destroying them as God had commanded. David had been lying to Achish for sixteen months about his activities on the battlefield (see 1 Samuel 27:8-12). Achish thought David was making himself a stench to the people of Israel by attacking his own tribe of Judah. Instead, David was slaughtering men, women, and children of Israel's other enemies and not bringing back any prisoners or plunder to Achish from those raids. David was making a stench of himself alright—to the Amalekites.

I don't think we can adequately comprehend the devastation of soul that David and his men felt on the third day of their walk to Ziklag. I have a memory burned into my brain—seared there by the smell of the smoldering ruins of a house fire we survived as a family when I was nine years old. I will never forget the sickening feeling of violation I felt as I looked on the charred remains of all my girlish treasures that were made completely unrecognizable because of the flames. Though I looked for clues to try to distinguish my beloved doll, Annie, from the melted mess before me, I could not see any trace of her. Oh, girlfriends, put yourself in David's sandals as you ponder this horrible scene we are looking at through the eyes of these exhausted men. Surely you have had a fire of your own. Maybe it was the day after your parents' divorce was final (or your own). Maybe it was the day you realized a long time dream was forever shattered. Maybe it was the miscarriage, still birth, or death of a beloved child. Perhaps it was when you were served papers about an impending lawsuit or foreclosure. Tragedy has a way of searing its imprint on our minds forever.

What were David and his men's reactions to the condition of Ziklag and their loved ones in verse four? Choose one:

Made a battle plan.   Returned to Gath for help.

Wept until they had no strength.

When was the last time you cried like this and why?

David had messed up. In his desperation to get away from Saul, he had taken matters into his own hands and had fled to Achish, knowing Saul would not follow him there. Although it looked as though things were going David's way for a while, his lack of seeking God's direction almost cost him his life and his future as the king of Israel in the land of the enemy. God's mercy supernaturally rescued David. David had lived a deceitful life for sixteen months, killing men, women, and children under Achish's nose. There was a price to pay for leaving the safety of the shadow of the Almighty for the sham of protection that Achish offered to David.

There are only two things a fire can do, sisters. One is to ravage us; the other is to purify us. Looking at verse six, who chose the ravaging of the fire and who chose the purifying power of the fire? What are the results of each choice according to this verse?

David's choice:

David's men's choice:

✳ Turn to Isaiah 54:16-17. What is God's purpose for the fires in our lives according to verse 17?

Sometimes, fires are the only way to get our attention when we are hurtling headlong down a path of destruction. Which of us as mothers would willingly let our child fall off the edge of a cliff? A good parent sets up obstacles and boundaries that will deter the child from danger. We do not take pleasure in the pain of disciplining our children and neither does our God! But sometimes, girlfriends, we can be so hard-headed that a fire is the only way to get our attention.

David's response to the fire and fear of realizing his wives and children were hostages is another reason why God called him a man after His own heart. You see, it was his response that mattered most. We are all imperfect. We stumble everyday. But it is what we do when we are confronted in our sin that determines whether we have godly character or not.

After consulting the Lord and receiving God's gracious assurance that all the wives and children would be recovered, what happened in 1 Samuel 30:9-10?

> Sometimes, fires are the only way to get our attention when we are hurtling headlong down a path of destruction.

Not everyone was able to help in the recovery. Some men had to stay behind because of their exhaustion. How gracious are we to those who do not fight our common battles alongside us? How could jealousy raise its ugly head in that situation?

Verses 11-16 almost seem out of place to me. David and his men found an Egyptian slave of the Amalekites in a field on their way to rescue their families.

What did David do to this man according to verse 11-12?

At first glance, a slave might be overlooked as useless to help their cause, but David could not leave this dying man on the field, even though the slave had clearly implicated himself in the burning of Ziklag. Our deliverance from and recovery of what the enemy has stolen from us depends on our treatment of those we meet along the journey. God can change our circumstances in a twinkling of an eye, but the true miracle happens when we can let go and choose to forgive someone who has caused us great pain. This forgiveness saves us from the corrosive bitterness of an unforgiving heart.

How did God reward the men for their graciousness to the Egyptian slave in verses 15-17?

How long did David and his men have to fight to recover their families and possessions according to verse 17?

What did they gain in the fight (verses 18-20)?

What adjectives does Scripture use to describe David's men in verse 22 in their reaction to those too exhausted to have joined them in the fight?

What good comes out of a season of being purified by fire? Along with his newly acquired wealth, David had replaced the poverty of a deceitful heart with the riches of compassion and brotherly kindness. I believe he chose to remember how well those left behind had valiantly fought with him in the past. These men were going to be invaluable to him in the kingdom that awaited him when he ascended the throne. The fire allowed David to realize how short-sighted he had been in the past sixteen months. Running to enemy territory can dull our senses and heighten our false sense of importance. I love what Matthew Henry said of this graciousness on David's part toward his men:

"Superiors often lose their authority by haughtiness, but seldom by courtesy and condescension." [1]

What is the last thing that David did in verse 26?

David's kindness to the towns mentioned in Judah would come back to repay him sooner than he knew it at that moment. Girlfriends, how has generosity on your part rewarded you later?

"Give, and it will be given to you. A good measure, pressed down, shaken together and running over, will be poured into your lap. For with the measure you use, it will be measured to you."

Luke 6:38

David's life was about to drastically change, although he had no way of knowing that at the moment. You and I never know when God is going to change the tide of our circumstances. We want to be found faithful when the fire is passed so that the lessons of the fire will not be consumed, but only the dross in our lives.

We want to be found faithful when the fire has passed so that the lessons of the fire will not be consumed, but only the dross in our lives.

Day Three: A Fool's Epitaph

One of the most memorable assignments I ever had in college was to write my own obituary. I was twenty-two years old, full of boundless zeal without knowledge. I conjured up as flowery a picture as I could imagine about the fictitious and wonderful life I had lived, hoping it didn't sound nauseating. In those few paragraphs summing up my entire life, I had painted a picture of a woman who had had it all. I had been successful both in my professional and personal life. I had been happily married, leaving behind devoted children and grandchildren after enjoying over fifty years of marriage. But as I look back on that assignment, I overlooked mentioning the area where success is most important—how I had lived my life for Christ.

In ten words or less, what would you want written on your grave stone as an earthly memorial to the life you had lived?

Do you think that those closest to you would agree with your assessment? Why or why not?

This is a really hard exercise, isn't it? I don't know about you, but something like this forces me to see the huge gap between what I wish I could say about me and what is really true. Those of us who are believers in Jesus Christ for our salvation know that life that is real life begins the moment our physical bodies die. But today I want us to ponder what kind of memorial these lives of ours are leaving in the sight of others.

Our lesson today takes us to a battlefield. All through this study we have seen jealousy's ugly face uncover itself in places that shocked and horrified us. Jealousy is insidious, subtle, and deadly. But the most tragic truth we have uncovered in the exposure of jealousy's many faces is that Saul fought the wrong enemy all along.

Who does Revelation 12:9-10 reveal to be the real enemy and what does he continually do?

Saul had faced many battles in his life. His confidence as a warrior in the early days of his kingship had inspired 330,000 men to fight victoriously against the Philistines. However, as he was dragged away by his envious desires, he started losing the most important battle of his life—the battle for God's favor. Don't think for one minute that living a life worthy of our calling in Christ Jesus is

WEEK EIGHT • A BITTER ENDING

not a battle. We have to die to ourselves daily. Because the good fight of faith is so exhausting and painful to our fleshly natures, we start seeing people as the enemy. The more Saul fanned the flame of jealous thoughts, the less he was able to see his sin and to see God in his circumstances. Jonathan, David, Michal, and Ahimlech became the enemy in his rebellious, unrepentant mind. Oh, sweet friend, I cannot emphasize strongly enough how dangerous is the poison of jealousy in our lives. Under its influence, we will go farther in sin than we ever thought possible.

Let's review our story. Saul and the troops of Israel are now marching toward Mount Gilboa to face Achish and the Philistine army with him. When Saul was unable to seek the voice of God through acceptable ways, he turned to speaking with the dead.

What do you think his emotional state was as he led his army into battle against the Philistines?

Terrified   Full of dread   Lonely   All of those emotions

Let's watch the ensuing battle by reading 1 Samuel 31:1-13.

What two horrible calamities became reality soon after the battle started according to verses 1-2?

Saul was the top general of the army of Israel. Already full of dread, the horror of watching his men being slaughtered in front of his eyes must have paled in comparison to witnessing the deaths of his three sons.

I don't have to guess what thoughts ran through Saul's head as he looked at the body of Jonathan. There are moments in my life that have been seared in my memory with the stamp of regret. And nothing can make me wallow in the pit of self-loathing more than when I dwell on regrets over mistakes I have made with my children. Something will happen to trigger a memory and I can be instantly transported by my guilt to the crushing my words caused in my children's eyes. I have never had to claim the grace of Christ and His forgiveness more than over sins I have committed in my mothering. Satan is the accuser.

What memories of regret in 1 Samuel 20:30-33 could Satan have been using to accuse Saul regarding his dead son?

Now Saul had to come to grips with the reality that jealousy had robbed him of what he wanted the most! We can try to rationalize our jealous thoughts and actions toward someone else as protecting our interests. Jonathan would never ascend the throne and neither would his two brothers. The terrible truth is that there is no greener grass on the other side of the fence. When we have to sin to protect what is ours, it will slip away from us. The surest way for you and I to lose everything dear to us is to grip so tightly that we quench and grieve the Holy Spirit to keep what may not be ours. Jonathan would never ascend the throne nor would his two brothers.

No living heir translated into no hope to the hardened heart of Saul. What did he ask his armor bearer to do for him in 1 Samuel 31:4.

What did Saul's actions in verse 4 cause in verse 5?

Write out verse 6 in its entirety here:

As the mournful winds of death blew over the slain on Mount Gilboa that day, the truth of Proverbs 11:29a was realized.

"He who brings trouble on his family will inherit only wind, and the fool will be servant to the wise."

Make no mistake about it, God's Word is the final authority on our actions. God will not be mocked in our choices of disobedience. Jealousy produces a bitter crop. The bitterness never stays contained, but always causes trouble to defile many (Hebrews 12:15).

Saul tried to pin David against the wall with his spear on three different occasions before David became a fugitive. What sad end did Saul come to according to 1 Samuel 31:9-10?

Saul, unknowingly, had written his own epitaph in a confession he made to David in front of the men who died with him on the battlefield that day. What was his epitaph according to 1 Samuel 26:21? Fill in the blanks:

> The surest way for you and I to lose everything dear to us is to grip so tightly that we quench and grieve the Holy Spirit to keep what may have never been ours at all.

"Then Saul said, 'I have sinned. Come back, David my son. Because you considered my life precious today, I will not try to harm you again.

_____ I have _____ like a _____ and have _____ _____.'"

We have all acted foolishly—not one of us has always made the right choices. Not all of us, however, are fools. David made a foolish decision to go into the territory of the enemy under Achish of Gath. That foolish decision not only affected him, but also the lives of his family and the families of the men who had become part of his army. When the fire of Ziklag came, however, David returned to the source of his strength in Jehovah. Saul, on the other hand, never did. Saul continued his manic, pride-infused, jealous foolishness until the very end of his life. The hardening of his heart resulted in a seared conscience that would not repent, even though he saw the error of his ways for brief moments. Oh, sweet friend, there is tremendous danger in only being stirred by the conviction of our sin when the stirring does not cause us to repent and change.

Rampant, unrestrained jealousy is more deadly to us than we could possibly imagine. Because of the blindness that it causes our souls, we can fail to see the greatest sin of all: we are fighting the sovereignty of God.

Saul had wrongfully assumed that David was his enemy. What do the following verses tell us:

"But the plans of the LORD stand firm forever, the purposes of his heart through all generations."	Matthew 1:1
"A record of the genealogy of Jesus Christ the son of David, the son of Abraham."	Samuel 2:25
"If a man sins against another man, God may mediate for him; but if a man sins against the LORD, who will intercede for him?"	Psalm 33:11
"The LORD said to Samuel, 'How long will you mourn for Saul, since I have rejected him as king over Israel? Fill your horn with oil and be on your way; I am sending you to Jesse of Bethlehem. I have chosen one of his sons to be king.'"	1 Samuel 16:1

> We have all acted foolishly—not one of us has always made the right choices. Not all of us, however, are fools.

What does 1 Chronicles 10:13-14 give as the reason for Saul's death? What does Isaiah 63:10 warn us about?

Saul made himself an enemy of God in his jealous pursuit of David. The Messiah, Jesus Christ, was going to come through the line of David, God's choice for a king. God the Father's purpose for David's kingship was for a far greater purpose than either Saul or David could have possibly imagined. David was the ancestor of the Savior of the world, God's own beloved Son. Saul's jealous actions and murderous rage against David were actually against God Himself, although I believe that was a truth Saul's hardened heart could not grasp. As close as Saul came on that mountain to catching the fleeing David on the other side, nothing was going to thwart the plan of God. Saul put himself in the most dangerous position a human being can be in. In the end, he died a coward's death on a field of slaughter next to the three sons for whom he had so desperately fought to keep the throne.

The Bible's definition for a fool is someone who says in her heart that there is no God (Psalm 14:1; 53:1). The way we live our lives is how we discover if we have a healthy fear of the Lord. We can give lip service that we love Jesus, but if we do not obey Him, our words are meaningless. Are our relationships contradictions of the love we profess for Christ? Have we chased someone into enemy territory by our jealous actions or words? Has our jealousy set us up as an enemy of God because we have discouraged someone else in his or her God-given purpose?

Our God is always the God of hope, sweet friend! The difference between a fool and one who acts foolishly is how the rebuke of God's Word is acted upon in each of those lives. There is a remedy for the fool who wants to leave his or her foolish ways. Listen to what our God says:

"If you have played the fool and exalted yourself, or if you have planned evil, clap your hand over your mouth!"   *Proverbs 30:32*

Our God is the One who makes all things new, the One who can create a pure heart and can renew a right spirit in us in place of the sin that was once there. There was a woman caught in a sinful act who deserved to be stoned for what she had done. Jesus did not condemn her. But He did say, "Go and sin no more." Let's run to make things right, apologize to the victim of our sin if God leads us to do so, and turn away from the destructiveness of a jealous heart. When we do, we will cease being enemies of our God and women after God's own heart.

> Let's run to make things right, apologize to the victim of our sin if God leads us to do so, and turn away from the destructiveness of a jealous heart.

205

Day Four: A Measurement of Growth

If we have memories from kindergarten on, we can probably pinpoint moments when jealousy has been our enemy. Either we have beckoned its evil face into the vacuum in our souls or we have stared at it in the eyes of another looking back at us. My guess is that we have been both jealousy's perpetrator and its victim, maybe even simultaneously. Life on this sin-sick planet provides a dichotomy on this subject. Someone is looking at our life right now thinking that we have it altogether. And we are looking at someone believing the same lie.

Let's remind ourselves of the pervasiveness of jealousy by writing out Ecclesiastes 4:4:

It is my firm belief that as long as you and I draw breath, we are going to have to fight against the vileness of jealousy that causes us and others to sin. No matter how mature we become in the faith, we are going to wrestle with the temptation of destructive, jealous thoughts. The apostle Paul discussed this frustration in Romans 7:18-19:

> "I know that nothing good lives in me, that is, in my sinful nature. For I have the desire to do what is good, but I cannot carry it out. For what I do is not the good I want to do; no, the evil I do not want to do—this I keep on doing."

> Someone is looking at our life right now thinking that we have it altogether. And we are looking at someone believing the same lie.

My son is playing on a baseball team of eleven and twelve-year-old boys. The height difference among the players is astonishing, with one boy being head and shoulders taller than others the same age. My son laments being left behind when it comes to the growth of his body. We have a wall in our family room that is a growth chart of permanent markings of each of our children. The only way my son can see that growth is occurring is to compare his current growth with the last time he measured his height.

Our lesson today gives us a growth chart of sorts, a measuring rod of how we are doing with the never-ending problem of jealousy. We are going to see ourselves through the stature of another today.

Please read 2 Samuel 1 and answer the following questions:

With whom had David just returned to Ziklag from fighting (verse 1)?

The Ziphites   The Philistines

The Moabites   The Amalekites

What was unusual in the messenger's appearance who came on David's third day home?

After identifying himself as an eyewitness of the battle and the fate of the Israelites and Saul, what did this man confess to doing for Saul in verses 9-10?

According to 1 Samuel 31:4, was this man giving a truthful account of Saul's last moments alive? Circle the correct answer:

True   False

Understanding that David's estrangement from Saul was well-known both inside and outside of Israel, what reaction did David have to learning of Saul's death in verses 11-12? Does this surprise you?

In your opinion, what was the Amalekite's motive for coming to David with his fabricated story?

What reason did David give for ordering his death in verse 16?

I think I can say, without hesitation, that whatever the informer was hoping to receive, the death sentence he got probably never entered his mind as a possibility. I believe he assumed that David's hatred for Saul was as intense as Saul's for David. He could not have been more wrong.

After reading the heartbreaking lament for Saul and Jonathan which David not only wrote, but required his men to learn (2 Samuel 1:17-18), list the surprising signs of growth in David toward his enemy:

Verse 19:

Verse 20:

Verse 23:

Verse 24:

Verse 25

David left the private
wounds which Saul
had inflicted on him
private. Could we do
the same?

I expected many reactions from David, but not this one. Saul's death meant the fulfillment of the promise of God made long ago through Samuel that David would sit as king on the throne of Israel. It meant the end of countless days of running from the deluded ruler, the end of fearfully looking over his shoulder, and sleepless nights spent on an uncomfortable cave floor in the desert. David could return to the life which had been stolen from him by Saul whose blind jealousy could not let either one of them rest. I honestly wonder if some of the tears that David shed were over what could have been had he and Saul been allies. The man after God's own heart never showed the spiritual growth in his own heart more readily than when tears of sorrow slipped from his eyes and soul over the demise of his ruthless enemy—the enemy he should have hated, but lamented over instead.

David refused to forget that Saul was the Lord's anointed. The Lord had been rejected by a people who wanted a king like the other nations. God gave Israel what they thought they wanted. Saul was not God's choice for a king for His beloved people, but God elevated Saul to a position of honor by anointing him through Samuel. In the worst of circumstances, David never allowed himself to forget that the Lord had placed Saul in that position, not the people of Israel. David understood that retaliation against Saul was rebellion against God's plan. Girlfriends, that is the heart of the wickedness of jealousy—rebellion against the lot that God has given to us.

Did you notice that David never shamed Saul in this lament for him? He could have mutilated Saul's memory to others as the Philistines mutilated Saul's body. He did not. He chose instead to remember what a mighty warrior Saul had been in battle against the enemies of Israel. How weak and cowardly we are when we have to bash someone else to elevate ourselves. David left the private wounds Saul had inflicted on him private. Could we do the same?

Instead of capitalizing on his weaknesses, David praised Saul's strengths. This may, at first glance, seem to be false flattery. I believe that many children have had fathers who have acted rashly in their presence, but I also believe that there are tender moments that must not be overlooked in the relationship between a parent and his or her child. We can falsely believe it is easier to throw the whole relationship out when we have difficult relationships with our parents. We can choose to forget the sacrifice and blessings of a fallible father. David remembered the affection he must have seen between Saul and Jonathan. Remember Jonathan's response to David after David first told him he suspected Saul wanted him dead?

"Never!" Jonathan replied. "You are not going to die! Look, my father doesn't do anything, great or small, without confiding in me. Why would he hide this from me? It's not so!"   *1 Samuel 20:2*

Finally, David praised Saul for the prosperity his kingship had brought to the people of Israel (2 Samuel 1:24). I believe that David's men knew that David was a man of grace through the final words he spoke over his enemy. Could we be known as women of grace that way, too? If we could be, I believe we would find the abundant life that Jesus promises all of us in John 10:10. We would start really living, knowing that God is going to be the final, righteous Judge. We can leave our hurts with Him where they can be healed in the balm of forgiveness that He will pour into our souls as a result of our relinquishment.

So how would you and I measure up on a growth chart of maturity in Christ, sweet friend? Have we won that hard-earned wisdom that has cost our flesh so much but allows us to leave the poison of our bitterness behind? I do not possess the ability by myself to forgive the ravages of my enemy, but my Jesus empowers me through His strength to do the impossible.

Girlfriends, this life with Jesus is hard—just plain, stinking hard sometimes. There have been times when I know this world would tell me I do not have to cooperate with Him. *After all,* I have fumed, *the wrong has been done to me.* I can think of a million reasons why I am justified in withholding forgiveness and clinging to my bitterness. And then I have heard Him quietly remind me:

"Shawn, how many times have I forgiven you? Do I hold against you what you have done against Me? How many times have you wronged Me?"

And I have stomped my foot as my well-thought-out arguments have crumpled to the floor around me. In the midst of my fuming, crying tantrum, I have heard His gentle whisper:

"Will you do it for Me?"

Will I do it for the One who has saved me from hell and the wrath of God that I deserve? Will I do it for the One whose mercies to me are new every morning, even when I have sinned appallingly against Him the day before? Will I do it for the One who has promised me that the riches of heaven are mine? Will I do it for the One who not only asks me to forgive but gives me the grace to do so? Will I do it for the One whose thoughts toward me are greater in number than the sand on the seashore?

Yes, Jesus, yes! my wounded heart sobs. I cannot find the strength within myself to obey You but through the grace You have given me which triumphs over my weakness, my hurt, and the bitterness of unforgiveness, I can obey for You. I have been forgiven much. Let me love much. Not for the sake of others, *but for Your sake.*

I have been forgiven much. Let me love much. Not for the sake of others, but for Your sake.

"But to each one of us grace has been given as Christ apportioned it."
Ephesians 4:7

Do you need to forgive the one who has made you the victim of his or her jealousy? Maybe you cannot find the strength within you to do that. The grace you need has been given in just the right amount by Christ Himself. If you do not possess the power to forgive, could you forgive for Jesus' sake? Use the space below, sweet friend.

Does the above confession make our circumstances change, my dear sister? No, but I will tell you what our obedience does. Refusing to let jealousy rule our hearts brings us hope, hope that does not disappoint. That hope gives us the ability to live with unmet desires in a way that pleases the One who has done so much for you and me. That is the good news of Jesus Christ.

And endurance (fortitude) develops maturity of character (approved faith and tried integrity). And character [of this sort] produces [the habit of] joyful and confident hope of eternal salvation.

Such hope never disappoints or deludes or shames us, for God's love has been poured out in our hearts through the Holy Spirit Who has been given to us.

While we were yet in weakness [powerless to help ourselves], at the fitting time Christ died for (in behalf of) the ungodly.
Romans 5:4-6 (Amplified Bible)

Day Five: Not Home Yet

Forty years after leaving their homeland of America to serve as missionaries in Africa, Henry Morrison and his wife were pulling into the port for the last time at New York Harbor. As Henry looked at the dock where the ship carrying them home was to pull in, he saw a large crowd awaiting the ship's arrival. Astonished at the excitement of the people in the port, Henry turned to his wife and said,

"They haven't forgotten about us!"

Unbeknownst to the Morrisons was the fact that their ship also carried President Teddy Roosevelt returning home from a hunting expedition to Africa. The crowd was in a frenzied state of excitement as President Roosevelt emerged from the ship. Deafening cheers from those welcoming the president engulfed the Morrisons as they slowly walked away from the ship, unnoticed, to hail a cab to take them to their one bedroom apartment. Not one person had been waiting in the vast crowd to greet the missionary couple on their return.

Henry Morrison fell into a depression as he tried to put the incident at the harbor out of his mind. After several weeks of wrestling with his feelings, he turned to his wife one day to confess his bitterness concerning the matter. Henry shared how dejected he felt as he compared the warmth of the crowd toward President Roosevelt returning from a hunting trip with the coldness of having no one to greet the Morrisons.

Mrs. Morrison encouraged Henry to go to the Lord with his sorrow, reminding her husband that God did not mind Henry's questioning Him over his feelings. Henry decided to take his wife's advice and quietly went into the bedroom and closed the door.

Henry Morrison poured out his grief to the Lord on his knees in the small room. He told the Lord that he felt it just wasn't right that the president had received such an enormous welcome when Henry and his wife had received rejection after faithfully serving God for forty years without complaining.

Several minutes passed before Henry returned to his wife's side. Mrs. Morrison wondered at the change in Henry's face. His expression was peaceful as he explained to her what had taken place in the bedroom between the Lord and him.

"The Lord settled it for me," Henry confided in his wife. "I told Him how bitter I was that the President received this tremendous homecoming, but no one even met us as we returned home. As I finished, it seemed as though the Lord put His hand on my shoulder and simply said,

'But, Henry, you are not home yet!'"[1]

Surely, you and I have felt unnoticed, haven't we? Jealousy is a symptom of a heart that does not believe she is significant in this world. I have lived through seasons where I have felt that those whose approval I was seeking the most did not seem to notice that I existed. Let's remind ourselves what all of us so desperately want more than anything else in this life by writing Proverbs 19:22 here:

Each time I was disappointed in the inability of a human being, a material possession, or a realized dream of mine to fill the aching void in my soul, my foot became more deeply entrenched in the hidden snare that Satan and life's difficulties laid in my path. I used to think the Bible was full of superspiritual people who always did the right thing in God's eyes. I rarely picked up the Bible because I thought that the words would condemn me and confirm how messed up I was. My presumption could not have been more wrong.

I don't know about you, but I need God to be big enough to handle this heart of mine when it does not feel like praising Him. If I cannot trust Him to love me despite my unlovable behavior, I cannot heal or grow. I need a savior to meet me at the point of my need, which may be so far from where I assume God would want me to be. In a world that accepts me for what I can contribute to make it look better than it is, I need someone who loves me because of who I am, not because of what I do or don't do. For so many years I did not realize that Jesus loved me in all of those ways.

> I need a Savior to meet me at the point of my need, which may be so far from where I assume God would want me to be.

The sad truth is that the world will never applaud you and me for making godly choices. You and I have lived enough of life to have come to that conclusion experientially. Jesus never told us that life with Him would be a continual joyride. He never deceived us. Summarize what Christ told us in the following passages:

Matthew 5:10-12:

Matthew 24:9:

John 15:19-21:

John 16:1-3

When the Lord first started laying the idea on my heart to write this Bible study, I wanted to find Biblical characters who handled jealousy well. I panicked as I realized the pages of Scripture were full of those who had fallen for jealousy's lies. There was only one person who quickly came to my mind as one who had lived in victory with unmet desires. This person was the unsung hero to me. He was the one who had every right to feel justified for the bitterness he refused to succumb to. He was the one who died without receiving the throne that his father lost through his rebellion and rabid jealousy—Jonathan.

What happened to Jonathan on the day of the battle according to 1 Samuel 31:1-2?

After reflecting on Jonathan's character, why do you think he joined his father in battle?

List what the Philistines did to Saul and his three sons in 1 Samuel 31:7-13:

I could sob over the injustice of Jonathan's demise. In a perfect world, the hero of the story would have lived happily ever after. Jonathan would have survived and lived a long and prosperous life. The same women who had praised David so lavishly after he killed Goliath would have recognized the stellar character Jonathan had displayed throughout his life as Saul's son. Instead, Jonathan's mutilated body was burned in a city named Jabesh and his ashes were buried under a tree. Jonathan's life was extinguished before the world realized whom they had lost. Isn't that the story of so many of our lives?

When have you wrestled with the injustice of your circumstances knowing you have tried to do what God has asked you to do?

Could it be possible, my darling friend, that you and I have a skewed perspective of what justice is? If we are looking to get justice in this life, we will be disappointed until the day we die. We cannot expect perfection to rule in an imperfect world filled with sinful human beings. Oh, but we do expect the world to give us what it cannot give, don't we? And because of that expectation, we end up feeling duped as we live in defeat over our unmet desires.

Listen to what the apostle Paul proclaimed in 1 Corinthians 15:19-20 (NLT):

And if our hope in Christ is only for this life, we are more to be pitied than anyone in the world. But in fact, Christ has been raised from the dead. He is the first of a great harvest of all who have died.

We are faced with a great temptation to believe that if we do not receive what we were hoping for in this lifetime, we have missed the opportunity forever. Lives lived in obscurity before the eyes of this world are intimately known before our heavenly Father. Contrast the following two passages of Scripture:

Psalm 90:9-10

1 John 2:17

We cannot expect perfection to rule in an imperfect world filled with sinful human beings.

The seventy or eighty years —perhaps more, perhaps less— which we have been given to live here on this earth are so minute in the light of eternity. One day, sweet sister, our God is going to right all wrongs. We will not be rewarded for our earthly achievements. They will be forgotten like grass that is cut and burned. What we will be rewarded for is lives that reflected God's glory. We will be exalted for dying to ourselves in these seventy or eighty years before we go to be with Jesus forever.

Jonathan was not noticed as he should have been before he died on a bloody battlefield. Jonathan chose to believe that Jehovah was his ultimate Judge. Heaven's perspective of this unsung hero is going to be vastly different than this cruel world's unjust system of reward.

All these people were still living by faith when they died. They did not receive the things promised; they only saw them and welcomed them from a distance. And they admitted that they were aliens and strangers on earth. People who say such things show that they are looking for a country of their own. If they had been thinking of the country they had left, they would have had opportunity to return. Instead, they were longing for a better country—a heavenly one. Therefore God is not ashamed to be called their God, for he has prepared a city for them. Hebrews 11:13-16

My beloved sister, each time we say no to bitterness over not having justice served and continue to walk humbly with Jesus, we show that we are just strangers here in this world. A stranger to this world does not desire man's fickle affection, but rather the incomprehensible reward of our soul hearing that our God is not ashamed to be our God!

Indeed, if we consider the unblushing promises of rewards promised in the Gospels, it would seem that our Lord finds our desires not too strong, but too weak. We are half-hearted creatures, fooling about with drink and sex and ambition when infinite joy has been offered to us. We are far too easily pleased, like an ignorant child who goes on making mud pies in a slum because he cannot imagine what is meant by an offer of a holiday at the sea.[3]
-C. S. Lewis

Like the overlooked, missionary Henry Morrison, have you and I forgotten that we are not home yet?

Have you and I forgotten that we are not home yet?

Antidotes For Jealousy's Poison

Long ago, in eternity past, God the Father and His beloved Son, Jesus Christ, along with God the Holy Spirit, decided to make human beings in their own image. A dilemma was introduced when they also decided to give their beloved creation a free will to ultimately seek the Godhead and find them, or to reject the Ones who had created men and women. Because of the holy Trinity's boundless love for their creation, Jesus Christ became a man so that He could fully understand the frailties of our humanness without ever sinning. Centuries before His birth of a virgin in the obscure Judean town of Bethlehem, the prophet Isaiah foretold what His life here on earth would be like:

1 Who has believed our message
and to whom has the arm of the LORD been revealed?

2 He grew up before him like a tender shoot,
and like a root out of dry ground.
He had no beauty or majesty to attract us to him,
nothing in his appearance that we should desire him.

3 He was despised and rejected by men,
a man of sorrows, and familiar with suffering.
Like one from whom men hide their faces
he was despised, and we esteemed him not.

4 Surely he took up our infirmities
and carried our sorrows,
yet we considered him stricken by God,
smitten by him, and afflicted.

5 But he was pierced for our transgressions,
he was crushed for our iniquities;
the punishment that brought us peace was upon him,
and by his wounds we are healed.   *Isaiah 53:1-5*

My sweet sister, do you know my Jesus? I always understood and believed that Jesus Christ was fully God, but I did not always understand that He was fully human—a Man who was despised and rejected by others, just like you and me. I did not understand that to prevent the wrath of God from falling on me, Jesus had to become sin on a cruel cross. Jesus has felt everything you and I have—the deepest sorrow and the greatest joy. He is unequaled in His power, His wisdom, and His love for those who believe on His Name for salvation.

This week we are going to look at five antidotes for the poison of jealousy. Jesus longs for us to experience the abundant life promised in John 10:10, but this life can only become a reality when we deny our fleshly desires and take up a cross to follow Him. Although the process is excruciating, the irony is that we will never feel more alive than when we die to ourselves and our preconceived ideas of who God is or how we think He should act toward us.

✳ **Day One:** The Narrow Gate

Can you believe where we have arrived? We have made it through to the end of the study! I cannot express to you the privilege it has been for us to take this journey together into a subject that is rarely talked about. Thank you for sticking with me during this roller coaster ride of highs and lows in the lives of Hannah, Samuel, Saul, Jonathan, and David. One of the most wonderful benefits Scripture gives us is the ability to observe real life situations through the Bible's pages and learn from them, even though we have never met the individuals we have studied. It is my fervent prayer that you and I will reap the rewards of the benefit of looking in on the serious mistakes of Saul which we have studied over the last eight weeks and determine, through the power of the Holy Spirit, not to repeat those sinful lapses of judgment in our own lives. On the other hand, I pray that we will act on those areas of obedience that we have seen in Hannah, Samuel, Jonathan and David and reap the benefits for ourselves.

Our goal in this study has been to realize that jealousy is a symptom of a heart that is broken in some area in our relationship with God. I have asked that the Holy Spirit would enable us to see that feelings of destructive jealousy we are struggling with are a symptom of unbelief in our hearts regarding the character of God.

I want to make a disclaimer about this last week right at the start. Just as I believe the study of the four core issues of a jealous heart presented in week one was not an exhaustive one, the five antidotes for jealousy's poison in this week's study are not being presented as the only five ways to combat jealous thoughts and actions. These five that we will examine this week come from my personal experience in the ongoing fight I am involved in to become more like Christ and less like sinful Shawn in the area of jealousy. I do not pretend to be an expert in the subject of jealousy, but only a fellow sojourner on this journey that I have been so honored to take with you.

My parents were the first people who had a relationship with Christ that I wanted for myself. Throughout my life as a child growing up in their home, I saw a lasting joy and deep trust in Christ that evaded me. I was convinced as a child that I needed to reach a certain age to have a consistent walk with Christ like they did. At age ten, twenty-two years old seemed so far away. My twenty-second birthday came and went, however, and I still had not found the satisfaction I was looking for in my relationship with Jesus. I then thought that maybe I would be content when I got married. No. Although God blessed me with a wonderful husband, Rob could not fill up the void I still felt in my soul. I convinced myself that when I had children I would somehow find the answer. After all, I thought that pregnancy and childbirth equaled maturity. Wrong! To my dismay, having children only showed me how unbelievably selfish and inadequate I was.

To compound my distress, my fear of totally surrendering to Christ was overwhelming. I had given my heart to Him to be my Savior, but making Him Lord of my life was not yet a reality. Total surrender was too confining or so it seemed. Christianity seemed full of rules and regulations and devoid of much fun. In my opinion, my sins were like an albatross around my neck. It was too great a risk to change. The thought of me having to review all my horrible acts and words pressed against me, backing me into a corner of condemnation and guilt. I tried to pacify myself by enjoying the brief mountaintop experiences with Christ that infrequently occurred before I plunged into the deadness of my apathy again.

Jesus' teachings during His life on earth are counterintuitive to my sinful flesh. His parables found in the New Testament often puzzled me. A teaching of His that I did not understand for so long was the one I would like to examine today.

Please read Matthew 7:13-14 and answer the following questions:

What does Jesus beckon each of us to go through (verse 13)?

Baptism   Church membership classes

A narrow gate   A broad road

How many find what Christ is beckoning us to go through?

Why is this true (verse 14)?

I was more than willing to be saved from hell by entering the narrow gate, but the thought of traveling down the narrow road that went out from there which led to life was a frightening prospect.

Although I did not realize my flawed perspective at the time, I was afraid of that narrow road that led away from the narrow gate. The word *narrow* troubled me. Synonyms for narrow in my mind were *confined*, *restrictive*, and *smothering*. I was more than willing to be saved from hell by entering the narrow gate, but the thought of traveling down the narrow road that went out from there which led to life was a frightening prospect. To me it was synonymous with rigid sacrifice. The narrow road demanded a squeezing and purging I was not willing to put myself through. Accepting Him as my personal Savior was a cost I was willing to make; however, pursuing His Lordship in my life lacked incentive for me because of the changes it would demand I make.

One blustery winter day in Chicago, I hit the wall. Eleven years ago, after the birth of my second baby in thirteen months, I was at the end of my rope. I had everything in my possession I had fooled myself into thinking would make me happy growing up. My fifteen month old son, my six week old daughter, and I were on the family room floor sobbing. I don't know what they were crying about, but I had come to the end of myself. God had somehow become a righteous Judge waiting to zap me. I knew of Him, but I didn't *know* Him. Out of the depths of my soul came the most desperate cry I had ever uttered. I was exhausted and was the most miserable I had ever been. It was not the most articulate prayer, but it came from the heart of a wayfaring stranger who wanted to come home. "Jesus… help me. I have seen you in my childhood. I have seen things that cannot be explained away by human reasoning in the Congo. If You are there, please, please, please come to me. I can't live like this anymore."

A consistent quiet time in God's Word had never been my experience. I knew this area in my life had to change. God's Word is powerful and effective. Like a double-edged sword, it has cut away the dead parts, just as a surgeon's scalpel would do. Has it hurt to go back and work through the disappointments and sin in my life? Yes, and sometimes I have thought I would die. But I am a living, breathing testimony of the same power that raised Christ from the dead which now lives inside of me. He has given me a new song, a new life.

He came! Jesus, my Redeemer, came for me that day. I was in the desert and as He said to Hagar after she had fled from Sarai in Genesis 16:7 so He asked me, "Shawn, where have you come from and where are you going?" I responded that I didn't know. I was scared. I had so much healing to do. He gently whispered to my heart, "There is no place that we will go that I have not gone before you. I will be with you. I will help you face it all. And we won't do all the healing at once. We'll just look at it a little at a time."

That day I decided to surrender to the Lordship of Jesus Christ was not necessarily full of drama or sudden change. No bells or whistles went off. It was an act of the will. My children were still crying, but I knew then that I had to change some habits in my life. I decided to stop hanging on to the narrow gate and start walking the narrow road. I cannot say that I even felt any different. Overwhelmed with two children in the middle of a Chicago winter that I knew would require me to stay housebound for several more weeks, and with no family nearby, the isolation was very real. The Lord confirmed to me that I had to make some drastic changes in my life, and I had to get into His Word. He gave the idea of giving nap-time to Him—my precious two hours of "me" time. I remember telling Him, "Lord, how can I fill two hours up with You? I can't even pray for five minutes without running out of things to say, for goodness' sake!" I am sure that He was amused with my excuses. I had this crazy notion that I had to figure out how to keep Him entertained (and me, too) for those two hours. I wondered how I could fill two long hours with Bible reading and prayer. At that point I realized He was asking for my obedience, not my creativity.

Rob brought home the *The One Year Chronological Bible* [1] right after that and I dove in with both feet. I loved that particular Bible because it gave me the exact passages to read for each day to enable me to read the whole Bible in a year. The major and minor prophets had scared me to death, not to mention the book of Revelation! The only time I even saw those books in the Bible was when I was flipping through to get to the familiar Psalms or the Gospels, but I had never before camped in the books of Habakkuk, Ezekiel, Nahum, or Zephaniah on purpose! I felt unintelligent and lost

Has it hurt to go back and work through the disappointments and sin in my life? Yes, and sometimes I thought I would die.

before I realized it was Satan who made me feel too ignorant to be able to understand those books. It is the Holy Spirit, my sweet sister, who helps us decipher God's Word. Our educational level or knowledge of theology has nothing to do with God's ability to give us His wisdom so that we may understand what we are reading. I saw time after time passages whose meaning had eluded me before become clearer to me as the words I read pierced my heart in the days following my commitment to make the Scriptures part of my everyday life.

Writing has always been one of my passions. I have kept a journal most of my life. It was natural for me to journal during my quiet time along with using my concordance and cross-referencing to see how other parts of the Bible supported what I was reading. But the most amazing discovery I made was when I committed to memorizing Scripture. I started writing verses on 3X5 cards and carrying them around with me all the time. I would look at the cards whenever I could, prop them up while I was filling the dishwasher, or put them on the washing machine while I was folding the laundry. I would find I could memorize as I walked through my daily routine, even with the kids around. It shocked me how quickly I was able to memorize that way, often repeating verses ten times or more. I am convinced that when we do what pleases God in our lives, He gives us capacity beyond our own ability to do His will.

Do not listen to the lie of Satan that you cannot memorize Scripture!

Do not listen to the lie of Satan that you cannot memorize Scripture! Where does this power come from according to Philippians 2:13?

These three things—reading, memorizing, and journaling—have been the catalysts for the change in me over the last eleven years. God's Word has absolutely revolutionized my life. His Word is my biggest delight. It has brought me such healing in so many places, places I didn't even know needed healing.

I need to ask you: Where else can we find so great a salvation? Who knows the very number of hairs on my head and who thinks thoughts about me which outnumber the grains of sands on the seashore, telling me that all of those thoughts are good (Psalm 139, Jeremiah 29:11)? Who else has engraved my name on His hands as well as in His heart (Isaiah 49:16)? Who else leads me through the valleys and darkness and promises me that all things in my life will work together for good because I love Him and I am called according to His divine purpose (Romans 8:28)! I can't begin to fathom His thoughts toward me in my human understanding. My sweet sister, does the narrow road leading from the narrow gate require sacrifice? Yes. Is it painful to our sinful flesh—yes! But I have come to realize that all the negative connotations were a mirage which I once associated with the narrowness of the road that leads to life.

Please write out Psalm 18:19. Why did the Lord do this for David according to this verse?

Surrendering to the Lordship of Jesus Christ in my life continues to bring me into the most freedom I have ever known. What I have discovered is that the restrictiveness I imagined I would experience if I surrendered my unmet desires to Him was the bondage from the shackles of my sin and unyielded heart. My obedience to walk the narrow road by way of the narrow gate allows me to experience the soul satisfaction I had never been able to find in anything or anyone of this world.

The best news of all is that God brings me into that freedom because of what His Son did on the cross. It is His delight in me that brings me into the spacious place, not anything I have done. What do I bring my Jesus? Righteousness that is like filthy rags and He gives me no condemnation in return (Isaiah 64:6, Romans 8:1-2). I come to Him with empty hands and heart and He tells me that I am a coheir with Christ (Romans 8:17) and that a place in heaven in promised to me, prepared by Christ Himself (John 14:2-3). I come to Him with a fallen, fickle, sinful nature and He comes to me with the shed blood of Calvary. He will throw my sin into the deepest ocean and remember it against me no more simply for my contrite confession (Micah 7:19). And Jesus lives forever to intercede for me as my faithful High Priest (Hebrews 7:24-26)! He rises to defend me against the enemy of my soul (Psalm 35:2-3).

What does Philippians 2:10-11 declare will happen one day?

Who, my sweet sister, has lordship in our lives? Every creature will submit to Jesus Christ one day, but I want bowing in submission to be my choice here on earth—now—while I have the will to decide. Yes, Jesus may require you and me to give up sinful habits that we are involved in, but the exchange is not for a smothering of our fun. Until we bow the knee and submit in obedience, the abundant life that Jesus promised us will continue to elude us. Until we stop conforming our minds to the pattern of this world and start to exalt His Word above any other form of counsel or unmet desire we have, we will continue to feel constricted in our unmet desires and experience a lack of peace in our lives.

❊ What did Jesus call Himself in John 10:9 and what did He promise would be the result if we acted upon His command in this verse?

What is keeping you from entering the gate and walking in freedom with Jesus?

How badly do you want the abundant life that Christ promises can be yours in John 10:10?

Are you willing to surrender to the Lordship of Jesus Christ? Why or why not?

Do we want to be saved from the lies of jealousy, my beloved friend? The antidote is walking through the narrow gate and continuing on the narrow road that few find. The paradox we will experience is that our longing for joy and freedom, the need we have to feel significant, and the spaciousness we have been searching for, are found by way of the narrow gate and road. Are you and I ready to let go of the narrow gate and start walking into the abundant life by making Jesus Christ Lord of our lives? The choice is ours.

Day Two: The Gift I Give Myself

I never understood who forgiving others was for. I seethed with bitterness over hurts I had received from others, long years after the actions had been committed against me. I plotted my revenge down to the very last detail toward the one who had hurt me. I carried out complete conversations in my mind with the other person, imagining my brilliant rebuttal for every possible refusal of the other's part to accept accountability for what had been done to me. In my imaginary world, the perpetrator of my pain would be full of shame over the sin as I turned a deaf ear toward their pleadings for forgiveness. I reasoned my actions would be justified because granting forgiveness would condone the anguish the person had caused me, right? The person needed to feel the pain they inflicted on me. I was never going to forgive, even if the forgiveness was begged for.

I carried a chip on my shoulder the size of a boulder as I sat and stewed over the whole sorry mess. Ironically, although I wanted that person to feel even a little of the hurt I was carrying around, I was the one who was in prison. So many hours were wasted in futile daydreams of revenge. As my mind would recount for the thousandth time what sin had been committed against me, my depression over the matter only deepened. Years later, I was still being held a captive to my perpetrator years later; a prisoner to someone who was not even aware of how much damage had been done. The person was not even in my life anymore, but I thought about the object of my bitterness every day. My anger shackled me in the chains of my unforgiveness.

Jesus spoke to masses of people in parables, but only explained the meaning of His words to those who had ears to listen. Let's read Matthew 18:21-35 and answer the following questions:

What was Peter's question of Jesus in verse 21?

What was Jesus' reply to Peter in verse 22? Choose one:

seven   seventeen   thirty-five   seventy-seven

What exceptions did Jesus tell Peter there were to forgiving his brother when his brother sinned against him in these verses?

No exceptions! Did you notice that forgiveness was required on Peter's part when his brother sinned against Peter? An apology was not even the prerequisite for forgiveness toward the brother who had wronged Peter. And if a brother sinned against Peter seventy-seven times, Peter was to forgive him *every time.* Sometimes my finite mind has a difficult time understanding God's ways of justice.

> I plotted my revenge down to the very last detail toward the one who had hurt me.

When have you felt it was within your right to withhold forgiveness from someone and why? According to these verses, were you justified in your actions?

How large was the debt the servant owed the master in verse 24 and what was the servant going to be required to do as payment?

What saved the servant from his deserved punishment according to verse 27?

What did the servant immediately go out and do after the debt had been forgiven?

How small was the fellow servant's debt to him?

Describe the similarity of the actions of both servants in verses 26 and 29. What were the outcomes of each one's actions in verses 27 and 30?

Who else was affected by the first servant's actions according to verse 31 and what did they do as a result?

What did the master do when he heard the report of all that had happened in verses 32-34?

In your opinion, was the master justified to do what he did to the first servant? Why or why not?

My dear sister, have you and I been living the torturous existence caused by our refusal to forgive a fellow human being when God, through the blood of Jesus Christ, has forgiven us of so much? We can be saved from the wrath of God through our salvation by Christ, sealed by the Holy Spirit until the day we go to be with Jesus, and remain a slave because of our bitterness toward others.

How has your unwillingness to forgive someone else imprisoned you?

Yesterday we talked about the truth that Jesus stated regarding many who refuse to walk the narrow road that begins after we enter the narrow gate. Forgiveness is not an option for someone who loves Jesus Christ. Forgiveness is not for the other person, my sweet friend! Forgiveness does not condone what has happened to us; it does not say that the wrong perpetrated against us was acceptable. Child molestation or abuse, rape, the smearing of our reputations through slander, being lied to or about, or the murder of a loved one is not okay with God. All of those things are sin. But if we as individuals are going to walk in liberty until justice is served either on this earth or in heaven, we must forgive those who have done these treacherous acts against us. Forgiveness is the gift we give to ourselves because forgiveness sets us free from the prison of bitterness.

What do the following Scriptures reveal about the sins of others toward us? Match the following verses with the correct reference:

Nothing in all creation is hidden from God's sight.   *Hebrews 4:1*
Everything is uncovered and laid bare before the
eyes of him to whom we must give account.

For God will bring every deed into judgment,   *2 Corinthians 4:5*
including every hidden thing, whether it is good or evil.

Therefore judge nothing before the appointed time;   *Ecclesiastes 12:14*
wait till the Lord comes. He will bring to light what
is hidden in darkness and will expose the motives
of men's hearts…

> Forgiveness does not condone what has happened to us; it does not say that the wrong perpetrated against us was acceptable.

We are not the judge, thank the Lord! We can be assured that our righteous Judge has seen and heard everything that not only our perpetrator has done to us, but also what we have done to others. The latter part of the previous sentence should cause us to be merciful and freely forgive them.

But what do we do about the anguish we may feel toward someone who has wronged us? Why would God allow that person to do such evil toward us? I believe until we can come to a satisfying conclusion about why God allows bad things to happen to us, we will never have peace in our hurt.

225

Genesis 37-50 tells us the story of Joseph, the boy who was sold into slavery in Egypt by his ten jealous brothers. After earning the respect of his master, Potiphar, he was wrongfully accused of attempted rape by Potiphar's lying, lust-filled wife. The reward Joseph received for his integrity in Potiphar's house was a two-year prison sentence. Joseph's vindication came through his God-given ability to interpet a troubling dream of Pharoah. One day's time saw Joseph rise to the highest position of power under Pharoah, the king of Egypt. The dream of the king foretold the famine which would affect all the world (Genesis 41:57), including Joseph's father and brothers who were living hundreds of miles away in Canaan.

Twenty years after being sold into slavery, Joseph's brothers came to Joseph, the man whom they had sinned so greatly against who now had the power to save their families from destruction. All of those years of separation did not allow the brothers to recognize Joseph. After returning from Canaan with their youngest brother Benjamin, the brothers were stunned to witness Joseph finally reveal his true identity to them.

Let's read Genesis 45:1-7. What did Joseph declare in verse five that speaks of his forgiveness toward his brothers?

We can either continue to believe the lie that God has abandoned us, or allow our own healing to occur by using our pain to bring glory to our God.

My darling friend, I am convinced that Joseph could not have said those gracious words of forgiveness to his brothers in Potiphar's house right after he had become a slave. I am confident that he wondered where in the world God was the first day the door of his prison cell clanged shut after he had been falsely accused by Potiphar's wife. Joseph and God had some huge issues to settle about what justice looked like to Joseph.

God has been so faithful to give me verses that speak directly to my deepest questions. I want to share three passages that have helped me greatly in understanding why God has allowed painful, undeserved hurts to happen in my life.

I would like us to read the following passages and answers the questions below:

Isaiah 54:16-17

According to verse sixteen, who created the destroyer and for what purpose in verse 17?

God has always been in control. Always. What He has allowed in our lives has been for our vindication! Our pain gives us the right to empathize with someone else who is in the pit we were once in and expose Satan for the liar that he is. We can either continue to believe the lie that God has abandoned us, or allow our own healing to occur by using our pain to bring glory to our God.

Isaiah 30:20-21

What does God give us in verse 20 and for what purpose in verses 20-21?

Affliction and adversity are the greatest teachers, my dear friend. Without these two, we will never have the scales removed from our eyes. We will not see God in our situation because we will have come to believe the lie that we don't need Him. The lessons we learn through affliction and adversity allow us to hear His voice and walk away from the broad road that will lead us to our destruction.

Genesis 50:20

Please write this verse here:

We must believe this is the truth, my sweet friend. Even if we have stepped into the net that life's disappointments has laid down in front of us, God's purpose is to use our pain for the saving of many lives. Girlfriend, this life is all about glorifying God, not ourselves. Until we get that through our heads, we will be disappointed continually. We must become less so that our Jesus can become greater.

But I have not even shared with you the most amazing reward of our forgiveness toward others. When I forgive, even when I do not want to, the following promise is mine to claim:

> *Dear children, let us not love with words or tongue but with actions and in truth. This then is how we know that we belong to the truth, and how we set our hearts at rest in his presence whenever our hearts condemn us. For God is greater than our hearts, and he knows everything.*
> *Dear friends, if our hearts do not condemn us, we have confidence before God and receive from him anything we ask, because we obey his commands and do what pleases him.*   *1 John 3:18-22*

When Satan the destroyer comes to me with his lies, trying to convince me that my own confessed sins are not forgiven, my heart will be set at rest in my God's presence because I have loved in action and in truth by forgiving my perpetrator. I am able to clearly hear the Voice of my God behind me because I have tasted and learned from the bread of affliction and the water of adversity, assuring me that my right as a forgiven child of my Abba is to refute the wicked, lying tongue of Satan. This is my vindication, sweet sister.

Let's leave the torture of our unforgiveness toward others behind! The rewards of our obedience are far more satisfying than the clutching of our hurts. Jesus is faithful. With His perspective, we will see our forgiveness of those who have hurt us as the gift we give ourselves.

Day Three: The Blessed Heart

We are looking this week at the antidote for the poison of jealousy. You have been asked repeatedly throughout the study to identify four core issues of a jealous heart.

List the four one more time here:

1) _____

2) _____

3) _____

4) _____

The jealous heart cries out desperately to be loved, to be accepted, and to have significance, while tragically believing something or someone on this earth can fill the void of those needs. We have all tried to find love, acceptance and significance in the things of this world and have found that they do not satisfy. We keep looking for the blessing of love, approval, and purpose in all the wrong places. Who wouldn't want to lay down the burden of not being worthy? Isn't that the wounded cry of the jealous heart, to be worthy to someone who believes that we are?

What does the psalmist ask of the Lord in Psalm 119:174?

 How do you think salvation and delighting in God's law are related to one another?

We will never find our soul's salvation by looking anywhere other than God's Word. I am aware if I miss one meal. If I miss two meals, my stomach starts to complain loudly. My physical hunger is very difficult to ignore. If I continued to not satisfy my hunger day after day, my body would eventually show the fact that it was starving. Oh sisters, a jealous heart is a starving heart. But the most tragic fact of all is that there is a feast set before us if we will just partake of it.

We are going to look at that table laden with soul-satisfying fare today. Let's turn in our Bibles to Ephesians 1:1-8 as the text for our lesson today.

What are the first blessings that the apostle Paul gives to his readers in verse 2?

In light of our study, why are grace and peace a balm for a jealous heart?

✳ How we are blessed in the heavenly realms according to verse three?

The jealous heart is ignorant of what is hers. The only condition for having these blessings is making Jesus Christ the Lord of our lives. There are no other conditions. Without Christ, the jealous heart will continue feeling threatened, unloved, rejected, and overlooked.

Let's analyze verses four through eight by comparing the blessed heart to the jealous heart. I will give the lies believed by the jealous heart; you provide what the blessed heart receives through believing God's Word as truth.

The Jealous Heart	The Blessed Heart
Believes that it was not chosen by God (verse 4)	Knows that it was chosen
Believes that it is unholy and guilty.	
Does not believe it belongs to anyone.	
Believes it must earn the favor of others.	
Has rarely experienced grace.	
Does not realize that forgiveness is in Christ's blood.	
Feels threatened in its poverty, so it hoards.	
Lives without wisdom and understanding.	

The jealous heart is ignorant of what is hers.

Which column above is most closely represents your belief system right now? Are you believing a lie or the truth of God's Word?

According to Ephesians 1:1-8, we have everything we need to ward off feelings of jealousy. If this is true, why do we followers of Christ still struggle with the green-eyed monster of jealousy? I believe that there are two reasons:
1) We were ignorant of all that is ours in Christ or
2) we choose not to believe that this passage is the truth.

According to Hebrews 5:2, how does God look at ignorance?

My life experiences dictate what is truth to me. It is very difficult for me to believe that which is not tangible to my five senses but must be experienced through the eyes of faith. When I look at the benefits of a blessed heart, I must honestly say that it is very easy for me to have a problem believing these blessings are mine. My fleshly nature wants to scream that what God declares is truth is not the truth. The apostle Paul was directed by the Holy Spirit to address this issue also in this letter to the Ephesian church.

What was Paul's prayer in Ephesians 3:17-19?

We are not capable of acknowledging the blessing of God in our lives without the power of Christ in us to deliver us from our jealous thoughts toward others

We are not capable of acknowledging the blessing of God in our lives without the power of Christ in us to deliver us from our jealous thoughts toward others. I must pray for this ability. It will not come naturally because my incomplete earthly knowledge cannot embrace spiritual blessings. I must have Spirit eyes, to believe and I must ask for those eyes.

I must be in God's Word daily. It must be food to me. As necessary as it is for me to eat nourish my body with physical food, I must feast on the Living Bread of Christ by reading and applying the truths of Scripture to my life. My starving spiritual soul will spend its energy trying to fill itself with that which cannot satisfy me. Every spiritual blessing in Christ Jesus is mine, but I have to believe that this is truth.

The pathway to realizing all that I have in Christ is through gratitude. How grateful are we in our lives? I am a pessimist married to the eternal optimist. God has a sense of humor in putting spouses together! My natural inclination is for my mind to go to the worst possible scenario and camp there in worry. Jesus specifically told His followers not to worry in Matthew 6. An attitude of gratitude is vitally important for us to be able to see God's generosity to us.

What do the following passages say about the power of gratitude in our lives?

Psalm 50:23:

Philippians 3:1:

Philippians 4:6-7

Colossians 3:15

Why is it a safeguard for me to rejoice? Because rejoicing keeps me from the downward spiral of futile thinking caused by my lack of gratitude. I must rejoice in all things, for this is the will of God for me in Christ Jesus. Being thankful keeps me from despair and the tragic inability to see my circumstances as the blessing His presence has the power to make them.

We must regularly remind ourselves of all that we have been given. The spiritual blessings that we have looked at today do not depend on how our socioeconomic status. The antidote for jealousy is to remember all that we have in Christ and to be thankful.

What would happen if we truly started believing that our Creator redeems, forgives, accepts, adopts, and loves us because that was His will and pleasure? Jealousy's pride says that I must have some part to play in each of the blessings He has given me freely in the One He loves. If I could somehow grasp how wide and long and deep and high is the love of Christ, this jealous heart could become a blessed heart.

Please join me here, sweet sister, in asking our God to make this a reality in our lives:

Because of God's glorious grace, we are accepted by Him in the Beloved Person of Jesus Christ!   **Ephesians 1:6 (NKJV)**

Being thankful keeps me from despair and the tragic inability to see my circumstances as the blessing His presence has the power to make them.

Day Four: Fighting the Good Fight

I would like us to start today's lesson by praying Ephesians 1:17-23 out loud, inserting the word "I" every time we see the word "you" in these verses. We must see this passage through the spiritual eyes of faith to enable us to believe that everything this passage of Scripture says we have in Christ is ours to claim. Let's take a moment and pray these verses, especially asking for hearts that will be sensitive to His voice.

Share any thoughts you heard from the Holy Spirit in your own heart as you prayed that passage over yourself:

A general in the armed forces never comes into his or her position overnight. Never. Each one of those medals on the uniform represents battles fought in the past. My beloved sisters, to do this life well with Jesus, we must realize that the Lord never makes us an instant success on the battlefield of life. I would love to think that by studying His Word about jealousy, I would be miraculously delivered of all jealous thoughts from now on. This is just not true. I will be confronted with jealousy and fall into its pit many times before I take my final breath. A general is not decorated for never being ambushed by the enemy, but rather for how he confronted that enemy. For as many honors as the general has received, the unseen defeats are twice or more times as many. We cannot let the enemy convince us that we have defeated him for good in this area. He will come back again. Expect him. But the wonderful news is that the lessons we have learned through the life of Saul can help us to be wiser in the fight. In fact, we have the opportunity to fight the good fight of faith in this area armed with the knowledge we have gained from the precious Word of God.

So how do we do this? We are going to look at a special relationship that the apostle Paul had with a man younger than himself named Timothy.

Let's read 1 Timothy 1:1-2 for and try to surmise their relationship. Answer the following questions:

Who does Paul declare himself to be in verse 1?

Who does Paul declare Timothy to be in verse 2 and what words does he bless him with?

The general is about to give instructions from their mutual Commander-in-chief to his beloved subordinate officer. Timothy was a leader in the church at Ephesus. Paul wrote two epistles (letters) to his special son in the faith,

> We cannot let the enemy convince us that we have defeated him for good in this area. He will come back again. Expect him.

232

bestowing on Timothy some of the lessons he had learned in the many spiritual battles he had fought. For context, let's read 1 Timothy 1:3-11. We will spend most of our study today on verses five and six.

Timothy found himself in the middle of some serious problems in his church. False teachers had arisen inside the church, which caused Paul enough concern that he wrote to Timothy twice about the problem. Timothy was faced with the undesirable task of supervising the church's affairs and appointing qualified church leadership to try to clean up the mess. Can you imagine the hot bed of controversy and jealousy that could have been directed at Timothy over this?

So what is Timothy to do? Paul sums up the solution and problem in verses 5 and 6. Because they are the key verses today, let's write both of them out here.

What is the common goal mentioned in verse five?

_____

How in the world is Timothy going to be a catalyst of love to a very unloving place? List the three attributes Paul gives in verse five:

1)_____ 2) _____ 3) _____

Purity takes the chaff off my eyes. With spiritual eyes, I can wait for God to bless me in His time.

We are going to look at these three attributes through the prism of fighting jealousy.

A Pure Heart

What is so remarkable about a pure heart? I believe that the other two attributes cannot be a reality in our lives without this being in place first. Jesus praised those with a pure heart during his sermon on the mount.

❃ What did He say a pure heart can do according to Matthew 5:8?

It will be shown mercy.   It will be forgiven.   It will see God.

Oh, beloved sisters, doesn't our jealousy spring from not being able to see God in our situations? I can easily see Him in the middle of someone else's life, but my distorted vision, blinded by jealousy, cannot see Him in mine. We cannot believe in a just, good, powerful, and trustworthy God that our hearts do not see. Being able to see God's goodness to me even though someone else has something that I want, need, or deserve is such an antidote for the poison of jealousy! Purity takes the chaff off my eyes. With spiritual eyes, I can wait for God to bless me in His time.

The key to changing an impure heart to a pure one is found in 2 Corinthians 4:2. Please write the verse out here:

What does Paul say we must do with those jealous thoughts when they invade our minds? We must renounce them. We have talked about how jealous fantasies of ours are rarely brought into the light of truth. They live and fester in the secrecy of our hearts and minds. Girls, we must renounce those out loud. When a jealous thought comes calling, I must say, "Jesus, I take this jealous thought captive and make it obedient to you (2 Corinthians 10:5). I renounce this falsehood. I will not believe that You are withholding anything good from me."

A Good Conscience

Remember the example of the general that I cited in the beginning? Generals are responsible for many others under them. They earn this sacred trust of others' lives through integrity and doing the hard thing, no matter what the personal cost is to themselves. They are invested in the lives of their men. That general started out in a lower rank and determined to do the next right thing in front of him or her. Those decisions were rewarded. Faithful days turn into reward.

But how do we know what pleases our God? Some of the most tender passages of Scripture are found in John 14-16, which is Jesus' farewell to His beloved disciples just before He went to His death on the cross. He was leaving them. They would no longer walk, talk, and minister together in the same way they had for three years. Jesus was returning to the Father, but He foretold the profound hope of the coming Holy Spirit. Let's read each of these passages and give the attribute and/or duty of the Holy Spirit in each passage:

John 14:16-19
The Holy

Spirit_____

John 14:26
The Holy
Spirit_____

John 16:7-11
The Holy
Spirit_____

Hebrews 3:7-12
The Holy Spirit _____

That last passage was very sobering. Everyone, whether they have believed in Christ for salvation or not, has a conscience. We who are in Christ have the Holy Spirit to convict, judge, and remind us. We must start recognizing His voice. That "voice" we hear, what we may falsely call our "gut instinct," is God the Father speaking to us through His Holy Spirit. The results of listening to His voice and not hardening our hearts are a clean conscience before God. Satan loves to taunt us with jealous thoughts and will be able to get us in the pit when we do not have a clear conscience. We cannot underestimate the horrible net that Satan plants for us to step into when we ignore the Holy Spirit's convicting voice. We must train ourselves to obey immediately. Otherwise, we are prey for the enemy of our souls.

A Sincere Faith

How important is faith to us in our good fight against staying in the pit of jealousy? Write out Hebrews 11:6 for God's perspective to that question:

Faith is perhaps the greatest antidote of all to jealousy. We cannot have the faith that pleases God without a pure heart and a good conscience. But, girls, this is where the rubber meets the road. So much of the crucified life is lived in the dark. Our circumstances scream at us constantly that we have the right to hold onto our jealous thoughts. We may get others to agree and help us feed that perspective.

What is faith according to Hebrews 11:1?

"Now faith is _____ _____of what we _____ for and _____ of what we do not _____."

> Our circumstances scream at us constantly that we have the right to hold onto our jealous thoughts.

Jealousy is unbelief in the justice, goodness, love, and trustworthiness of our God toward us. To start fighting the good fight, we must be willing to say to the Lord that He knows what He is doing. And if we don't believe what we say with our mouths, we beg Him to help us in our unbelief. Because of His infinite power, our God is capable of changing our circumstances in a second. He could instantly give us our heart's deepest longing, but we wouldn't appreciate His power without the wrestling through with Him that our unmet desires requires of us. We wouldn't learn to love Him without the trial of having to believe He is who He says He is when our circumstances don't change. Faith dares to believe what seems to be unbelievable. And nothing pleases Him more than when we, with a deliberate act of our will submitting to Him, live by faith.

This life is a fight. Armed with the weapons of a pure heart, a clear conscience, and a sincere faith, we can live at peace with our unanswered questions in this lifetime and leave jealousy in the pit where it belongs.

Day Five: His Name is Jealous

We have made it to the last day of our study! If this is the first time that you have ever done an in-depth Bible study, just imagine a thundering round of applause from me over your dedication and diligence to such a huge undertaking. I cannot tell you how honored I have been to share these past nine weeks with you examining a character flaw that has caused me more heartache and confusion in my life than I can express. Thank you, sweet sister, for taking this journey with me into the inner recesses of a jealous heart. My deepest prayer is that we may we be wiser women for the lessons that we have learned along the way.

As you have probably concluded by now, I have loved to ask questions of you throughout the study. Ask anyone who knows me well and he or she will tell you that I ask many questions in conversation. I have found that a good question asked can be the start of a fascinating and enlightening conversation. I hardly enjoy anything more than to be a part of those kinds of exchanges between two or more people.

Please read Exodus 34:10-14. I am about to ask you the most important question of the study. Drumroll, please! Ready? Okay, here it is:

After verifying who is speaking in Exodus 34:10, what does God call Himself in verse 14? Choose one:

Almighty

Righteous

Jealous

Merciful

Had you ever known that God called Himself that before? Please check your response:

___yes   ____no

Are you shocked? You might be thinking, *How can a holy God give Himself that name?*

Now I am going to ask you another question:
What does Genesis 1:27 reveal?

We are made in God's image.   God was very pleased.

We were created on the sixth day.

> My deepest prayer is that we may we be wiser women for the lessons that we have learned along the way.

Jealousy is a part of the holiness of God. Based on the fact that God is a jealous God, the conclusion can be made that jealousy *can* be a godly emotion. Because we are made in the image of God, we share emotions that God Himself feels. Jealousy is a God-given emotion. The big difference between us human beings and God is that He never sins when He feels those emotions. You and I know ourselves too well to think that we could ever be perfect in our emotions without sinning.

The Merriam-Webster's Online Dictionary defines the word *jealous* in this way:

1: a) intolerant of rivalry or unfaithfulness;
   b) disposed to suspect rivalry or unfaithfulness
2: hostile toward a rival or one believed to enjoy an advantage
3: vigilant in guarding a possession [2]

Our God is passionately jealous for our devotion, but has no sin in His Person to taint that emotion. We, on the other hand, are sin-filled. While we are full of darkness and evil, there is no darkness in Him at all. His jealousy for us is driven by agape love—that love which is hostile toward the destructive path we take when we look to others or material possessions to fill His place in our lives. God is vigilant in guarding us. His possessive nature, unlike our human nature, does not smother, crush, or enslave us like the pursuit of someone or something of this world will. Walking in the obedience of His command to love Him only, offers us true freedom and the ability to satisfy that empty hole in our souls. Unlike human beings, God has no ulterior motive to lure us in and abuse us. In fact, loving Him is the only place we are going to fill the raging need within us to trust, be loved, know true goodness, and have our demand for justice met, even when life is not fair.

I just want you to think through this with me. You do not have to be involved in a relationship with the opposite sex to know that one of love's attributes is a desire for time, attention, and affection from the one we love. I was the oldest sibling of four children in my family growing up. I can remember, clearly, how jealous I felt when I believed my parents were giving more attention to my brothers and sister than I felt they deserved. If I felt any doubt that my parents did not love me as much as my siblings, it was enough to turn my world upside down, causing me to act disrespectfully and unloving toward them.

And now I come back to the question that I have wrestled with for years, but have never been able to answer satisfactorily until recently: Can you and I live with unmet desires successfully and allow jealousy to be part of our lives? The answer to that question is one I have come to realize through the lives of the heroes (Hannah, Samuel, Jonathan, and David) we have studied in depth these last nine weeks. The astounding conclusion I have come to is that making **God's jealous desires for us and others** our own is the way to achieve the abundant life we have been longing for. The common denominator in all four heroes' lives was the decision to be jealous for the Lord. That Godly jealousy became their source of strength through the temptations that they each faced.

> Our God is passionately jealous for our devotion, but has no sin in His Person to taint that emotion.

Hannah's struggle with infertility was a battleground many of us are sadly familiar with in our own experience. Hannah's despair over her situation led her to choose the wrong plan of action to try to cope with her sadness. She did not eat; she felt misunderstood by her husband, which led her to feel isolated and alone in her pain. Through Penninah's vindictiveness, Hannah became jealousy's victim. But Hannah found triumph in her situation when she allowed the "bitterness of her soul," caused by her heartache, to propel her into the presence of God in His sanctuary. Hannah's jealous desire for God's will to be done in her life provided victory for her soul. Hannah's pursuit of Him overshadowed her difficult home situation as she left the injustice of her barren womb with the One who eventually fulfilled her unmet desire. In the process of the struggle, she learned that the presence of God was better than the presents of God.

Samuel faced the heartbreaking reality that all of us have faced—feeling unloved and unneeded by others. There is nothing like the bottomless pit of rejection to rock our once-safe and predictable worlds. Samuel had the right to refuse the people their request for a king to rule over Israel. He could have argued a compelling case and refused to step down until his death. Instead, he brought his rejection before God, who assured Samuel that He loved him and was well-pleased with Samuel's character. My sweet sisters, Samuel was jealous for God's love more than the love of men; the latter always proves to be a snare for us (Proverbs 29:25). For us to know true, unfailing love—the kind that does not mislead or disappoint us—we must learn to follow Samuel's example. The Creator of the universe *is* love (1 John 4:8). God does not just display attributes of love to us, nor is that love conditional. We never have to question whether He loves us as much today as He did yesterday or when we first came to believe in His Son, Jesus Christ. God is not a man who gives love on the condition of what we can do for Him. He loves us because His essence is love. He cannot do otherwise. Although Samuel may have been ousted from his position over Israel, his need for love was satisfied in the bottomless fathoms of God's love for him. God's love was enough.

One of the greatest destroyers of trust is sin-tainted jealousy. Jonathan was thrust into a position none of us would desire. Saul's jealous raging against David killed the trust between the king and his son. Jonathan could have gotten caught up in the web of deceit in which Saul tried to make him a player. What allowed Jonathan to choose to stand with truth, although it cost him the abuse of his father and, ultimately, the crown? Jonathan trusted in Jehovah. Time and again, Jonathan submitted and trusted in God's plan for his future (see 1 Samuel 23:16-18). Although Saul proved to be unstable and unpredictable in his thoughts and actions toward his son and others, Jonathan continued to put his trust in the One whose ways were higher than his ways and whose thoughts were higher than his thoughts (Isaiah 55:9). Oh, sisters! Let's be jealous for the ability to trust that Jesus Christ is our refuge, even when all is chaos in our lives.

What sustained David's belief in the goodness of God during the years he spent as a fugitive in caves and deserts? David had to decide what he would believe about God's character early in his life with a household that did not recognize his value. The net Satan carefully laid down was exposed to David because David chose to believe God was good. The shepherd boy spent years alone in the lowly job of looking after sheep. David could have frittered the hours away in bitter thoughts toward his family members, stewing in his jealousy over being the youngest son, doing the meanest of chores. Instead, he chose to use the solitude to praise Jehovah. And because of that attitude, God gave David the thrill of knowing that His hand was the one which guided the stone flung from his slingshot which found its target in the heads of the lion, the bear, and, ultimately, the Philistine giant. Although his fear threatened to overwhelm him, the still, small voice of God sustained David as he ran from hiding place to hiding place during Saul's maniacal pursuit. Girlfriends, we can train our ears through righteous living to hear the same Voice, because surely our God has been good to you and me. Although the shadow of Saul's betrayal threatened to extinguish David's hope, David continued to make the choice to encourage his soul in God. Only the Lord knew the depth of David's devotion and the cost it had personally written on his soul to be able to write the words of Psalm 13:6.

Please write out Psalm 13:6 here:

Can you and I, at this very moment, write the same from a heart that really means those words? Share your answer here:

Dear sisters, I cannot say this strongly enough: Unmet desires are a part of this life on planet earth.

Dear sisters, I cannot say this strongly enough: Unmet desires are a part of this life on planet earth. If you and I have come to believe that God has somehow duped us and given us the shaft, we are believing a lie from the pit of hell. Jesus assured us that our lives would be full of trouble, but we are to take heart for He has overcome the world and given us the power to be victorious. Satan, in the meantime, is doing all he can to make us forget that truth through our unmet desires and the lies of our jealous hearts. As we end our time together in the magnificent Word of God, my prayer has been that when we encounter strife within our own hearts, which we cannot easily understand, we will ask ourselves if the disease of jealousy has infected a deeper heart wound in our understanding of God's character. If we are the victim of another person's jealousy, may we see that hurt from the refuge provided to us by our God who sees and knows everything.

We have exposed many ugly faces of jealousy in this study. We have watched the slow self-destruction of a man named Saul who was given everything he needed to rule righteously and yet threw it all away because of a rebellious heart that would not be grateful for what he had. Instead, he squandered his family's trust, lived a miserable existence, and spent his life trying to crush an enemy who only lived in his deluded mind. Please, Jesus, keep us from a wasted life!

I must ask us one more time: How do you and I live with unmet desires? We expose the sin-tainted face of our jealousy to the One whose Name is Jealous and let Him quiet us with Himself (Zephaniah 3:17). What happens when we allow ourselves to be jealous for what Jesus Christ is jealous for us? I believe the answer to that question is revealed in 2 Corinthians 3:17-18:

For the Lord is the Spirit, and wherever the Spirit of the Lord is, there is freedom. So all of us who have had that veil removed can see and reflect the glory of the Lord. And the Lord—who is the Spirit—makes us more and more like him as we are changed into his glorious image. *(NLT)*

The freedom we will have to live at peace with our unmet desires will come as we allow Jesus to remove the veil of jealousy from our hearts, making us more like Him as we are changed into His glorious image. Now *that*, my dear friend, is something to be jealous for!

I love you!

Shaun

Shaun

 ## My darling friend,

Before you were born, your Creator planned out a life for you that would ultimately lead you to Jesus Christ. You may have been raised in church and have tried to live a good life. You also may be exhausted and disillusioned with having to try to be good enough to be worthy of love. Until you have settled the most important question you will ever wrestle with, your heart will continue to search for something or someone in this world that can never fill the void you know is there.

I want to share with you the best news you will ever hear. You are deeply loved by a God whose love for you is unfailing and unconditional. You do not have to do anything to make yourself worthy of this love. You only need to accept the gift of salvation he offers to you through His Son, Jesus Christ.

The apostle Paul was inspired by the Holy Spirit to write the following truth:

"That if you confess with your mouth, "Jesus is Lord," and believe in your heart that God raised him from the dead, you will be saved. For it is with your heart that you believe and are justified, and it is with your mouth that you confess and are saved. As the Scripture says, "Anyone who trusts in him will never be put to shame."

Romans 10:9-11

Do you want the abundant life that Jesus Christ offers in John 10:10 to all who believe on Him for salvation? The first step toward that life is in asking Jesus Christ to become your Savior. He doesn't want a perfect life to be surrendered to Him. He will accept you as you are. If you are ready to have Jesus be the Lord of your life, please pray this simple prayer:

God,

I know that I am a sinner. I believe that Jesus Christ died on the cross for my sins and that you have raised Him from the dead. I want to surrender my life to the Lordship of Jesus Christ from this point on. Thank you for saving me and for loving me with a love that will never fail me. Give me a desire for You and Your will that surpasses any other desire I have in my life.

In Jesus' Name,

Amen

May I have the privilege of welcoming you as my sister in Christ? Please tell a fellow Christian what you have done and get involved in a Bible-believing church. I cannot tell you how thrilled I am over your decision. I would love to hear about how the Lord brought you to Himself at esengoministries@aol.com. God bless you!

End Notes

Week One: Four Core Issues of a Jealous Heart

1   Christian psychologist and author, Larry Crabb, Ph.D, is the one who introduced me to rethinking my definition of God's blessings in my life through the reading of his book, *The Pressure's Off.* I must give Dr. Crabb credit for asking his readers whether God's blessing is in His presence or in His presents. Thank you, Dr. Crabb, for such a life-changing book and encouraging me to want God's presence over anything He could give me materially.

2   Skoglund, Elizabeth. *Bright Days, Dark Nights: With Charles Spurgeon in Triumph and Emotional Pain.* (Grand Rapids: Baker Books, 2000), 167-168.

3   Brown, Driver, Briggs and Gesenius. "Hebrew Lexicon entry for Shiyloh". "The KJV Old Testament Hebrew Lexicon".www.biblestudytools.net/Lexicons/Hebrew/heb.cgi?number=7887&version=kjv>."

4   Brown, Driver, Briggs and Gesenius. "Hebrew Lexicon entry for Shiyloh". "The KJV Old Testament Hebrew Lexicon".www.biblestudytools.net/Lexicons/Hebrew/heb.cgi?number=7886&version=kjv>.

5   Barker, Kenneth et al., *The NIV Study Bible.* (Grand Rapids: Zondervan, 1985), 375.

6   Brown, Driver, Briggs and Gesenius. "Hebrew Lexicon entry for Sh@'owl". "The KJV Old Testament Hebrew Lexicon". www.biblestudytools.net/Lexicons/Hebrew/heb.cgi?number=7585&version=kjv>.

Week Two: Straight Down A Twisted Path

1   Henry, Matthew. "Commentary on 1 Samuel 8". "Matthew Henry Complete Commentary on the Whole Bible". <http://bible.crosswalk.com/Commentaries/MatthewHenryComplete/mhc-com.cgi?book=1sa&chapter=008>. 1706.

2   Henry, Matthew. "Commentary on 1 Samuel 9". "Matthew Henry Complete Commentary on the Whole Bible". <http://bible.crosswalk.com/Commentaries/MatthewHenryComplete/mhc-com.cgi?book=1sa&chapter=009>. 1706.

3   Ibid, 1706.

4   Henry, Matthew. "Commentary on 1 Samuel 10". "Matthew Henry Complete Commentary on the Whole Bible". <http://bible.crosswalk.com/Commentaries/MatthewHenryComplete/mhc-com.cgi?book=1sa&chapter=010>. 1706.

Week Three: Portraits of a King

1   Youngblood, Ronald, et al., *Nelson's New Illustrated Bible Dictionary.* (Nashville: Thomas Nelson Publishers, 1995), 774.

2   Henry, Matthew. "Commentary on 1 Samuel 10". "Matthew Henry Complete Commentary on the Whole Bible". <http://bible. crosswalk.com/Commentaries/MatthewHenryComplete/mhc-com. cgi?book=1sa&chapter=010>. 1706.

3   Bruce, F.F., *New International Bible Commentary.* Grand Rapids: Zondervan Publishing House, 1979.

Week Four: The Ugly Turn of Disobedience

1   MacDonald, William, *Believer's Bible Commentary.* (Nashville: Thomas Nelson Publishers, 1995), 305.

2   Spurgeon, Charles, "Psalm 105:19: Trial By The Word." Metropolitan Tabernacle Sermons. www.spurgeon.org/sermons/1277.htm

Week Five: Under His Jealous Eye

1   Brown, Driver, Briggs and Gesenius. "Hebrew Lexicon entry for Shalowm". "The KJV Old Testament Hebrew Lexicon". <http://www. biblestudytools.net/Lexicons/Hebrew/heb.cgi?number=7965&version=kjv>.

2   Henry, Matthew. "Commentary on 1 Samuel 17". "Matthew Henry Complete Commentary on the Whole Bible". <http://bible. crosswalk.com/Commentaries/MatthewHenryComplete/mhc-com. cgi?book=1sa&chapter=017>. 1706.

3   "rash." Dictionary.com Unabridged (v 1.1). Random House, Inc. 31 Aug. 2009. <Dictionary.com http://dictionary.reference.com/browse/rash>.

Week Six: Fugitive of a Hardened Heart

1   "Mobutu Sese Seko," Microsoft® Encarta® Online Encyclopedia 2009. http://encarta.msn.com © 1997-2009 Microsoft Corporation. All Rights Reserved. http://encarta.msn.com/encyclopedia_761578969/Mobutu_Sese_ Seko.html

Week Seven: In Enemy Territory

1   Henry, Matthew. "Commentary on 1 Samuel 23". "Matthew Henry Complete Commentary on the Whole Bible". <http://bible.crosswalk.com/Commentaries/MatthewHenryComplete/mhc-com.cgi?book=1sa&chapter=023>. 1706.

2   Brown, Driver, Briggs and Gesenius. "Hebrew Lexicon entry for Q@lalah". "The KJV Old Testament Hebrew Lexicon". <http://www.biblestudytools.net/Lexicons/Hebrew/heb.cgi?number=7045&version=kjv>.

3   Spurgeon, Charles, "Psalm 105:19: Trial By The Word." Metropolitan Tabernacle Sermons. www.spurgeon.org/sermons/1277.htm

4   Reinberg, Steven. 16 July 2009. "Many Veterans Need Mental Health Care." American Journal of Public Health. 31 August 2009. http://www.medicinenet.com/script/main/art.asp?articlekey=103877

5   Spurgeon, Charles, "Psalm 105:19: Trial By The Word." Metropolitan Tabernacle Sermons. www.spurgeon.org/sermons/1277.htm

Week Eight: A Bitter Ending

1   Henry, Matthew. "Commentary on 1 Samuel 30". "Matthew Henry Complete Commentary on the Whole Bible". <http://bible.crosswalk.com/Commentaries/MatthewHenryComplete/mhc-com.cgi?book=1sa&chapter=030>. 1706.

2   Kroll, Woodrow. *Facing Your Final Job Review: The Judgment Seat of Christ, Salvation, and Eternal Rewards.* (Wheaton: Crossway Books, 2008), 81-82.

3   Lewis, C.S. *The Weight of Glory.* (New York: HarperCollins Publishers, 1949), 26.

Week Nine: Antidotes For Jealousy's Poison

1   "jealous." Merriam-Webster Online Dictionary. 2009. Merriam-Webster Online. 31 August 2009<http://www.merriam-webster.com/dictionary/jealous>

NOTES

NOTES

NOTES